# The Romance of Origins

# The Romance of Origins

## Language and Sexual Difference in Middle English Literature

Gayle Margherita

University of Pennsylvania Press

Philadelphia

Library of Congress Cataloging-in-Publication Data
Margherita, Gayle.
    The romance of origins : language and sexual difference in Middle English literature /
Gayle Margherita.
        p.      cm.
    Includes bibliographical references (p.) and index.
    ISBN 0-8122-3217-8. — ISBN 0-8122-1502-8 (pbk.)
    1. English literature—Middle English, 1100–1500—History and criticism.    2. English
language—Middle English, 1100—1500—Sex differences.    3. Sex differences (Psychology)
in literature.    4. Feminism and literature—England—History.    5. Women and literature—
England—History.    6. Psychoanalysis and literature.    7. Authorship—Sex differences.
I. Title.
PR275.S49M37    1994
821'.109—dc20                                                                    94-12610
                                                                                      CIP

Cover: Labyrinth from the floor of the cathedral at Chartres. Photo Fiévet, Chartres,
France. Reprinted by permission.

*To John Tanke*

# Contents

# Preface

It is the premise of a recent award-winning science fiction novel that in the future historical research will make use of time travel, thereby eliminating the historian's troublesome reliance on textual records in recovering the "real" of history. The heroine of Connie Willis's *Doomsday Book* is an Oxford undergraduate who returns—so she assumes—to the year 1320 in order to experience the English Middle Ages first-hand.[1] A few days prior to her voyage, however, a long-dormant virus emerges from a medieval archaeological site—coincidentially, from the remains of the town she herself will have visited during her sojourn. The "tech" who is responsible for the "drop" contracts the virus, becoming ill just as she is about to be sent back. Chronological "slippage" occurs, and she ends up in 1348 instead of 1320, at the precise time and place when/where the Black Death reached Oxford. Owing to illness at both ends of the journey, she cannot return home as planned; disease links past and present as historiography cannot. The "moral" of the story is not unexpected: the heroine is forced to give up her romantic fantasies about the past in the face of its nasty and brutish realities, but discovers what is noble and, yes, universally human in the doomed medievals she comes to know. A similar idealizing movement occurs in the present, and the confrontation between life and death, past and present ultimately results in a transcendence of the historical difference on which the journey was predicated.

The triumph of idealist over materialist "readings" of the Middle Ages is as predictable as it is inevitable given the generic presuppositions of mainstream science fiction. More significant for our purposes, however, is the sense in which this contemporary fantasy about the medieval past shares the epistemological and metaphysical assumptions of many of the current historicist readings of the Middle Ages, specifically the assumption that only two readings of the past are possible, and that these readings cannot really speak to one another in any meaningful way. Either the medieval period is irreducibly different and "other," or it is fundamentally the same, linked to our own historical context by philosophical, linguistic, and/or psychic "universals" that resist any historical specification. The ongoing debate as to whether or not psychoanalytic or deconstructive readings are methodologically "appropriate" to the study of medieval texts, whether or not feminism can speak to a period that was institutionally grounded in a theologically-sanctioned misogyny, and so on, inevitably returns to this binarist metaphysical paradigm. The problem is compounded by economic and institutional issues that are specific to our own historical and cultural context: I refer to the fact that, in colleges and universities in North America and Britain, medieval studies may be in danger of disappearing altogether. Conservative medievalists argue that the recent emphasis on cultural and post-colonial studies, combined with the "transhistorical" demands of "literary theory," are pushing medieval literary studies out of the curricular picture. On the other side of the political divide, some theoretically-oriented medievalists argue that traditional medieval courses have ceased to speak to the present, and are therefore keeping students away in droves. The fact that most of this discussion has taken place at conferences and in electronic discussion forums rather than in print suggests that the issue has thus far evoked emotional responses that are uninflected by any rigorous analysis. That this debate over sameness and difference, historicism and "presentism" effaces other differences that adhere to our understanding of both past and present has been noted by an increasing number of medievalists, however. Drawing on poststructuralist and materialist theoretical paradigms, as well as a formidable knowledge of medieval literary and cultural history, these scholars have begun to interrogate the conditions of historical meaning in terms that efface neither the specificity of the past nor the urgent political and philosophical concerns of the present.

Nevertheless, the field of medieval literary studies continues to be haunted by the notion that deconstructive and psychoanalytic readings of the Middle Ages are "transhistorical" and totalizing, as traditional philological or neo-traditional historicist readings are not. At the conceptual heart of this argument is the assumption that history, as an irreducible origin that stands outside language, is itself transhistorical. If the demand to historicize is, as Fredric Jameson has asserted, "Marxism's only transhistorical imperative," then any attempt to read or write "historically" will always remain excessive in relation to a notion of history that is not subject to historicity, a history that is transcendent and extra-semiotic.[2] In opening his introduction to a recent collection of historicist essays by medieval literary scholars with Jameson's command to "always historicize," Lee Patterson links the medievalist's understanding of history to the dialectical imperative that subtends Marxist literary theory.[3] Similarly, David Aers has drawn on Marxist economic theory in attempting to create a social context for medieval texts, distancing himself in the process both from "poststructuralizing assertions" that deny the existence of extralinguistic reality and from "literary scholarship," which "tends to ignore the material foundations of medieval culture."[4] For both scholars, history and materiality are foundational and primary, the thingly origin from which language and literature emerge, and to which the rigorous scholar must return them. This romance of the origin pits "history" against "literariness" in a dialectical struggle whose synthetic resolution holds out the promise of return and of moving not, as Hegel would have it, to the realm of Spirit that is the end of History, but rather to the equally transcendent space that exists outside language: the end, if you will, of literature.

If we wish to move beyond this reductive and unadventurous oppositional frame, it seems to me that we must begin to engage more honestly with the issues and challenges posed by a post-structuralism that seeks to unsettle the notions of *archē* and *telos* that underwrite most historicisms, and to restore the historicity to history. Far from foreclosing the possibility of history, deconstruction and psychoanalysis offer frameworks whereby we might begin to read and write different kinds of histories—to interrogate, for example, the fantasmatic construction of fascism, the connection between pathology and theology in mystical texts, the ways in which fantasy and reality are mutually implicated at precise moments of historical trauma or crisis. Perhaps more important, these theoretical interventions pose the question of history in an ethical sense. What is the at stake in the notion of an extralinguistic origin, when our understanding of origins is so dependent on assumptions about gender, race, and class? How do literary conventions and genres encode the "drama of the origin" in ways that sustain and/or subvert the metaphysical presuppositions and psychic fantasies that in turn sustain patriarchal, nationalist, and aristocratic hegemony? How does the public/private opposition inform what "counts" as history? To what extent, in short, does our historical memory depend on a strategic "forgetting" of the conditions of historical meaning?

In his case history of the Wolf Man, Freud asserted that "dreams are another kind of remembering." In this book, I will make a similar claim: literature is another kind of history. As the condensations and displacements of the dream-work enable us to both remember and forget psychic trauma, so the tropes that constitute "literature" are the culturally-specific traces of histories remembered and forgotten, of a past that is uncannily both familiar and strange. Following the work of Derrida, Lacan, Freud, and the the feminists who have engaged with their work most rigorously, I begin this book with the assumption that to historicize is the most historical of acts: that historicist reading and writing are historically embedded interventions, and that in effacing this fact we risk merely repeating/re-enacting the most conservative assumptions that have characterized the periods we study. Despite claims to the contrary, the myth of "presentism" carries with it the notion of an inviolable and recoverable "truth" about the past as a moment of pure presence and univocity. It is a profoundly moral assertion; carried to its logical conclusion, it both derives from and implies the belief in one God, one nation, one law. Anything in excess of this "oneness" is precisely that: a supplement that threatens the moral integrity of the past, and thus of the present. Any notion of history that does not efface the traces of its own historicity endangers this moral system in that it calls into question the transcendence of History as the epistemological and philosophical expression of the Word, the Fatherland, the Truth. My intention is to unsettle the univocity of these concepts by problematizing the question of history both within and around medieval literature. Because deconstruction and psychoanalysis are the theoretical systems most concerned with the problem of origins per se, they are the most obvious methodological point from which to initiate such an inquiry.

It is my own historically-specific contention, moreover, that medieval writers were as troubled by this issue as we medievalists are, and that the problem of history is bound up with the problem of femininity in medieval texts. This is not, however, a book about "women in medieval literature." Several excellent books have been, and continue to be, written on this subject—perhaps someday I will write one as well. My emphasis now, however, is on sexuality and representation rather than on gender and experience. The division here is clearly between two competing traditions within feminism itself (although there are certainly more than two): one rooted in the notion of woman's essential "otherness," the other committed to an exploration of that otherness as a condition of logocentric thinking. This book intends to explore the category of "the feminine" as it emerges through various literary conventions, in the hopes of articulating the political and material "stakes" in the business of representation, in criticism as well as in literature.

This book has its own history as well: it is the product, in many ways, of the intellectual atmosphere of the 1980s, inflected with some of the

emerging concerns of this decade. It is also a product of my very traditional early training as a medievalist, although my teachers might not recognize their influence here in an obvious way. My early study of medieval
language, genres, and theology are the foundation upon which this admittedly highly theoretical book rests; it is a testament to the flexibility and
durability of these concerns within the field that *The Romance of Origins*
could be written at all.

It may be said, and probably will be, that for all its concern with
history, this is not a very "historicist" book; this is inarguably true. As an
exercise in time travel, this work uncovers more paradoxes than any good
science-fiction story would allow. Lacking any "net" for filtering out paradoxes and anachronisms, my apparatus is, empirically speaking, far inferior to the one that carried Connie Willis's heroine back into the medieval
past. Nevertheless, my historical fantasy shares something with hers: in
both cases, there is something in excess, something that eludes the gaze of
empirical science and its technology. It is perhaps not coincidental that
attacks on theory from within medieval studies have occasionally resorted
to the language of pathology; whenever we encounter the past, there is
danger of "infection" on both "ends" of the journey. It may be that the
only way to escape this unpleasant fate is to stop thinking in linear terms.
Recent science fiction films have begun to play around with this idea that
the past may need the future as much as the future needs the past, that is,
that we are subject to what critics of science fiction have called a "time-
loop paradox." The premise of many of these "time-loop" stories is that
our interventions in the past are necessary to our continued existence, and
that the past itself is ongoing, never finished. This is, of course, Freud's
notion as well—through the inevitable mediation of language, we are constantly engaged in re-membering our own histories. Only the melancholic
has ceased to re-present the past to her- or himself, retreating into a silent
mourning for an object lost on the linear continuum of time. Some would
argue that only faith, the belief in transcendence, can restore speech—and
thus hope—to the melancholic subject. I would like to resist that sublimating turn away from materiality in suggesting another possibility—
namely that, if the past is never finished, then it is never lost.

# *Acknowledgments*

Like most books, this one has gone through several permutations, and there are people to thank at every stage. Linda Waugh first awakened my interest in semiotics and language, and Mary Jacobuş provided both inspiration and guidance in my early ventures into the related fields of psychoanalysis and feminist theory. Winthrop Wetherbee supported this project from its inception, offering valuable criticism and much-needed encouragement. Equally important, he respected this work, and its author, enough to disagree with both at times; my genesis as a scholar owes a good deal to his example and support. R. A. Shoaf has supported and encouraged young scholars in the field for many years; his interest in and engagement with my work in its various stages helped me to see that there was an audience for this kind of inquiry. I should like to say, also, that the importance of *Exemplaria* in sustaining and promoting debate and difference in the field of medieval studies cannot be understated; all of us who have attempted to bring theoretical considerations to bear on medieval texts owe a debt of gratitude to the editors of this significant and groundbreaking journal. Peter Travis offered insightful and generous comments on the manuscript in its nearly-final version; his suggestions helped me to see that there were issues at stake here which I hadn't considered, and which had to be addressed before the work could be considered finished. Other readers read and commented on individual chapters at specific points: Allen Frantzen took the time to offer detailed and extremely useful comments on Chapter Five, Linda Lomperis and Sarah Stanbury helped me to clarify Chapter Four as part of their anthology *Feminist Approaches to the Body in Medieval Literature* (University of Pennsylvania Press, 1993). Thomas Hahn was a helpful and affirming reader of Chapter Four in its early stages. J. P. Hermann's comments were invaluable in re-thinking Chapter Two prior to its appearance in *Exemplaria* several years ago. I would also like to thank two anonymous readers: the reader for *Exemplaria* who offered such rigorous commentary on the psychoanalytic material in my *Troilus* chapter, and the more curmudgeonly—but nonetheless helpful—reader of the essay on Chaucer's *Duchess*, which appeared in the Lomperis/Stanbury anthology. Needless to say I didn't always follow the paths these readers suggested, but quite often I did, and the book is better for it.

I am grateful to Alfred David for his support of my work and his invaluable friendship; I am extremely fortunate to have such a committed teacher and intellectually honest scholar as a friend and colleague. Jerry Singerman has been an insightful and patient editor; his enthusiasm for the project helped sustain my own. I would also like to acknowledge my debt to the innovative work of several medievalists with whom I engage, and occasionally disagree, in these pages. R. Howard Bloch, Carolyn Dinshaw, Louise Fradenburg, and Lee Patterson have had a significant, if indirect, role in the genesis and development of this project—I'm grateful to these and other scholars for the somewhat daunting precedent they have set in formulating new questions for the field as a whole. I'd also like to thank my good friend Bill Hughes; his emotional and financial support made my undergraduate education possible. I'm grateful to Linda David, for friendship and coffee breaks; to my family, for giving me a sense of humor that keeps me from taking myself too seriously; and to Atli and Frieda, for comic relief. I also thank Eva Valenta, for commiseration and "French that gets results," and Luke Bouvier, for priceless bibliographical assistance. Most of all, I thank John Tanke, who cheerfully read every word of this book more times than either of us would like to remember. Without his love, friendship, and good sense this book would never have been written.

Portions of Chapter 2 appeared in an earlier form in "Desiring Narrative: Ideology and the Semiotics of the Gaze in the Middle English *Juliana*," *Exemplaria* 2,2 (October 1990): 355–74. Copyright © 1990 by the Center for Medieval and Early Renaissance Studies, State University of New York at Binghamton. Permission to reprint this material is gratefully acknowledged.

# Introduction: The Psychic Life of the Past

This book has a dual agenda; it seeks to foreground the epistemological question of origins in rethinking the ethical and political basis of aesthetic judgments, and to interrogate some of the ideologies of "medievalism" from a feminist and psychoanalytic perspective. Since the field of medieval studies is to a great extent informed and determined by its vexed relationship to the concept of history-as-origin, these concerns are closely related. It is my contention that the problem of origins is, in medieval literature and criticism, linked to that of sexual difference: in texts as "qualitatively" different as the Middle English *Juliana* and Chaucer's *Troilus and Criseyde*, the fetishized body of woman comes to stand in for the divisions and losses whereby the historically-specific speaking subject is constituted. In short, sexual difference is installed as a defense against the potentially de-stabilizing effects of other, prior differences and divisions; for both medi-eval writers and their modern readers, historical difference is the most troubling and irreparable of these.

It is perhaps owing to the chronological structure of the literary ca-non that medieval literary studies is so troubled by the question of origins. As the beginning of nationalism and its vernacular literatures, the medieval period is the historical progenitor of western humanism. Medieval writ-ers are themselves not unaware of this burden; Chaucer, Dante, and the Gawain-poet are merely the most canonical exemplars of the medieval lit-erary obsession with history and the genesis of tradition. Chaucer in particular is conscious of the difficulty of building a vernacular poetic tra-dition on the fragmentary remains of classical precedent; his awareness of this dilemma is reflected in the persistence with which the problematics of beginning and ending, the issues of memory and translation return to dis-rupt his narratives.

Given the narcissistic dimension of the critical enterprise, it is not surprising that medievalists are similarly troubled by anxieties about origins. The volumes of source studies generated by medievalists since

the nineteenth century attest to the scholarly obsession with the philological, generic, exegetical, and archaeological beginnings of medieval literary texts. As is most often the case with obsessions, this one has been
characterized by a fetishistic investment in the object of study itself, and
a denial or negation of the loss that necessarily structures the modern
reader's relation to the past. In his *Preface to Chaucer*, D. W. Robertson
argues that we must protect the integrity and innocence of the past from
the potentially contaminating influence of the present:

> we must guard against the very natural tendency of critics to project modern
> "truths" concerning the nature of beauty and art on a past which was entirely
> innocent of these "truths."[1]

Robertson's acknowledgment of the essential otherness of the Middle
Ages is simultaneously undone by his implicit assertion that the difference
or gap between past and present can be methodologically bridged through
accurate contextualization. For Robertson, this confrontation between an
innocent past and a potentially corrupting present centers on the question
of aesthetics; here, as so often, aesthetic and historical concerns are shown
to be intimately related.[2]

More recently, neo-historicist critics such as Lee Patterson have re-
asserted the privilege of context in political terms. For Patterson, contextualization restores history as the "absent cause" of literary production;
the historicist critic figuratively gives a voice to the political struggles that
literature at once preserves and effaces.[3] Robertson understood the critical
act in terms of restoration or preservation of a theological and historical
"truth" that is untroubled by internal divisions or contradictions; for the
Christian historicist reader, the literary fantasy is merely a symptom of or
metaphor for the monolithic historical reality it conceals. Patterson's historicism is based on subtler and more provocative assumptions, assumptions that are nonetheless rooted in a dialectical framework that links
Marxist materialism to Christian dualism. A significant portion of this
study will be dedicated to an exploration of the conditions of dialectical
thinking, and to the ways in which sexual difference enables the negations
and annulments essential to dialectical synthesis and transcendence in both
secular and sacred historical configurations. I will ultimately suggest that
the opposition between secular and sacred history that grounds recent
historicist readings is finally untenable: dialectical thinking is itself theological thinking, insofar as both insist on the abjection/effacement of a
privatized and corporealized Other, she who becomes the guarantor of

patriarchal and collectivist fantasies about history and knowledge. My aim here is not to undermine the political aspirations of recent collectivist interventions, but rather to unveil some of the unacknowledged presuppositions that have informed the dialectical imperative.

Throughout this project, I argue that history as an epistemological category is inseparable from the problematics of representation, or, more specifically, from fantasy and figuration. In exploring this assumption, I rely heavily on psychoanalytic theory as the critical discourse that speaks most precisely to problems of memory, fantasy, and tropological substitution. This methodological foundation allows me to insert sexual difference into the dialectic of past and present, as a disruptive third term that breaks up the narcissistic mirroring of traditional criticism. My analysis of medieval texts is set against my readings of works by Sigmund Freud, Jacques Lacan, and Julia Kristeva, in an effort to explore the problematic but intimate relationship between sexual and originary fantasies.

Invariably, these readings return to the role of the mother within oedipal and preoedipal configurations. According to Freud, the oedipus complex brings with it the paternal interdict whereby the subject is denied access to the mother's body. The maternal body is always already lost to the subject, and thus becomes the focus of nostalgia; within psychoanalytic theory, the pathogenesis of both melancholia and hysteria is linked to this originary loss. The oedipal triangle always bears the troubling traces of the preoedipal dyad: an archaic state of plenitude and immediacy, an idyllic moment of union with the maternal object. This edenic fantasy is at the heart of all "golden age" mythologies. It is hardly surprising that the idea of a "first fall" from grace should derive from our own originary fall from the womb into the world, from plenitude into lack and desire.

If it is the realization of lack—the so-called castration complex—that initiates the oedipal drama and prescribes its patriarchal outcome, it is the mourning for the lost object relation that gives rise to figuration itself. For Freud, the spectral figure of the mother grounds fantasies based on substitution: both the fetishist and the implicitly male child of the *fort-da* scenario are reacting to the troubling psychic intersection of mother, loss, and lack.[4] Yearning for lost plenitude, the fetishist denies his knowledge of the mother's castration, while the artist/child of the *fort-da* game "masters" loss through representation.

In Lacan's re-reading of Freud, the lost object relation is metaphorically linked to the loss of the real, or the referential world, that is the necessary consequence of the entry into language and signification. The gap between signifier and signified is the index of our "fall" into language, or, in Freudian terms, our castration. For Lacan, this symbolic castration exceeds sexual difference even as it seems to install it. The difference between masculine and feminine is put in place by representation in an effort to affirm the metaphysical hierarchy of the signifier/signified relation, or, more precisely, to disavow the "incessant sliding of the signified under the signifier."[5] Because the perception of woman's anatomical lack only makes sense within a metaphysical system that privileges the order of the visual, the originary myth of castration covers over a loss prior to the installation of sexual difference, and prior to the scopophilic scenario: a division between the word and the thing, or between language and reference.

It is in the writings of Julia Kristeva that the conceptual relation between loss and representation is most precisely theorized. In particular, her work on abjection (*Powers of Horror*) and melancholia (*Black Sun*) uncovers what the works of Freud and Lacan merely imply: the sense in which figuration unfolds as a response to loss and privation, preserving traces of the lost object relation in its own moments of desiring excess. Her work foregrounds the intimate connection between bodies and signifying systems. Because corporeal pleasures must be controlled and ordered in specific ways in order to facilitate discourse, all representational systems encrypt a sublimated corporeality that can only be acknowledged in rare moments of poetic and mystical expression. The polymorphous pleasures of the preoedipal child, linked to the maternal body, are necessarily lost with the entry into language. This split between the maternal body and the subject can only partially be healed or covered over through language; when language fails absolutely to perform this reparative function, melancholic asymbolia ensues.

In uncovering the maternal function as the unstable component of the oedipal triangle, these theoretical texts juxtapose the "pathological" conditions of nostalgia and melancholia with the problematics of sexual difference, thus providing a methodological way into the troubling connections between loss, figuration, and fetishism in the medieval and critical texts I have chosen to discuss here. If there is a primary aim or fundamental logic to the project as a whole, it lies in my effort to elucidate the sense in which the problem of history is bound up with the problem of body, or, more precisely, the sense in which sexual difference as an effect of lack is made to stand in for historical difference as an effect of loss.

Implicit, and occasionally explicit, in this discussion is my reliance on the important work of feminist theorists of the past two decades. My essentially Lacanian re-reading of Freud's texts is indebted to the precedent, if not always the conclusions, of theorists such as Jane Gallop, Mary Jacobus, Juliet Mitchell, and Jacqueline Rose, as well as the feminist film theorists Mary Ann Doane, Laura Mulvey, and Kaja Silverman. These scholars have negotiated the once-treacherous impasse between feminism and psychoanalysis.[6] My efforts to bridge the similarly forbidding chasm between feminist/psychoanalytic theory and medieval studies are predicated upon their insights into the ways in which libidinal investments and power relations structure sexual identity within representation such that woman becomes the privileged site of desire and prohibition. Emphasizing the mediating function of fantasy and psychic drives in establishing the subject's relation to language and culture, feminist psychoanalytic theory acknowledges the unconscious as "something in excess" that confounds any positivist or essentialist notion of sexual identity.[7]

Psychoanalysis also has much to offer to our understanding of the ethical and epistemological questions of history. Well before he had elaborated his theory of the unconscious, Freud began to interrogate the referential status of memory and memorialization. In both *Project for a Scientific Psychology* and *Studies on Hysteria*, he suggested that the subject can "remember" events that never actually happened. Owing to what he calls *Nachträglichkeit* (which we may translate as "belatedness" or "deferred action"), psychic constructions can take on the status of significant memories.[8] These fantasmatic "memories" are the result of repetition, whereby an early event that was not traumatic at the time is reconfigured in relation to a later event that recalls it to the unconscious mind. Many years after its original occurrence, a relatively insignificant incident can belatedly be "remembered" as a highly traumatic event. As Freud puts it,

> Here we have the case of a memory arousing an affect which it did not arouse as an experience, because in the meantime the changes [brought about] by puberty had made possible a different understanding of what was remembered. . . . We invariably find that a memory is repressed which has only become a trauma by deferred action [*nachträglich*].[9]

In another early essay, Freud introduces the concept of "screen memories" as non-referential substitutes for repressed materials or fantasies that are withdrawn from consciousness. Screen memories are largely fabrications, bearing an "emotional value that does not properly belong to them, but rather to what they replace."[10] These concepts, together with the more elaborated theories of melancholia and identification, can, I think, provide the basis for a substantial rethinking of the relationships between history, politics, and knowledge both in and around the field of medieval studies, a rethinking that will compel us to acknowledge the historicity of history, or more precisely, the historical contingency of historicist reading and writing.

At the heart of this methodological contention is the notion of transference, figured in Lacanian theory as the mirror within which we misrecognize ourselves as autonomous and historically coherent subjects. The mirror stage creates the illusion of an historical and historicizing subject in a way that is nonetheless alien to the logic of chronology. There is no specific "time" when the mirror stage happens; it cannot be located on any linear continuum. Both anticipation and retroaction issue from it in ways that cannot be sorted out in temporal terms: both past and present are "produced" through this moment of stasis and self-delusion. What the mirror stage chiefly and most relentlessly produces is the concept of an origin, a moment of unity and plenitude that can only be recovered "historically," that is, by moving backward on the linear plane that the mirror has mapped out for us. As Jane Gallop has pointed out, the mirror stage constitutes the subject "through anticipating what it will become, and then this anticipation is used for gauging what was before."[11] This moment of illusory wholeness and autonomy only makes sense in terms of a previous fragmentation and dependency, which in turn look back to an originary state of presence and non-differentiation. Most important, the mirror produces an illusion that veils its own illusory nature; we are not re-presented through the mirror, because the mirror has generated the fantasy of a self that is outside it, that is exterior, objective—a subject who knows. In short, this historicizing speculum effaces the trace of its own historicity precisely by insisting on chronology, on the "truth" of the past and the inevitability of the future. It is the fantasy that produces what we have come to know as reality.

Our relation to history is always produced through the imaginary moment of transference, whereby we see the past in terms that actually have more to do with our investments in and anxieties about the present and future. Since its invention in the nineteenth century, medieval studies has reflected the nationalist aspirations, racial fantasies, and/or sexual anxieties of its practitioners.[12] Latter-day medievalists are no more exterior or objective than their predecessors: feminist, materialist, and Christian ideological assumptions structure our specular relation to the past in ways that are both conscious and unconscious. While most medievalists would admit to these conscious investments, few seem willing to acknowledge that the unconscious invariably intervenes in our own historicist interventions such that a purely empirical and "innocent" relation to the past becomes an ideological and methodological impossibility. Part of my aim in writing this book is to explore the ways in which unconscious assumptions about sexuality work to both sustain and subvert our ideologically-specific relation to medieval texts, as well as our notions of what it means to be a medievalist today.

This understanding of the unconscious as a psychic force that subverts historical and social determinations of sexual and political identity and meaning provides the basis for my admittedly unorthodox choice of primary materials. The first three chapters of this project submit to analysis several hitherto disregarded or undervalued medieval literary artifacts, all of which have been associated in traditional criticism with excess and transgression. My readings focus on the function of corporeality and figuration in each text, or, in the case of the lyrics, group of texts. Thus my reading of Margery Kempe's *Book* emphasizes Margery's "corporealizing" of figural language and her identification with maternal figures throughout her autobiography. In discussing the little-known *Life and Passion of Saint Juliana*, I am interested specifically in the ways in which voyeuristic and fetishistic textual strategies work to sustain as well as subvert the hagiographer's theological and ideological agenda. Similarly, my analysis of several of the secular Harley Lyrics uncovers the link between figural excess and feminine *jouissance*: for the Harley poet or poets, the instability of language is invariably allied with the mythic sexual excesses and instability of woman.

In all these texts, the problem of language and body allies itself conceptually with the problem of origins. Margery's alienation from writing as expressed in the proem to her *Book* literalizes what Lacan has identified as woman's "exclusion from the nature of things which is the nature of words." Her insistence on the *mater*iality or libidinal component of figural language can be understood as an effort to mitigate this exclusion by returning to the body as the irreducible origin of signification. This nostalgic fantasy is, of course, just that; nevertheless, it enables her to insert herself into a patriarchal and exclusionary theological narrative, and to overcome the paralyzing melancholia and asymbolia with which her story begins.

For the author of the *Juliana*, the hagiographic narrative provides the diegetic frame for yet another nostalgic fantasy, having to do with the ethnic and linguistic origins of the English language. The text's conspicuous exclusion of romance vocabulary and its reassertion of the alliterative compositional meter work to inscribe a nostalgic ideal of Englishness within a fantasy of Christian origins. As Juliana's body remains inviolate or "unwemmed," so the English language, cleansed of its Anglo-Norman "supplements," would seem to retain an implicitly pre-conquest integrity that the courtly heathen, Eleusius, is unable to subvert. The female saint's body is the central object over and through which this drama of power and resistance is played out. If her virginity bespeaks a longing for lost wholeness and plenitude at the ethnographic level of the text, however, the violent fragmentation and dismemberment of her body (*lich*) ensures her typological relation (*lichnesse*) to Christ, and her place in sacred history.

My decision to include the Harley lyrics in this analysis derived initially from my assumption that the move from body to metaphor that the hagiographic text dramatizes so well is endemic to the lyric, and particularly to the love-lyric, wherein figural language circulates around an empty center, the place of the idealized and always-absent lady. Within the canonical lyric, the feminine body becomes the excuse for the fetishistic substitutions that ensure the lyric poet's place in the patriarchal continuum of poetic tradition, just as in the hagiographic genre the abjection of the feminine or feminized body attests to the triumph of *logos* over temporality, of the Word over the Flesh. Religious metanoia or conversion, as the ideological focus of the hagiographic text, is thus linked to turning or troping of a more explicitly discursive kind; both conversions represent a turn from figure to figure of speech—from *lich* to *lichnesse*.

In light of these generic assumptions, I decided to turn my attention to a set of lyrical texts which critics have deemed "least likely to succeed" in a bid for canonical status: the Harleian love-lyrics. Condemned for being unsophisticated, excessive, and even "riotous" in their transgression of courtly convention and manipulation of figural language in general, the Harley texts would seem to expose or unveil what remains repressed and uncanny in canonical courtly lyrics: the prurience and violence that underpins the discursive conventions of medieval romance, and the sense in which courtly idealization is sustained by what Kristeva has called the "erotic cult of the abject."[13]

What is most troubling about poems such as "Annot and John" and "The Fair Maid of Ribbesdale" is their inability or refusal to annul dialectically or sublimate the feminine body behind the trope: the pleasure in the signifier is inextricable from a voyeuristic pleasure in the body itself. Rhetorical excess is made synonymous with feminine *jouissance*; femininity is revealed to be the symptomatic condition upon which the semiotic system of courtly romance is constituted. Structured as lacking, woman stands in for what Lacan has identified as the *pas tout* of any system of representation: the idea, as Jacqueline Rose puts it,

> that there is no such system, however elaborated or elevated it may be, in which there is not some point of impossibility, its other face which it endlessly seeks to refuse—what could be called the vanishing point of its attempt to construct itself as a system. [14]

Because the Harleian texts are explicitly parodic, conscious of their generic context and its assumptions, they expose the "points of impossibility" in the courtly system, the points at which the cultural and discursive cohesiveness of romance ideology yields to the dispersing and fragmenting impulses of the libidinal drives that sustain it; the point, in short, at which woman as idealized object is shown to be, simultaneously and unparadoxically, a despised and feared abject.

Here, too, femininity is symptomatic of the courtly system's vexed relation to the question of origins. To the extent that the feminine body is installed in representation as a defense against the excesses and "points of impossibility" that subvert conventional systematization, it/she also points toward the ineluctable yet unapprehensible materiality of signification: the libidinal drives that threaten socially and aesthetically sanctioned paradigms, even as they sustain them. The playful transgressiveness of the Harleian poems, their insistence on the intimate connection between word play and sex play, foreground the psychic ambivalence at the heart of courtly ideology. Within the courtly lyric, longing for the lost object relation always carries with it a repudiation of the abject as the symptom of the object's failure to ensure the integrity of the discursive system that "speaks" the subject-as-poet.

There is another aspect of the Harley poems I discuss that makes them an appropriate "borderline" between the extracanonical and canonical portions of my study. Many of them are staged explicitly as an exchange between the male poet and another man. In several of the lyrics, the reader/hearer is asked to join the poet in a moment of specular pleasure, as the woman's body is exposed, piece by piece, to the desiring look of the poet and the "third party" to whom the poem is addressed. In his essay "Jokes and Their Relation to the Unconscious," Freud suggests that, in the obscene or "exposing" joke (*entblößender Witz*), woman is merely the excuse for an erotically charged exchange between men; these jokes are, predictably, most effective when the woman is *not* present.[15] This Freudian paradigm has much to offer to our understanding of these parodic and voyeuristic love lyrics. In light of Freud's essay, the specifically rhetorical pleasure generated by this sort of scopophilic exchange can be conceptually linked to what Eve Sedgwick has identified as the "male homosocial desire" that sustains patriarchy.[16] The "riotous" lyric, like the dirty joke and, for that matter, the prurient hagiographical text, exposes the female body to the male look. In so doing, however, it also reveals something of the homoerotic subtext of a patrilineal and patriarchal literary system that is parasitically dependent on a rhetorical "traffic in women."[17]

As I stated at the outset, one of the goals of this study is to bring marginal or extracanonical texts to bear upon a feminist analysis of canonical ones. There are several assumptions behind this endeavor. Psychoanalytic theory after Lacan has claimed that the unconscious represents a challenge to the dualist metaphysics and hierarchical epistemological structures of Western culture. As the locus of undecidability and plurality, of something in excess of "pure reason," the unconscious preserves that which ideology and morality would have us repress. Perhaps most disconcerting and subversive from a dualist and empiricist point of view is the ability of the unconscious to transgress the boundary between the body and the word, or between self and other: hysterics, paranoiacs, and melancholics all share an inability to maintain culturally imposed distinctions between inside and outside.

This inability or failure to maintain binary oppositions is also characteristic of the marginal texts I have chosen to explore here. Both Margery Kempe's *Book* and the Middle English *Juliana* ultimately fail to uphold the dualist metaphysical assumptions mandated by Christian ideology, while the Harley poems I examine remain essentially trapped in their own moments of specular desire, unable to attain the *Aufhebung*— or sublimation of ma(t)ter—that lyric generically promises. It is my contention that extracanonical texts are in many cases the "unconscious" of canonical ones, and that through their excesses and transgressions of conventional registers and hierarchies, we may read more clearly what has remained "uncanny" in works that traditional criticism has deemed great.

As a work of feminist criticism, then, this study sees the project of "reading from the margins" in somewhat broader terms. If feminist analysis assumes a commitment to reading the marginalized other within representation, it seems not only logical, but politically necessary, to extend this confrontation between literature and the other into the larger realm of aesthetic theory, such that it might encompass not only questions of gender per se, but also larger epistemological dilemmas of which sexual difference is often only a textual symptom. In juxtaposing the problem of sexual difference with that of aesthetic judgment, this project seeks to explore the points of intersection between sexual and aesthetic marginality, and, in so doing, to suggest some ways in which feminist theory might contribute to a rethinking of the canon of medieval texts, as well as the function of gender in those texts.[18]

My focus on the issue of canonicity also represents an attempt to move beyond the qualitative judgment, even apologism, that has often colored the traditional medievalist's relation to her or his object of study. Although many volumes have been written on Chaucer, Langland, and the Gawain/Pearl-poet, the much larger corpus of metrical romances, mystical treatises, and hagiographical texts has thus far failed to inspire many innovative critical studies. For the most part, these "lesser" texts have been condemned for their poverty of invention and/or lack of sophistication and subtlety; the limited scholarly attention they have received has focused exclusively on philological or linguistic problems. Moreover, this attitude has not been confined to scholarly journals: it has also been institutionalized as a pedagogical position. These "other" texts are the wayward children of the field, the ones who didn't turn out as well as one had hoped. Consequently, they are seldom studied, even at the graduate level. As students we were given to understand that, however interesting they may be as historical documents or linguistic records, hagiographical or mystical texts are not truly "literary," not "good" poetry or prose. Questions about the intellectual and aesthetic basis of these judgments seem always to elicit phrases like "universal human significance" and "timeless truth": *The Life and Passion of St. Juliana*, after all, cannot be compared with the *Canterbury Tales* or the *Troilus*.

Since the advent and currency of post-structuralist theory, the critical community has been made aware of the extent to which canonicity as a value judgment depends on canonical readings, readings that work to suppress those aspects of a given literary artifact which do not affirm closure, transcendence and univocity. An emphasis on meaning as such has shifted to an emphasis on the conditions of meaning: the philosophical and aesthetic assumptions that subtend the notion of literary greatness. For feminist theorists, this new emphasis continues to point the way to an understanding of the place of the feminine and the marginal within normative aesthetics as disseminated by academic institutions and their members. "Universality" and "timelessness" are not sexually neutral concepts. On the contrary, they are axiological terms that carry with them the sexual and political hierarchies of a patriarchal and phallocentric cultural order.[19]

It is with this emphasis in mind that I have staged this "confrontation" between much-studied Middle English texts and those deemed to be somehow insufficient or unimportant. My aim is not to denigrate Chaucer, whose work has given me more pleasure and insights over the years than that of any other poet, nor is it to argue for the "comparable worth" of Margery's *Book*, the *Juliana*, and the Harley Lyrics, although I find these texts fascinating in their own right. Instead, I see these marginal texts as a means of inserting a degree of oppositionality into the poetry of Chaucer and the Gawain-poet, of uncovering the gaps and resistances to canonical reading within an inarguably canonical text such as the *Troilus*.

In short, I would like to explore the conditions of possibility for reading "extracanonically," to read the moments of desiring excess and points of impossibility within texts that traditional literary history has taught us to esteem. Using these marginal works as a model for this kind of reading, I am operating from the assumption that medieval literature, as such, still has a lot to teach us about medieval literature. I am also arguing that redefining the canon cannot be limited to changing its content; we must simultaneously interrogate the structures that produce canonical systems and sustain their exclusionary strategies. The fact that the Norton Anthology editors were moved to include Margery Kempe as well as Chaucer and the Gawain-poet was significant, but not sufficient. Unless we find a way of making these texts speak to one another, canonical revision will be, like school integration, only a partial success.[20]

That this study can only be the beginning of such an endeavor is clear. Conscious of these limitations, I have confined the second half of the project to an analysis of three Middle English poems: *The Book of the Duchess, Troilus and Criseyde*, and *Sir Gawain and the Green Knight*. In a sense, these poems represent the canonical poet's investigation of the problems of canonicity; all three speak to and of the issue of poetic inheritance, the epistemological dilemma of origins, and the role of sexual difference in resolving or giving closure to these literary problems. In Chapter Four, I read *The Book of the Duchess* as a narrative about the loss of the real, the foreclosure of the world of objects, wherein poetic speaking originates. By identifying woman (the lost Lady White) with the lost real, the poet is able to displace the origins of his discourse from the realm of ma(t)ter to that of the father: from the world of objects to that of "olde stories." In *Troilus and Criseyde*, the lost real becomes identified with the lost classical tradition of the Trojan Saga. I argue that Criseyde inherits the place of Lady White, insofar as she comes to stand in for the poet's anxieties about literary history. The classical tradition, represented in the poem by the figure of Hector, is set against medieval romance conventions throughout the text. Criseyde's body becomes the object of exchange in a poem self-conscious of the traffic in women that sustains romance narrative. Through Criseyde, Chaucer the historiographer confronts Chaucer the romancer: her duplicity metaphorically reflects the generic "doubleness" of the work itself.

In both these poems, women occupy a space similar to that of the absent love-object in the Harleian lyrics. That is to say, both Lady White and Criseyde provide implicit sanction for the homosocial bonding that grounds and sustains the patrilineal system of textual production and inheritance. *The Book of the Duchess*, like the *Troilus*, is in some sense the story of generative collaborations between men: the narrator of the *Duchess* and the rhetorically masterful Black Knight prefigure Troilus and Pandarus as diegetic models—albeit ironic ones—for other, metadiscursive collaborations between Chaucer and his classical or continental forebears. Chaucer the poet is conscious, it seems to me, of the role of sexual difference in justifying and sustaining these collaborations; Lady White and Criseyde will have their Chaucerian successors in Emelye and the Miller's Alisoun, women who are explicitly installed as fetishized objects of exchange within the libidinal economies of romance and fabliau, respectively.

I have included *Sir Gawain* because it foregrounds many of the same issues as Chaucer's *Troilus*, but with a difference. Like the *Troilus, Sir Gawain* stages an implicit confrontation between the linear/historical assumptions of epic and the digressive pleasures of romance, a confrontation that speaks to and of the role of sexual difference in sustaining the patriarchal and patrilineal agenda of both genres. I argue that *Sir Gawain* encodes a reading of Virgil's *Aeneid*, a reading that emphasizes the feminine and maternal threat to the paternalization of origins. Gawain's ability to rhetorically master the feminine Other is specifically linked to the threat of castration and privatization; his digressive "dalliance," like Aeneas's, endangers the patrilineal/patriarchal culture he represents. Once again, discursive excess, the inability of signs to *refer* to any extrasemiotic reality, is allied with the notion of feminine corporeal excess; women are therefore "blamed" for Gawain's failure and, by implication, for the signifying excesses of both the pentangle and the Court's reputation. My reading focuses finally on the disturbing and belated insertion of "Morgne þe goddes" as a moment of epistemological undecidability, a rupture in the ideological and axiological system of the medieval narrative. This seemingly "gratuitous" return to the feminine/maternal origin of both sin and signification constitutes an open-ended challenge to the aristocratic and paternalist assumptions of both the medieval romance and its epic/historical context. Both marginal and central, placed at the end but responsible for the beginning of the poem-as-game, Morgan prefigures Margery Kempe in challenging the metaphysical and ideological basis of canonical reading. To the extent that it restores the connection between the feminine body and the origin, then, *Sir Gawain* allows for the possibility of a reconceptualization of the problematic of beginnings, and perhaps a rethinking of the epic/paternalist fantasy of history.

In tracing the connections between originary and sexual fantasies in these medieval works, this project asks finally that we interrogate further the epistemological barrier between ontogeny and phylogeny, a barrier that recent historicist work seems at pains to reinforce. Drawing on those Freudian essays that seem to call the boundary between cultural and psychic life into question, I argue that these medieval texts problematize the relation between public and private, or historical and psychic, in ways that literary criticism has thus far failed to take into account. In the 1970s, feminists took a stand against this exclusionary binarism by contending that "the personal is political." My own feminist literary analysis acknowledges its debt to this earlier transgressive assertion in asking that we consider the ways in which psychic life intrudes, unbidden, into public life. Historicity is always, in some sense, rooted in psychic fantasy; the *Troilus* testifies to the difficulty with which the boundary between public and private is sustained.

In an effort to address this issue in both medieval and contemporary critical texts, I preface my reading of the *Troilus* with a reading of some of the most recent and provocative historicist work in the field. My analysis focuses on the sense in which sexual difference works to sustain the barrier between public and private in the medieval poem as well as in recent literary-historicist writing. Ultimately, I suggest not that we abandon the question of history, but rather that we acknowledge, as Chaucer seems to, the ethical and political implications of historicity as a discursive position. Only then, it seems to me, can we avoid losing sight of the future in our pursuit of the past.

# 1. Margery Kempe and the Pathology of Writing

Like many works of literary criticism, this one begins with a fantasy of identification. In choosing to begin this project with a chapter on Margery Kempe's *Book*, I am conscious of the sense in which my narrative (mis)-recognizes itself in hers. For a feminist reader of the Middle Ages, this imaginary relation to the *Book of Margery Kempe* is perhaps inevitable. Margery's attempt to inscribe her own story into the patriarchal narrative of sacred history seems to prefigure the situation of the feminist medieval-ist, who must continually negotiate her/his way through the predomi-nantly conservative and masculinist field of medieval studies.

Given this parallel, it is perhaps not surprising that feminist work in the field has taken its cue from Margery's *Book* in several respects: most notably, in reading Christian theology with an emphasis on the feminine and the maternal. Works such as Caroline Bynum's *Jesus as Mother*, pub-lished as recently as 1982,[1] provided what I take to be the first paradigm for a feminist re-reading of the Middle Ages. Focusing on feminine im-agery in the writings of medieval mystics and holy women, Bynum's book, like Margery's, turns the traditional understanding of medieval theology "up-so-down" by uncovering a maternal metalanguage outside the hege-monic and paternalist discourses of the institutional Church. For Margery as for the feminist reader, this inversion or reversal of gender hierarchies at the tropological level opens up a space within Christian ideology, a space within which the female authorial voice can potentially be heard.

In the pages that follow, I will be discussing this authorial strategy of inversion in more detail. Ultimately, I will argue that although Margery Kempe essentially "pioneered" this feminist answer to the phallocentrism of Christian theology, her *Book* strains the limits of Christian historicist reading, in that it challenges the very conditions of meaning within the Christian signifying system. Margery's autobiography transgresses the theo-logical boundary between the Word and the Flesh, as well as the episte-mological barrier between textual fantasy and historical reality. It is thus

an appropriate place from which to begin a critical narrative that seeks—
among other things—to interrogate the binarist thinking that sustains the
literary canon, and continues to separate "literature" from "history."

In the *Book of Margery Kempe*, as in any autobiography, the question
of history is implicit. The autobiographical text foregrounds the difficulty
of reconstructing the past, and the problematics of origins per se: the beginning of a textualized life is always an aesthetic decision. For Margery
Kempe, the dilemma of memory and the indeterminacy of origins constitute real obstacles to the autobiographical project. Her illiteracy and
consequent reliance on scribal mediation[2] alienate her from the writing
process, and from her own reminiscences. The proem to her *Book* seems
to echo Chaucer's own vexed relation to the problem of beginnings in its
emphasis on the mediation of tropes and the condensations and displacements of memory:

> Thys boke is not wretyn in ordyr, every thyng aftyr oþer as it wer don, but
> lych as þe mater cam to þe creatur in mend whan it schuld be wretyn, for it
> was so long er it was wretyn þat sche had for-getyn þe tyme & þe ordyr
> whan thyngys befellen. (5)[3]

> (This book is not written in order, every thing after another as it was done,
> but just as the matter came to the creature's mind when it was to be written
> (down), for it was so long before it was written that she had forgotten the
> time and the order when things occurred.)

For Margery as for Chaucer (as we shall see in later chapters), the
genesis of narrative is inseparable from an originary forgetting of "þe tyme
& þe ordyr whan thyngys befellen." Autobiography mirrors fiction in
engendering a series of figural substitutions that re-member the gap left
by an inaugural loss—the loss of memory as the only link to the historical real.

In fact, the proem to the *Book* envisions the autobiographical project
specifically in terms of recuperation. Margery's difficulty in finding a scribe
is compounded by the fact that her first amanuensis dies before the project
is completed, leaving her with a text that is neither "good Englysch ne
Dewch." The continuity of the project comes to depend on a restoration
of the mother-tongue, from which writing has alienated her:

> Than had þe creatur no wryter þat wold fulfyllyn hyr desyr ne ʒeue credens
> to hir felingys vn-to þe tym þat a man dwellyng in Dewchlond whech was
> an Englyschman in hys byrth & sythen weddyd in Dewchlond & had þer
> boþe a wyf & a chyld, hauyng good knowlach of þis creatur & of hir desyr,

meued I trost thorw þe Holy Gost, cam in-to Yngland wyth hys wyfe & hys goodys & dwellyd wyth þe forseyd creatur tyl he had wretyn as much as sche wold tellyn hym for þe tyme þat þei wer to gydder. And sythen he deyd. Than was þer a prest whech þis creatur had gret affeccyon to, & so sche comownd wyth hym of þis mater & browt hym þe boke to redyn. Þe booke was so euel wretyn þat he cowd lytyl skyll þeron, for it was neiþer good Englysch ne Dewch, ne þe lettyr was not schapyn ne formyd as oþer letters ben. Þerfor þe prest leued fully þer schuld neuyr man redyn it, but it wer special grace. (4)

(Then the creature had no writer who would fulfill her desire, nor give credence to her feelings, until the time that a man living in Germany—who was an Englishman by birth, and afterwards married in Germany and had there both a wife and a child—having good knowledge of this creature and of her desire, moved, I trust, through the Holy Ghost, came to England with his wife and his goods, and lived with the said creature until he had written as much as she would tell him during the time that they were together. And afterwards he died. Then there was a priest for whom this creature had great affection, and so she talked with him about this matter and brought him the book to read. The book was so poorly written that he could make little sense of it, for it was neither good English nor German, nor were the letters shaped or formed as other letters are. Therefore the priest fully believed that no one would ever be able to read it, unless it were by special grace.)

The original text, neither one language nor another, is suspended on a borderline where reading is no longer possible. The project of writing the past becomes bound up with problems of reading and translation as Margery's efforts to re-member her story are mediated and "defferyd" at every turn. The rhetorical struggles of the proem prefigure the spiritual struggles of the *Book* itself: the necessity for linguistic mediation undermines Margery's rhetorical authority before her story begins, just as social and ecclesiastical mediators will continually undermine her mystical vocation within the diegesis proper.

The proem to the *Book* problematizes the relation between language and reference to such an extent that it asks to be read allegorically. Margery's narrative, like the sacred scripture it wishes to emulate, begins with a "fall" from immediacy and plenitude into alienation and difference. The author's dependence on scribal mediation literalizes the alienation from experience that is the condition of autobiographical writing: the *Book of Margery Kempe*, like the biblical text, begins as a story of loss.

Not surprisingly, the remainder of the *Book* is structured as a movement toward re-appropriation and re-integration. In attempting to recover the feminine and corporeal within an alien system of signification, Margery's text unveils the nostalgic subtext of Christian theology, the maternal and libidinal component of Christian discourse that sustains and occasion-ally subverts patriarchal law.[4] That this nostalgia presents itself as autobio-graphical reminiscence rather than, say, lyrical effusion, has contributed to the controversy that still surrounds the *Book*. Autobiography by its very nature effaces the boundary between body and spirit and subverts the epis-temological distinction between history and aesthetics.[5] Lyric, on the other hand, sublimates its nostalgic yearnings in metaphor, placing libidi-nal or corporeal signifying traces in the service of a transcendent univocity, an "artifice of eternity." Canonical mystical writings are thus those that rely most consistently on lyrical or metaphoric expression; needless to say, Margery's un-lyrical *Book* is seldom included among these.[6]

In the remainder of this chapter, I will be exploring the *Book*'s subver-sion of tropological and gender hierarchies, as well as its troubled relation to the theological system it inscribes. We will see that, in Margery's text, the body is always implicated in the genesis of the Word, and the world of ma(t)ter continually invades the paternal realm of the spirit. The *Book*'s peculiar insistence that corporeality is ultimately redemptive asks that we reassess the ethical assumptions that have hitherto structured our acts of reading and interpretation. Given the text's power to subvert traditional paradigms, it is no wonder that many medievalists, trained not only in the referential value of history, but also in the hermeneutic authority of Chris-tian doctrine, have had such a difficult time coming to terms with the work, resorting time and again to diagnosis rather than interpretation.

My own reading will interrogate the assumptions that have continued to pathologize Margery's text, focusing on the relationship between writ-ing and pathology both in and around the *Book*. Ultimately, I will follow Margery's example, working, as she puts it, "up-so-down" in allowing the *Book* to read its readers. It is my hope that this strategy of inversion will open up some new possibilities for feminist reading in the field, as well as contributing something of value to current debates centering on the re-lated questions of canonicity and sexual difference.

## The Pathologized Text

Prior to 1934, when Hope Allen first identified the Butler-Bowden MS as the lost *Book of Margery Kempe*, Margery was known only through the excerpts of her *Book* published by Wynkyn de Worde in 1501. The selections were re-issued in 1521 by Henry Pepwell, and again by Edmund Gardener

in 1910. The passages were obviously chosen for their conventional mystical sentiments, and can best be described as inoffensive. The pre-1934
Margery belongs to the contemplative tradition of Julian of Norwich;
Pepwell's edition even adds the word "ancress" after Margery's name. It is
one of history's ironies that the wish/curse uttered by a disapproving old
monk in Chapter 13 of the *Book* became a reality. Upon hearing that Margery "wyl boþe speke . . . & heryn of [God]," the monk reproves her: "I
wold þow wer closyd in an hows of ston þat þer schuld no man speke
wyth þe" (27). His wish proved prophetic. For five centuries, the bois-
terous and garrulous Margery was relegated to the status of "devoute
ancresse."

When she finally came out of the cell to which history had confined
her, Margery was greeted with the sort of offended superiority that might
attend the sudden appearance of a long-lost relative who has very bad
manners and needs a bath. In short, the excitement over the discovery of
a lost medieval text turned quickly to shock and hostility. As a result, little
has been made of the *Book* as autobiography; instead, the text itself has
been eclipsed by the personality, or rather the perceived pathology, of its
author. Although she was later to revise her initial assessment, Hope Allen
could not avoid concluding that Margery was "petty, neurotic, vain, illit-
erate, physically and nervously over-strained."[7] Father Herbert Thurston,
who wrote several reviews of the Butler-Bowden translation for the Catho-
lic periodicals *The Month* and *The Tablet*, repeatedly noted what he called
Margery's "terrible hysteria," a pathology "revealed in nearly every page
of the narrative portions of the *Book*."[8] His opinions are later echoed by
David Knowles, who compares Margery unfavorably with Julian of Norwich, noting the "large hysterical element in her personality,"[9] and by
Wolfgang Riehle, who deems her "pathologically neurotic."[10]

More recently, the *Book* has passed into the hands of critics whose
readings reflect some sort of feminist orientation. Maureen Fries's reaction
is fairly typical of the liberal feminist readings of the text: she lays many of
Margery's woes at the door of "male-dominated society," and laments the
fact that "women mystics were second-rate in religious experience as in
everything else."[11] Hope Weissman offers a "typological and psychohis-
torical" reading of the *Book*. She observes that Margery's story bears significant resemblance to "the case histories of hysterical women analyzed
by Freud in his early career," but sees this hysteria as "also symptomatic of
repressive social and sexual attitudes, and of rigidly defined sex roles."[12]
More recently still, Sarah Beckwith has attempted to approach the *Book*

from the standpoint of Marxist and psychoanalytic theory. Her fascinating and influential analysis of mysticism as an ideologically-contained phenomenon proposes Margery's text as a particularly striking example of the sense in which women's mystical writings succeed in changing "the terms but never the structure." She concludes with a socialist call-to-arms, urging feminists to interrogate "the structures of power, the boundaries and definitions that enforce marginality onto women."[13]

We can discern a pattern in these responses. For the most part, the earliest reactions to the *Book* were negative. For reasons we will explore presently, Margery's autobiography was initially seen as a symptom of her neurosis, a "sick" text that reflects the pathology of its subject/author. The feminist readers cited above return, in a sense, to the view of the *Book*'s early audience, in that they acknowledge the fact of Margery's pathology; they differ from the early reviewers only in that they insist on a recognition of the socio-political causes of her "illness," what Weissman calls the "social and sexual repression in the late medieval world."[14]

Strangely enough, both the early reviewers of the *Book* and the feminists who have lately claimed it for their own have reduced the text to a mere symptom, a manifestation either of Margery's hysteria, or of the pathologically misogynistic culture which the text inscribes. There are several reasons for this paradoxical alliance. Liberal feminism, rooted in an empiricist intellectual tradition, has traditionally privileged "women's experience," often effacing the production of the text in its assertion of a continuity between life and literature. As Mary Jacobus has pointed out, it is a view that asserts a mimetic relation between women's writing and the (ultimately knowable) social/historical reality within which it takes place.[15] In the case of Margery's *Book*, it is the reality of medieval misogyny that is laid bare. In this positivist scheme, Margery herself becomes the quintessential feminine subject, the essence of female culture in opposition to the hegemonic forces that would suppress and deny it. The text, then, is little more than a record of feminine trauma, a symptom of a larger historical and cultural malaise.

Not all responses to the *Book* have been negative, however. A third approach, which I will call "historicist," has attempted to redeem the *Book* on religious and historical grounds. Since the appearance of Caroline Bynum's influential study, *Holy Feast and Holy Fast*, this Christian historicism has become the dominant academic discourse in the field of women's spirituality; as such, it warrants closer examination. In its early manifestations, the historicist approach to the *Book* looks more like apologism; many of the readers in this "second wave" see themselves as Margery's defenders, even champions. In one of the earliest book-length studies, Katharine Cholmeley commends Margery's "exactness of memory and intensity of feeling."[16] Eric Colledge emphasizes her virtues while downplaying her "suggestibility"; he offers possible sources for some of her mystical experiences in an attempt to place her within the tradition of late medieval mysticism.[17] E.I Watkin claims that Margery's sincerity eclipses that suggestibility, which he calls "morbid"; he, too, sees the spiritual validity of Margery's experience as the central critical issue of her *Book*.[18]

This perspective was revived during the last decade, which saw a renewed interest in women mystics in general, and Margery in particular. In her book *Mystic and Pilgrim: The Book and the World of Margery Kempe*, Clarissa Atkinson places Margery within the tradition of affective piety as revealed in the words and deeds of women mystics such as Catherine of Siena and Dorothea of Montau.[19] Atkinson acknowleges that modern definitions of hysteria may be "helpful in the interpretation of Margery Kempe," but cautions that "modern judgments about 'normal' and healthy sexuality are not applicable to medieval Christians, whose values, socialization, and world view were so unlike our own."[20] Caroline Bynum, who includes Margery in her study of food practices and body image in the lives of women saints and mystics, also takes pains to de-pathologize women's spirituality. She also sees the resolution of this dilemma in accurate contextualization:

> Those who have felt it necessary to defend the past (always a risky undertaking) have . . . had either to take the offensive and blame institutions or individuals who "oppressed" women or to ignore the full range and extremism of the self-torturing behavior and concentrate on other aspects of women's spirituality. But when we place even the most extravagant fasting and self-mutilation in its medieval context it is not clear that such behavior was rooted either in self-hatred or in dualism.[21]

According to Bynum, diligent scholarship can strip away the veils of modern prejudice that insists that self-mutilation and starvation are pathological behaviors; by amassing enough empirical evidence, one can accurately re-construct the "medieval context" that will recuperate these strange behaviors for a canonical history. Her book also makes clear, however, that empiricism can only de-pathologize these phenomena by yielding final and transcendent authority to Christian doctrine:

> The notion of substituting one's own suffering through illness and starvation for the guilt and destitution of others is not "symptom"—it is theology.[22]

In fact it is theology that gives transcendent closure to the vast amount of archival evidence Bynum advances; the self-imposed suffering of women mystics ultimately works to affirm "the humanity of God."[23] In this way, her study elicits and finally contains the disturbing phenomenon of religious masochism within theological, and thus institutional, boundaries.

It is not my intention to undermine the value of either of these studies. Atkinson's book was the first detailed and scholarly work on Margery's *Book* to emerge since its re-discovery, and Bynum's *Holy Feast* is a fascinating study that has already inspired a good deal of important work on the subject. At the same time, I think that the nervousness with which both authors approach the issue of pathology is telling; clearly there is more at stake here than either is willing to admit. If Margery's weeping fits are motivated by hysteria rather than piety, if the self-starvation of medieval holy women is anorexia and not, as Bynum would have it, an effort to "realize all the possibilities of the flesh,"[24] then the entire phenomenon has no place in canonical history except as a collective madness that most frequently afflicted women. To admit that these ascetic practices constituted a pathological aberration to the linear movement of historical "progress" is very nearly an admission that the medieval period was itself "sick," and that we who are medievalists partake of its pathology.

If, on the other hand, these phenomena "are theology," then they affirm the traditional understanding of literary history, which locates the origins of Western vernacular literature in Christian doctrine. Christian theology, which affirms the immaterial Father as origin as against the corporeal mother, provides divine sanction for political as well as literary systems based on patriarchy. To invoke theology as a means of hermeneutic closure is thus to maintain the pure presence and absolute exteriority of the Middle Ages as the origin of the patrilineal system of descent upon which the literary canon is founded. The medievalist becomes a sacerdotal mediator between a purely supplementary present and the thousand-year "originary moment" of vernacular literature. In such a system, medieval history must retain a referential value, or risk confronting the epistemological dilemma of origin; in giving up the ideological investment in reference, the historian of mysticism is forced to come to terms with the potentially pathological issues of nostalgia and loss.

Christian historicism thus fulfills a precise ideological function for medievalists, as for the institution of criticism in general: it allows both reader and "context" to remain exterior to the work in question, while simultaneously enclosing the entire discussion within a theological system that seems to be irreducible. It is also very problematic from a feminist perspective. Studies such as Atkinson's and Bynum's work to sanctify, or at least valorize, marginal historical figures such a women mystics by inscribing them into the androcentric narrative of canonical history. As representatives of "true" as opposed to "institutional" Christianity, however, women mystics can only naturalize the paternal mystery which is the theological justification for patriarchy. Mystical or feminine *jouissance*, as Jacques Lacan has asserted, has ever been man's connection to "the good old God of all times."[25] Following Lacan, I would argue that historicist readings of feminine piety which do not question the conditions of meaning within the Christian signifying system ultimately work to contain the phenomenon within repressive epistemological boundaries.

This is precisely the point at which Karma Lochrie's recent book, *Margery Kempe and Translations of the Flesh*, seeks to intervene. Influenced to some extent by the work of Hélène Cixous, Lochrie argues that

> the woman writer potentially occupies the site of rupture, where excess and unbridled affections threaten the masculine idea of the integrity of the body. . . . Kempe brings this fissure into language—into the text—thereby destabilizing it and at the same time offering a place for access to the sacred. The textual fissure which mirrors the psychic one occurs between written and oral texts in Kempe's narrative. (6)

Lochrie's analysis reflects some of the assumptions of *écriture féminine*, whereby the notions of fragmentation, excess, and transgression that adhere to the category of "the feminine" within the symbolic order carry with them the potential for subversion and disruption. In affirming Margery's "rupture" of the misogynist religious culture within which her *Book* must necessarily be inscribed, Lochrie gestures toward a restructuring of the aesthetic and epistemological assumptions that have hitherto informed both literary and historical assessments of the text and its author. Although Lochrie does not engage with the issue of pathology per se, the characteristics she celebrates are precisely those that led earlier readers to "diagnose" and disparage the *Book*: Margery's excess of affect, her continual efforts to authorize or legitimate her mystical experiences, and her corporealization of spiritual matters.

Nevertheless, Lochrie herself seems occasionally uncomfortable with the subversive role she has ordained for the *Book*. Her discussion of Margery's transgressive excesses explicitly privileges speech over writing, and in so doing seeks to move the text beyond the semiotic realm and—by

implication—beyond history. This reading exists side by side with an effort to place the *Book* within a cultural context; drawing on the work of
Bynum, Atkinson, and her own impressive knowledge of theology and
exegesis, Lochrie creates a textual landscape for the *Book* that contradicts
her repeated assertions that the mystic's text "does not rely on either textual or institutional authorization of its statements," that in fact "the mystical text severs itself from the institutional discourses which are grounded
in textual authority."[26] For Lochrie, Margery is at once beyond the reach
of written culture and dependent upon textual paradigms. In a sense, her
book mirrors Margery's own, in that it encodes a desire to affirm the subversiveness of the mystical moment as well as a desire to contextualize
mystical excesses within a cultural context that cannot truly be separated
from institutional and hegemonic imperatives. Moreover, in asserting a
privileged relation between mystical utterance and theological truth, Lochrie effectively reasserts the metaphysical hierarchies that legislate not only
the irreducible difference between speech and writing, but also between
affect and reason, inside and outside, female and male.[27]

It may be the case that any analysis of the subversiveness of the *Book*,
or of mystical theology in general, will find itself mired in the same paradoxes and impossibilities that have made Margery's text so difficult to cate-
gorize and so troubling to read. Mysticism, even "feminine" mysticism,
remains bound by the assumptions and injunctions of medieval Christian
theology; despite the best efforts of feminist medievalists, women will always be the "dangerous supplement" within the Christian system. In spite
of its internal contradictions, however, Lochrie's analysis is a significant
and ground-breaking one; it lays a foundation for the consideration of the
*Book* in its own terms, and for a reassessment of the epistemological and
theological assumptions that have conditioned and, in some sense, con-
founded our response to the text. Nevertheless, to the extent that she, like
the majority of the *Book*'s feminist readers, declines to engage with the
signifying imperatives of medieval Christianity itself—imperatives that
cannot be fully disengaged from the institutions that enforce them—her
analysis cannot disavow the gender-specific violence that both subtends and
results from the ideology of sacrifice and the metaphysics of sublimation.

One way a feminist reader might begin to question these representational conditions (and their inarguably material effects) would be to invert
Caroline Bynum's interpretive strategy, that is, to read mystical theology
through the issue of pathology. By blurring the boundary between body
and word, as Lochrie so persuasively argues, Margery's "mysterical"[28]

autobiography invites such a reading. Since the *Book* is also obsessively concerned with the problematics of linguistic mediation, however, it asks that we explore this theo-pathology as the condition of a narrative, operating within a system of representation that has its own teleological agenda. With this goal in mind, my reading will follow a different direction than that taken by either the "pathologists" or the Christian historicists, taking a necessary detour through the troubled history of hysteria.

## Hysteria and *Hystera*

Although quite a bit has been written in recent years about the Freudian hysteric, the subject of hysteria is still a touchy one for feminists. Much of the feminist debate over the historical status of the hysteric has centered on Freud's aborted analysis of the patient he called Dora;[29] some feminist readers have seen Dora's resistance to the analysis as heroic, while others claim that this resistance ultimately either serves or is contained by what Toril Moi calls a "phallocentric epistemology."[30] It is a third approach that most interests me here, however. Feminist theorists such as Jane Gallop, Mary Jacobus, and Jacqueline Rose, influenced to varying degrees by Lacan's rereading of Freud, see the hysteric's (and thus the analyst's) relation to language as the most salient feminist issue in the Freudian case histories. Rose points out that, in the case of Dora, Freud's theory of the unconscious was brought into irreconcilable conflict with his theory of sexuality.[31] Since the unconscious is "structured like a language," the two opposing constituents in this conflict are in fact language, as the site of loss (of the real), and femininity, which Freud's patriarchal and empiricist bias led him to see as a "real" and thus unproblematic category. In brief, because Dora resisted Freud's reading of her desire as heterosexual and genital, she revealed what Freud's theory had repressed: that sexuality is as ambivalent and multiple as the unconscious itself. In the footnotes and postscripts to Dora's case, Freud acknowledges his failure to recognize the homosexual aspect of her desire as a "failure to master the transference in good time."[32] Too late (for Dora), Freud attempts to locate the origin of hysterical identifications in an unresolved preoedipal attachment. The conflict in his own theoretical apparatus is "saved" by this gesture toward a prior, extralinguistic moment: Dora's hysteria derives from an anachronistic attachment to the *hystera*, or, more precisely, to the body of the mother.[33]

Nevertheless, the paradoxes and contradictions of Freud's own texts reveal the extent to which the subject's relation to language is precisely what is at stake in both the hysteric's narrative and that of the analyst. Hysterical narrative here mirrors autobiographical narrative; from Freud's and Breuer's collaborative work, *Studies on Hysteria*, we learn that hysterics, like autobiographers, "suffer mainly from reminiscences."[34] Hysteria is a kind of nostalgia played out on the body, a body which in turn becomes a text since, as Freud points out, it is the symptom that generates "those case histories that read like short stories."[35] The symptom becomes a "tropological substitution," a metaphor for a trauma whose origin has been repressed and thereby lost. The "cure" depends on the recovery, through narrative, of this lost originary moment. Because of its dependence on language as a way of reading the body, however, the analysis inevitably finds itself trapped in the twists and turns of figuration, unable to maintain its exteriority from the disease itself. Thus the hysteric's anxiety about origins invariably transfers itself to the analyst; both the hysterical narrative and the secondary "story" that seeks to explain it unfold as a series of disavowals and displacements, a deferral of the closure that can only be obtained by recovering the specular moment of pathogenesis, the "exciting cause" of the illness. The hysteric's discourse, like that of the autobiographer, effaces the border between subject and object, creating a fiction in which the analyst shares. Paradoxically, the regressive narrative promises to restore the boundary between sign and referent—between the symptom and the event—while simultaneously taking the reader or hearer further from the origin she or he seeks.

Assuming, then, that the originary trauma can be recovered, one is compelled to ask the question Freud himself could not answer: is the trauma a "real" content, or is it, too, a fantasy? Freud's initial assumption that hysteria resulted from an actual seduction by the father was later revised into a "seduction fantasy"—a move that shifted the "blame" for the illness from the paternal figure to the hysteric herself. Nevertheless, after Dora's case made it clear that attachment to the mother was more to the point, Freud insisted on the reality of the pathogenic event:

> And now we find the phantasy of seduction once more in the pre-Oedipus . . . but the seducer is regularly the mother. Here, however, the phantasy touches the ground of reality, for it was really the mother who by her activities over the child's bodily hygiene inevitably stimulated, and perhaps even roused for the first time, pleasurable sensations in her genitals.[36]

Seduction by the mother "touches the ground of reality," while seduction by the father—or the analyst—is merely metaphoric or symptomatic.[37] The analyst's exteriority depends upon the irreducibility of the category of mother; she is called upon to sustain the artificial distinction between fantasy and reality, a distinction that continually threatens to topple the theoretical apparatus.

Several feminist theorists have used the idea of a preoedipal or imaginary relation to the mother as the conceptual basis for an alternative theory of feminine sexuality which nostalgically privileges the mother-child dyad. As the hysteric's "nostalgia for the mother" plays itself out as symptom, the body becomes the site of a subversive narrative that constitutes a heroic resistance to the symbolic order. The hysteric's transformation of body into text is mirrored in the work of Luce Irigaray, while Julia Kristeva affirms the extra-linguistic moment of primary narcissism as the genesis of a modernist aesthetic. For Kristeva, the maternal body is a border that "[unsettles] the symbolic stratum." In Irigaray's work, the feminine body remains "elsewhere" vis à vis paternal law,[38] while Kristeva's theory of the maternal focuses on the significative traces of the libidinal drives, whereby the preoedipal situation "irrupts" into the normative oedipal configuration.

The seductive threat of the maternal is a metaphor for the instability of language itself, its pathological tendency to slide back into the materiality from which it derives, and finally into silence. This threat, which remains on the periphery of Freudian theory, is most fully explored in Kristeva's work, where the maternal becomes a condition of language and representation, a space and a series of processes whereby the Flesh maintains its hold on the Word. For medieval Christianity, as for Kristeva, the mother is a metonymy for woman, a metonymy that sustains the impertinent metaphors for a human god. Eliciting and containing desire for the mother within a discourse of paternity, Christianity invokes humility and passivity while simultaneously pursuing its own institutional imperative: a paradox strikingly evident, for example, in the life and works of Bernard of Clairvaux.

Where does this leave the hysteric, or her medieval precursor, the woman mystic? If, as Freud has argued, "hysteria and linguistic usage alike draw their material from a common source,"[39] then a theory of hysteria might very well point the way to a theory of writing or of representation, in which the mother remains a troubling, if peripheral, presence. The homosexual-maternal aspect of hysterical subjectivity is thus pathological to the extent that it refuses to reduce the maternal to a condition of paternal discourse. The alternative, which haunts Kristeva's work, suggests that by "taking verbal expressions literally," by returning the mat(t)er to language, one may find the impertinence of metaphor intolerable, as did Breuer's patient Anna O., who, taking the metaphor of *Muttersprache* literally, found herself hopelessly alienated from her own language.[40] The question that remains for feminism, then, is whether or not there exists an alternative to the preoedipal imaginary and the "mute border" of Kristevan theory. In other words, is it possible to write across or through the maternal body without being reduced to inarticulacy and finally to silence? Is "women's writing" possible, or must it always write its own impossibility? This, I believe, is the central issue of *The Book of Margery Kempe*, to which I now return.

## Writing "Up-so-down"

Margery begins her story by juxtaposing two images of origin: one corporeal or "auto-biological," the other linked to Christian history and to language. The narrative proper begins with a birth: a parturition, or splitting, which marks the beginning of Margery's alienation from her previous life. The experience of birth is followed by a period of mental illness, a fact that has led several readers to diagnose Margery's text as a symptom of post-partum depression.[41] A closer reading reveals that it is not the birth, but rather an encounter with the clergy that drives Margery "over the edge":

> & þan, what for labowr sche had in chyldyng & for sekenesse beforn, sche dyspered of hyr lyfe, wenyng sche mygth not leuyn. And þan sche sent for hyr gostly fadyr, for sche had a thyng in conscyens whech sche had neuyr schewed be-forn þat tyme in alle hyr lyfe. . . . And, whan sche was any tym seke or desesyd, þe Deuyl seyd in her mende þat sche schuld be dampnyd, for sche was not schreuyn of þat defawt. Wherfor, aftyr þat hir chyld was born, sche . . . sent for hyr gostly fadyr . . . in ful wyl to be schreuyn of alle hir lyfe-tym as ner as sche cowde. &, whan sche cam to þe poynt for to seyn þat þing whech sche had so long conselyd, hir confessowr was a lytyl to hastye & gan scharply to vndernemyn hir er þan sche had fully seyd hir entent, & so sche wold no mor seyn for nowt he mygth do. And a-noon, for dreed sche had of dampnacyon on þe to syde & hys scharp repreuyng on þat

oþer syde, þis creatur went owt of hir mende & was wondyrlye vexid & labowryd wyth spyritys half ʒer viij wekys & odde days. (6–7)

(And then, what with the labor pains she had in childbirth and the sickness that had gone before, she despaired of her life, believing she might not live. Then she sent for her spiritual father, for she had a thing on her conscience which she had never revealed before that time in all her life. . . . And when she was at any time sick or disturbed, the devil said in her mind that she should be damned, for she was not shriven of that fault. Therefore, after her child was born, . . . she sent for her spiritual father . . . fully wishing to be shriven of her whole lifetime, as nearly as she could. And when she came to the point of saying that thing which she had so long concealed, her confessor was a little too hasty and began sharply to reprove her before she had fully said what she meant, and so she would say no more in spite of anything he might do. And shortly thereafter, because of the dread she had of damnation on the one hand, and his sharp reproving of her on the other, this creature went out of her mind and was amazingly vexed and tormented with spirits for half a year, eight weeks and odd days.)

The trauma of giving birth is linked to an unnamed sin, a sin that ultimately plays a significant role in the genesis of the narrative itself. We are reminded here of yet another original—and originating—sin, which, according to Christian myth, forever bound woman to desire and to the body, excluding her from the signifying system which she (paradoxically) brought forth through her transgression. In the Book of Genesis, Eve's sin reveals the lack which language must always seek to "clothe" in trope.[42] Eve's transgression justifies placing women at the site of an absence that language denies; by confining women within representation, men fantasize their exteriority from it, thus veiling their own discursive inadequacies. In the Christian system, women can only escape their historic culpability through the institutional Church, which offers priestly mediation for the forgiveness of sins. In this first chapter Margery is literally caught between the theologically-justified suffering of her own maternal body, and the institution that promises, and finally refuses, to mitigate that suffering by eliciting a cathartic narrative. Like the hysteric's analyst, the "gostly fadyr" of Margery's story is ultimately implicated in the disease of his patient.

More important, however, is the sense in which this first chapter links the concept of an original sin to the materiality of the feminine body, thereby evoking the "gostly" or theological solution to the problem of origins. By refusing to choose between maternal (corporeal) and paternal (scriptural) geneses, however, the narrative locates itself at the intersection of linear materiality, figured as metonymy, and transcendent theology, bound to metaphor.[43] It thus unfolds as a series of paradoxes which can be seen as a materialization of metaphor and, more broadly, a maternalization of sacred history.

Margery has often been criticized for "sensualizing" the spiritual; like the hysteric, she tends to move freely between the figurative and the literal. After the failure of "gostly" mediation, we find Margery comforted, very literally, by the "manhood" of Christ:

> &, whan sche had long ben labowrd in þes & many oþer temptacyons þat men wend sche schuld neuyr a skapyd ne levyd, þan . . . owyr mercyful Lord Crist Ihesu, . . . worshypd be hys name, neuyr forsakyng hys seruawnt in tyme of nede, aperyd to hys creatur whych had forsakyn hym in lyknesse of a man, most semly, most bewtyuows, & most amyable þat euyr mygth be seen wyth mannys eye, clad in a mantyl of purpyl sylke, syttyng up-on hir beddys syde, . . . (8)

> (And when she had long been tormented by these and many other temptations, so that people thought she should never have escaped from them nor lived, then . . . our merciful Lord Christ Jesus . . . worshipped be his name, never forsaking his servant in time of need—appeared to his creature who had forsaken him, in the likeness of a man, the most seemly, most beauteous, and most amiable that ever might be seen with man's eye, clad in a mantle of purple silk, sitting upon her bedside, . . . )

The return of what is repressed in the concept of a "gostly fadyr," that is, the body of Christ, comforts Margery as her confessor would not, and she becomes "stabelyd in hir wittys & in hir reson." The incident is paradigmatic of the tropological inversion that will become the dominant narrative strategy in the *Book*. Privileging the sensual over the spiritual, the metonymic over the metaphoric, she reacts against a paternal discourse that makes the flesh the price of the word.

For Margery, figural language always bears a moral content, one which she is not above manipulating for her own ends. For example, by dismantling the Pauline metaphor of a "marital debt," she is able to begin a life of chastity despite her husband's reluctance to give up his legal right to her body. She effectively buys back her figurative debt by paying her husband's literal ones, thereby exposing the politics of the trope and turning it to her own advantage:

> "Sere, yf it lyke ȝow, ȝe schal grawnt me my desyr, & ȝe schal haue ȝowr desyr. Grawntyth me þat ȝe schal not komyn in my bed, & I grawnt ȝow to qwyte ȝowr dettys er I go to Ierusalem. & makyth my body fre to God so

þat 3e neuyr make no chalengyng in me to askyn no dett of matrimony aftyr þis day whyl 3e leuyn, & I schal etyn & drynkyn on 3e Fryday at 3owr byd-dyng." (25)

("Sir, if it please you, you shall grant me my desire, and you shall have your desire. Grant me that you will not come into my bed, and I grant you that I will pay your debts before I go to Jerusalem. And make my body free to God, so that you never make any claim on me demanding any conjugal debt after this day as long as you live—and I shall eat and drink on Fridays at your bidding.")

Margery's obsession with the sin of swearing throughout the *Book* can also be understood as an insistence upon the moral value of figural language. She echoes Chaucer's Parson and Pardoner in her condemnation of "hem þat slen [Christ] euery day be gret othys swearing." Here as elsewhere in medieval literature, swearing by Christ's body parts is seen as rhetorical dismemberment; the swearing of "gret othys" uncovers the connection between linguistic and material violence.

Where her own body is concerned, however, Margery again prefig-ures the Freudian hysteric in demanding to be read metaphorically.[44] Early in the *Book*, she relates a vision in which Christ tells her to replace the hair shirt on her back with a hair shirt in her heart, for he prefers an internal-ized asceticism to "alle þe hayres in þe world." Her white clothes, too, are a plea for a metaphoric reading of virginity, a plea her visions answer when Christ assures her that she is valued no less for having lost her maiden-hood. It is interesting that his reassurance contains an acknowledgment of the political realities of married life for women:

"3a, dowtyr, trow þow rygth wel þat I lofe wyfes also, and specyal þo wyfys whech woldyn levyn chast, *3yf þei mygtyn haue þer wyl*, & don her besynes to plesyn me as þow dost, for þow þe state of maydenhode be mor parfyte & mor holy þan þe state of wedewhode, & þe state of wedewhode mor parfyte þan þe state of wedlake, 3et dowtyr I lofe þe as wel as any mayden in þe world." (49)

("Yes, daughter, but rest assured that I love wives also, and especially those wives who would live chaste *if they might have their will*, and who make an effort to please me as you do. For though the state of maidenhood be more perfect and more holy than the state of widowhood, and the state of widow-hood more perfect than the state of wedlock, yet I love you, daughter, as much as any maiden in the world.")

He further asserts that virginity is not merely a state of the body, but also of the spirit:

"&, for-as-mech as þu art a mayden in þi sowle, I xal take þe be þe on hand in hevyn & my Modyr be þe oþer hand, & so xalt þu dawnsyn in hevyn wyth oþer holy maydens & virgynes." (52)

("And because you are a maiden in your soul, I shall take you by the one hand in heaven, and my mother by the other hand, and so you shall dance in heaven with other holy maidens and virgins.")

This strategy of inversion, this materialization of spirit and metaphorization of body, works against the binary logic of Christian theology. Margery's own body, de-materialized and de-eroticized, is in effect replaced by the eroticized body of the text, which in turn breaks down the metaphoric system whereby institutional religious texts are usually constituted. By turning the Christian signifying system "up-so-down," the *Book* creates ruptures in that system, gaps within which the female authorial voice can be inscribed.

These systematic inversions operate at every level of the text, subverting not only the hierarchy of metonymy and metaphor, but also the configurations of sexual difference. The strategy of inversion becomes particularly problematic when it acts upon Margery's secondary identification with hagiographic figures. Shortly after her initial conversion to religious life, she is tormented by lecherous thoughts. In yet another literalization of the abstract, Margery's temptation is embodied as a young man who becomes a type of Christ. Significantly, the temptation is connected to both the feast and the church of the saint who shares Margery's name, Margaret of Antioch. Margery's failure to conquer her own sexual desires is thus set against Margaret's triumph over lechery and the devil:

In þe secunde 3er of hir temptacyons yt fel so þat a man whech sche louyd wel seyd on-to hir on Seynt Margaretys Evyn be-for euynsong þat for anything he wold ly be hir & haue hys lust of hys body, & sche xuld not wythstond hym, for, yf he mygth not haue hys wyl þat tyme, he seyd, he xuld ellys haue it a-noþer tyme, sche xuld not chese. (14)

(In the second year of her temptations it so happened that a man whom she liked said to her on St. Margaret's Eve before evensong that, for anything, he would sleep with her and enjoy the lust of his body, and that she should not withstand him, for if he might not have his will that time, he said, he would have it an other time instead—she should not choose.)

It is interesting to follow the mutations of hagiographical motifs in this section of the text. Initially, Margery, like Margaret, is confronted with the unsolicited attentions of a man, which threaten to escalate into rape ("sche xuld not wythstond hym"). The young man's moral position becomes more ambiguous, however, and Margery loses the right to see herself as Margaret's successor:

> And, whan euensong was do, sche went to þe man befor-seyd þat he xuld haue hys lust, as sche wend þat he had desyred, but he made swech symyla-cyon þat sche cowd not knowe hys entent, & so þei partyd a-sondyr for þat nygth. (15)

> (And when evensong was over, she went to the said man, in order that he should have his will, as she believed he desired, but he dissimulated such that she could not understand his intent, and so they parted for that night.)

Finally, the entire situation is inverted, as Margery assumes the role of seducer, and the young man that of victimized saint:

> At þe last thorw inoportunyte of temptacyon & lakkyng of dyscrecyon sche was ouyrcomyn, & consentyd in hir mend, & went to þe man to wetyn yf he wold þan consentyn to hire. And he seyd he ne wold for al þe good in þis world; he had leuar ben hewyn as smal as flesch to þe pott. (15)

> (At last—through the importunings of temptation and a lack of discre-tion—she was overcome and consented in her mind, and went to the man to know if he would then consent to have her. And he said he would not for all the wealth in this world; he would rather be chopped up as small as meat for the pot.)

The references to Saint Margaret and the use of hagiographical motifs foreground the importance of sexual difference in this scene. Margery's "vnstabylnes" in this situation places her in the role of Margaret's male oppressor and would-be rapist, Olibrius, while the young man's "sta-bylnes" and willingness to suffer dismemberment rather than yield ally him with Margaret herself.[45] Through the mediation of hagiographic conven-tion, that is, through language, moral instability leads to unstable sexual identities. Margery's illicit desire here involves her in a deviant identifica-tion with the male antagonist of popular legend. A reassertion of moral order is also a reassertion of proper sexual identifications; even here, where Margery is "shown up" by a man, the ego-ideal is feminine and implicitly maternal.[46]

Throughout the *Book*, Margery sees herself as the filial inheritor of a feminine textual tradition. Her primary identification with the mother, to which I will return presently, is complemented by a secondary identi-fication with hagiographic heroines and women mystics. Where hagio-graphic convention is operative, however, the *Book* becomes mired in conflicting authorial systems. Because hagiography serves the ecclesiastical state apparatus and thus the ideological system of patriarchy, it can only superficially affirm feminine discursive autonomy. It is only by bypassing hermeneutic mediation, which endows hagiographical texts with a figurative or connotative value, that Margery is able to misrecognize herself in women saints such as Margaret and Katherine of Alexandria (see below). As we shall see in the next chapter, popular hagiography works to affirm the binary opposition between a feminine corporeality and a masculine immateriality: it dramatizes the making of the theological metaphor. Margery's narcissistic engagement with popular legends thus depends upon a refusal of saintly heroines as signifiers in a second order of signification. In short, the *Book*'s relationship to hagiography is based upon the "matter" rather than the (exegetical) "sense" of the Katherine and Margaret legends, upon their denotative rather than connotative value. Within the *Book*'s textual system, Katherine and Margaret represent feminine discursive potency and moral superiority, rather than a corporeal femininity which must be sacrificed to ensure the continuity of the theological Word.

The *Book*'s indebtedness to popular hagiography is perhaps most strikingly evident in the section dealing with Margery's trials and imprisonments for Lollardy. Her first trial, before the Mayor of Leicester and numerous clergy, is clearly modeled on the life of Katherine of Alexandria, whose triumph over the pagan Maxentius derived in large part from her rhetorical skills. Immediately after Margery's arrest, she is brought before the Mayor and, in keeping with hagiographical convention, asked about her lineage:

> þan þe Meyr askyd hir of what cuntre sche was & whos dowtyr sche was: "Syr," sche seyd, "I am of Lynne in Norfolke, a good mannys dowtyr of þe same Lynne, whech hath ben meyr fyve tymes of þat worshepful burwgh and aldyrman also many 3erys, & I have a good man, also a burgeys of þe seyd town, Lynne, to myn husbond."(111)

> (Then the Mayor asked her from which (part of the) country she came, and whose daughter she was. "Sir," she said, "I am from Lynn in Norfolk, the daughter of a good man of the same Lynn, who has been five times mayor of that worshipful borough, and also an alderman for many years; and I have a good man, also a burgess of the said town of Lynn, for my husband.")

Compare Katherine's response to a similar question from her tormentor Maxence, as it appears in the early Middle English version of the legend:

Ha onswerede & seide: / "ʒef þu wult mi nome witen, / ich am Katerine icleopede. / ʒef þu wult cnawen mi cun, / ich am kinges dohter; / Cost hehte mi feder; / & habbe ihauet hiðerto / swiðe hehe meistres."[47]

(She answered and said: "If you want to know my name, I am called Katherine. If you want to know my lineage, I am a king's daughter. Cost was the name of my father, and I have had hitherto very distinguished masters.")

Katherine declares her lineage equal to that of the King, and Margery echoes her in matching the Mayor's rank with that of her own father. The connection between Margery and Katherine is made explicit in the Mayor's response:

"A," seyd þe Meyr, "Seynt Kateryn telde what kyndred sche cam of & ʒet ar ʒe not lyche, for þu art a fals strumpet, a fals loller, & a fals deceyuer of þe pepyl & þerfor I xal haue þe in preson." (111–12)

("Ah," said the Mayor, "Saint Katherine told of what kindred she came, and yet you are not alike, for you are a false strumpet, a false Lollard, and a false deceiver of the people, and therefore I shall have you in prison.")

Later the Mayor reveals a fear that again echoes the Katherine legend. As Katherine converted the King's wife Augusta, so Margery is accused of luring wives away from their husbands, and, in particular, of upsetting the social hierarchy by sowing domestic discord among the nobility:

" . . . þu cownseledyst my Lady Greystokke to forsakyn hir husbond, þat is a barownys wyfe & dowtyr to my Lady of Westmorlonde, & now hast seyd j-now to be brent for." (133)

(" . . . you advised my Lady Greystoke to leave her husband, and she is a baron's wife, and daughter to my Lady of Westmorland. And now you have said enough to be burned for.")

Here, again, Margery's reading of the legend remains at the denotative level; noble saints and lower class servants alike share the rewards of Christian faith in virtually every hagiographic text. Nevertheless, as I will argue in the next chapter, the texts themselves ultimately propagandize on behalf of the institutional Church, appropriating the discursive power of the female saint and the mythic classlessness of the early Christian sub-culture for the very material ends of the Church Militant. By refusing both exegetical and ideological interventions on behalf of patriarchy and ecclesiastical power, Margery's *Book* asserts the existence of a counter-cultural canon of texts, a canon to which it hopes to belong.

This other canon constitutes what Michel Foucault has called a counter-memory; [48] in Margery's case, it is a memory informed by desire for and identification with the mother. It is clear, moreover, that the desired maternal figure is not the prediscursive mother of Kristevan theory. What Margery envisions is a matrilineal system of textual inheritance. "Bride's Book," the writings of Mary of Oignes, the legends of Katherine and Margaret are all re-membered in Margery's text: her maternal ideal exists within language and within history. Because her *Book* is ultimately an attempt to establish a maternal metalanguage, her fantasy is not of the preoedipal mother, but rather of a mother who is also bound by the symbolic order: the mother, perhaps, of Freud's "negative oedipus complex." [49]

In *The Ego and the Id*, Freud proposes the coexistence of a negative and a positive oedipus complex as a way of explaining "the bisexuality originally present in children." [50] The negative oedipus complex has as its object-choice the same-sex parent, while the positive version represents a culturally-sanctioned heterosexual alignment. The negative oedipus complex thus provides an explanation for the hysteric's attachment to the mother, as revealed in Dora's case. Freud's work on femininity, however, is marked by a refusal to decide between the negative oedipus complex and the so-called "pre-Oedipal phase," which gradually gained ascendancy in his theory. Kaja Silverman has eloquently argued that this shift is linked to Freud's assertion, in "Female Sexuality," of a referential value for the maternal seduction scene, a facticity which distinguishes it *temporally* from the paternal seduction fantasy through which he discovered the positive oedipus complex. [51] At issue here is whether or not the girl's attachment to the mother has a role to play within representation and language, or whether it must remain a prediscursive originary myth, accessible only as an unspeakable and futile nostalgia. If the mother is bound to the real, she is irretrievably lost with the accession to language. If, however, the homosexual fantasy has a part to play within the symbolic order, as a desire which "challenges dominance from within representation," [52] as Silverman puts it, then the establishment of a maternal metalanguage is no longer an impossibility. In my view, it is this constructive negativity, an effect of symbolic castration and loss but also an image of possibility within it, that structures the textual fantasy of Margery's *Book*.

After the initial reference to childbirth, Margery has very little to say about her relationship to her fourteen children. Maternity is displaced from body to affect; Margery's identification with mothers and participation in scenes highly charged with maternal pathos take the place of her own maternal experiences, about which we hear almost nothing. She is called "mother" by nearly every sympathetic male she meets, and she occasionally calls younger men "son." Those who are kindest to her treat her, we are told, with the consideration due a mother. God is both mother and son to her: he comforts her and calls her "dowtyr," but also tells her that he "wyl be louyd as a sone shuld be louyd wyth þe modyr" (90). The activity of mothering also informs Margery's relations with other women. She mothers the Virgin Mary in her visions, making her a "good cawdel," to comfort her for the loss of her son (195), while the Virgin assures her that she will treat her with maternal solicitude as well:

> "And, dowtyr, wete þu wel þu xal fyndyn me a very modyr to þe to helpyn þe and socowr þe as a modyr owyth to don hir dowtyr & purchasyn to þe grace & vertu." (175)

> ("And, daughter, know that you will find me a true mother to you, to help you and succor you as a mother ought to do for her daughter, and obtain for you grace and virtue.")

Motherhood links her to Saints Anne, Elizabeth, and Mary, as well as to women she meets on her travels. When she is in need, other women fulfill the role of mother to her, as she does, on other occasions, to them. This "maternal subculture" is set against the dominant patriarchal social system Margery continally finds antipathetic. Women are Margery's real audience when she speaks of religion; consistent with her *mater*ialization of "gostly" images, it is other women rather than the angels of hagiographic convention who sustain her in prison:

> þan stode sche lokyng owt at a wyndown, tellyng many good talys to hem þat wolde heryn hir, in so meche þat women wept sor & seyd wyth gret heuynes of her hertes, "Alas, woman why xalt þu be brent?" Than sche prey'd þe good wyfe of þe hows to ʒeuen hir drynke, for sche was euyl for thryste. And þe good wife seyd hir husbond had born a-wey þe key, wherfor sche myth not comyn to hir ne ʒeuyn hir drynke. and þan þe women tokyn a leddyr & set up to þe wyndown & ʒeuyn hir a pynte of wyn in a potte & toke hir a pece, besechyng hir to settyn a-wey þe potte preuyly & þe pece þat whan þe good man come he myth not aspye it. (130–31)

> (Then she stood looking out at a window, telling many good (i.e., moral) tales to those who would listen to her, so much so that women wept bitterly, and said with great heaviness of heart, "Alas, woman, why should you be burned?" Then she begged the good wife of the house to give her a drink, for she was extremely thirsty. And the good wife said her husband had taken

away the key, because of which she could not come in to her, nor give her a drink. And then the women took a ladder and set it up against the window, and gave her a pint of wine in a pot, and brought her a cup, begging her to conceal the pot and cup, so that when the man came back he might not notice it.)

Margery is particularly drawn to women in need. In one case, she comforts a woman whose situation parallels her own after the birth of her first child. A man comes to her as she prays in the Church of Saint Margaret, despairing because his wife, who "was newly delyueryd of a childe," was "owt hir mende" (177–78). Unlike the "gostly fadyr" of the first chapter, Margery comforts the distressed woman, who eventually "herd hir spekyn & dalyin wyth good wil wyth-owtyn any roryng er crying." Margery herself receives similar treatment from women she meets on her travels:

> Whan þes good women seyn þis creatur wepyn, sobbyn, & cryen so wondir-fully & mythtyly þat sche was nerhand ouercomyn þerwyth, þan þei or-deyned a good soft bed & leyd hir þerup-on & comfortyd hir as mech as þei myth for owyr Lordys lofe, blyssed mot he ben. (78)

> (When these good women saw this creature weeping, sobbing and crying out so amazingly and so mightily that she was nearly overcome by it, then they arranged a good soft bed and laid her upon it, and comforted her as much as they could for our Lord's love—blessed may he be.)

The feminine subculture that haunts the periphery of the text is clearly structured on the mother-daughter paradigm, and Margery herself alternates between the two roles vis-à-vis other women throughout.[53]

By contrast, her relationships to men are either strictly maternal or adversarial: there are no positive paternal figures in the *Book*. She mothers both her husband, who regresses to infancy late in life, and her "protectors," who invariably need her more than she needs them. Moreover, the homosocial relationships between men in the text suffer by comparison to those between women. In Chapter 27, for example, Margery's scribe finds himself unable to sustain either a paternal relationship to a young man or a filial bond to an old one, whom he initially calls "father." Both attempt to cheat and deceive him, and he is forced to acknowledge that Margery's intuition about them was correct. In addition to validating Margery's insight, this segment serves to discredit the patrilineal system of writing from which she is excluded. Masculine exchanges break down as the would-be son absconds with his "father"'s money, and the would-be father fails to confer the promised book (text) upon his "son" (55–58). It is significant that, on the one occasion when Margery falls victim to a woman who attempts to steal from her, the incident ends on quite a different note: the woman returns Margery's ring and begs her forgiveness (78–79). The patrilineal system of textual inheritance and exchange here yields to what would seem to be its maternal opposite: a discourse between women.

Here again, it is clear that the *Book* is constructed as reversal—a turning "up-so-down"—of the paternal law of discourse, which (paradoxically) relegates women to the periphery of history by denying them authorial or diegetic exteriority. In both the canonical and extracanonical texts we will explore in the remaining chapters of this study, the illusion of male discursive autonomy depends upon a strategic relegation of women to the interior of the mimetic circuit. In this way, symbolic castration—the lack that accompanies the entry into language—is projected onto the female body as object of the look. Through metaphor, the male look becomes allied with the divine gaze,[54] and thus with presence, while the feminine body bears the burden of lack or absence, standing in for the instability of language itself.

Consistent with this strategy of inversion, Margery's visions reverse the traditional paradigm by placing women on the outside of specular moments in which men are objects of the look. Her visions have a distinctly cinematic feel. On one occasion, she joins Mary in witnessing Christ's crucifixion, gazing at the spectacle of his torture in a manner similar to that of the inscribed male spectator in legends of female saints:

> And a-non aftyr sche saw hem drawyn of hys clothys & makyn hym al nakyd & sithyn drewyn hym forth a-forn hem as it had ben þe most malefactowr in al þe worlde. & he went forth ful mekely a-forn hem al modyr-nakyd as he was born to a peler of ston & spak no worde a-geyn hem but leet hem do & sey what þei wolde. And þer þei bowndyn hym to þe peler as streyt as þei cowde & beetyn hym on hys fayr white body wyth baleys, wyth whippis, & wyth scorgys. (190)

> (And soon after, she saw them pull off his clothes and strip him all naked, and then drag him before them as if he had been the greatest criminal in the world. And he went on very meekly before them, as naked as he was born, towards a pillar of stone, and spoke no word against them, but let them do and say what they wished. And there they bound him to the pillar as firmly as they could, and beat him on his fair white body with rods, with whips, and with scourges.)

Perhaps the most striking example of this interiorization of masculine fig-
ures occurs in Chapter 59, in which Margery, momentarily estranged from
God, is tormented by demons who inflict pornographic visions upon her.
In her hallucination, she is forced to look upon the genitals of priests:

> Sche sey as hir thowt veryly dyuers men of religyon, prestys & many oþer,
> bothyn hethyn & Cristen comyn be-for hir syght þat sche myth not en-
> chewyn hem ne puttyn hem owt of hir syght, shewyng her bar membres vn-
> to hir. (145)

> (She saw, as it really seemed to her, various men of religion, priests and many
> others, both heathen and Christian, coming before her eyes so that she could
> not avoid them or put them out of her sight, and showing her their naked
> genitals.)

Here the most "exterior" of figures, the "gostly fadyr," is enclosed within
the fantasy of representation and forced to uncover the sexual desire that
the law, like the priestly robe itself, attempts to veil. Margery's fantasy
circumscribes the sacerdotal mediator, just as the hysteric's narrative im-
plicates its analyst, as autobiography (another type of regressive fantasy)
interiorizes its reader.[55]

By inverting patriarchal paradigms, the *Book* attempts to open up a
place for the female authorial voice, and for a counter-canonical literary
tradition modeled on the mother-daughter dyad. Again, what distinguishes this model from the preoedipal configuration is its insistence on
the author's—and thus the reader's—problematic relation to language.
Several of the chapters dealing with Margery's travels abroad echo the
proem in their emphasis upon language as loss, a loss which can only be
restored through divine intervention. Margery's travels take her far from
her mother-tongue, just as the project of writing alienates her from her
experience, from the referential world, in the proem. Reading and writing
are only possible through "special grace"; meaning is lost without faith.
For Margery Kempe, however, faith manifests itself in negativity and a
transgression of the boundaries that inform more "lyrical" or metaphoric
modes of mystical expression. In her *Book*, the possibility of women's writing rests upon this negativity, or more specifically, upon a refusal of the
paternal interdict that makes the mother's absence a condition of meaning
within language.

The *Book*'s assumption that language both anticipates and exceeds
the subject, that authorial exteriority is an effect of discourse rather than
its origin, precludes the fantasy of a preoedipal, "feminine" language, a

language that is purely oral, immediate, and, as Karma Lochrie suggests, "[authorized] . . . by the realm of experience."[56] Its insistence on
the maternal as a condition of representability, however, pleads for a discourse of maternity, albeit one based on inversion, on a turning "up-so-
down" of tropological hierarchies. These would seem to be antithetical
strategies: the one originating in absence and loss, the other suggesting at
least the possibility of presence and plenitude. This tension within the text
is most apparent in the segments dealing with Margery's "roaring and
crying." Indeed, the scenes of weeping are a nodal point in the text.
On the one hand, they are a point of entry into its libidinal economy:
as Clarissa Atkinson points out, tears are Margery's "spiritual capital."[57]
With tears she buys grace for herself and for others; they manifest her
childish contrition as well as the maternal pathos so prevalent in late
Gothic piety. As a weeping mother, Margery takes her place beside Rachel
and her typological fulfillment, the Virgin Mary. Her tears isolate her
from her fellow Christians, and from men in particular, more effectively
than an anchoress's cell. On the other hand, her tears are the "vanishing
point" of the text: the point at which language, always unstable, finally
devolves into inarticulate sound.[58] Paradoxically, then, Margery's weeping
both stands in for the instability of language *and* claims a place for her
within the teleological narrative of Christian history. Maternity here inter-
sects with history—and thus with patriarchy—in an explicit and unset-
tling way.

In a sense, the paradoxes and contradictions of the *Book of Margery
Kempe* prefigure those of feminist theory. Her "counter-canon" insists on
the right to remain within the framework of sacred history, while simultaneously overturning the tropological and sexual hierarchies in which that
history is grounded. Feminist psychoanalytic theory also situates itself
within an androcentric discursive universe (a fact which is deplored by
some empiricist feminists) but with a difference. The feminist reader, as
Mary Jacobus points out,

> [opens] the gap between petrifying sameness and repeated identity, installing
> herself as the reader-in-between; her feminist reading is the reading of cor-
> respondences which are always near misses. . . . Less a triangulation than an
> internal differentiation,the feminist reader holds open a gap which would
> otherwise render her invisible in the seamless continuum of masculinist criti-
> cal and theoretical reading, whether such masculinist reading takes the form
> of the duality of narcissistic reflection or the imaginary unity (identity) of
> two-in-one.[59]

Margery's inscription of the maternal within the paternal discourse of medieval Christianity is likewise an internal differentiation rather than a triangulation, in that it operates at the tropological as well as the thematic level of the text. Returning the repressed matter-that-is-mother to the metaphoric system of Christian theology, her *Book* uncovers the difference that is latent in similarity, the maternal figure behind the paternal figure of speech. It is not surprising that, for virtually all of its readers, the *Book* exists as a rupture in the seamless continuum of history, a pathological aberration to an otherwise unproblematic narrative of origins.

It has been my contention throughout this study of Margery's text that a feminist reading—and particularly a feminist reading of medieval literature—must engage with the problem of origins. Following the *Book*'s example, I have attempted in this first chapter to begin a larger discussion of the ideological significance of originary narratives, and to focus—as the *Book* seems to—on the impossibility of sustaining authorial control over textual origins. Like both Margery Kempe and Julia Kristeva, I believe that one must problematize the notion of origins if one is to in any way "unsettle the symbolic stratum." At the same time, I am aware that there is still a good deal more to be said about the *Book* from a theoretical perspective; this reading should be understood as an effort to initiate rather than foreclose further dialogue. I have focused specifically on two issues throughout: that of tropological mediation and what I have identified as Margery's maternalist negativity. These issues are linked in that they foreground the problem of origins as an effect of loss: loss of the real in representation, and loss of the mother through the entry into language. As we shall see in the remaining chapters of this book, authorial anxiety about loss and linguistic instability inevitably seeks to project itself onto the feminine—or feminized—body. The feminist writer must create other strategies; this project, like Margery Kempe's autobiography, is an attempt to do just that.

## 2. Body and Metaphor in the Middle English *Juliana*

Very little has been written about medieval hagiography in general, still less about the three early Middle English legends known as the Katherine Group. The legends of Saints Katherine, Margaret, and Juliana are found together in two manuscripts: MS Bodley 34 and MS Royal 17A, which date from the first quarter of the thirteenth century. The texts are linked linguistically as well as thematically; together with the treatises known as the *Ancrene Riwle* and *Hali Meidenhad*, they represent an attempt at linguistic standardization.[1] Written during a period of Anglo-Norman cultural and linguistic hegemony, these legends usually exclude romance vocabulary, simultaneously affirming Christian ideology and Anglo-Saxon ethnic identity. They have a specific ideological agenda, which would link faith and Englishness, theology and (the English) language.

This narrative strategy leads to more than a few contradictions. Positioning itself against courtly/romance ideology, the hagiographical text foregrounds the violence that subtends courtly discourse. By placing this violence in the service of Christian allegory, however, it also uncovers the generic similarity or mutual reflexivity of these two seemingly exclusive discursive systems. As hagiography depends on the specular strategies of romance in carrying out its ideological/allegorical agenda, so courtly romance conceals a subtext of aggression and violence equal to that of the Katherine texts.[2] It is this paradox, this blurring of generic boundaries, that makes the Katherine legends, like Margery's *Book*, so troubling and so fascinating. In the pages that follow, I will explore the violence and violations of one of the Katherine texts: *The Life and Passion of St. Juliana*. The *Juliana*, like many of the legends of virgin martyrs, can be read as a drama of origins; it represents the sacrifice of the feminine or feminized body that enables the transcendence of *logos*, or, in Lacanian terms, of the paternal metaphor.[3]

The problem of origins has a particular urgency in the Katherine legends, moreover, that it lacks in others of the genre. Seeking to establish a relationship between the genesis of the Faith (the early Christian world) and the "true" or original English language, these legends have a specifically rhetorical investment in the epistemological question of beginnings, an investment that is inseparable from the historical context of the texts themselves. Within the *Juliana*, ecclesiastical and secular political concerns find themselves in uneasy alliance against the hegemonic discourses of Anglo-Norman England. The "anti-romantic" hagiographic text becomes the means whereby the Roman Church may enlist the Anglo-Saxon aristocratic minority in its ideological struggles with the too-independent Norman rulers of Britain.

At the same time, the secular and material concerns of that same disenfranchised minority are endowed with theological significance. As we shall see, the *Juliana* inscribes a nostalgic ideal of Englishness within a fantasy of Christian origins, a fantasy whose coherence and ideological efficacy depend upon the violent fragmentation and abjection of the feminine body. Juliana's body is the central object over and through which relations of power and resistance are played out. Torn apart at the hands of the "courtly heathen" Eleusius, it stands in for the imaginary body of the English nation, fragmented under the linguistic hegemony of a conquering people. There are thus two allegorical systems at work here, both of which illustrate the intimate connection between bodies and signifying systems. The English language is shown to transcend the dissolution of the social and political body wherein it originates, just as the typological relation between the female saint and Christ is predicated upon the violent sublimation of her feminine flesh. In some sense, then, the *Juliana* allegorizes the putative triumph of *logos* over temporality—a triumph that is, as I will argue throughout this chapter, parasitically dependent on the violent imposition of sexual difference, whereby a transcendent meaning is extracted painfully from the broken surface of the body itself.


## Romance and Abjection: A Question of Origins

In her appendix to the EETS edition of the *Juliana*, S.R.T.O. d'Ardenne notes with a certain romanticism the text's concern for linguistic origins:

> And although we find [the *Juliana*] on the whole brought up to date, a literary equivalent of good colloquial language, a speech of ladies' bowers and the halls of the gentle, it is garnished with ancient English ornament—with alliteration, and a copious flow of words, used often for the pleasure, which

the ancient poets themselves knew, of unlocking the ancestral *word-hord* and bringing out old treasures which moth and rust had spared.[4]

In a moment of imaginary misrecognition, the editor's nostalgia mirrors that of the text; the legend, like the "ancient English ornament" it purports to recover, takes on the privileged status of a lost archaic object—an object, moreover, associated with pleasurable feminine enclosures, with "ladies' bowers and the halls of the gentle," "copious" flows, and forgotten treasure-chests.

D'Ardenne's feminization of the text as archaic object is, I think, significant in light of the *Juliana*'s own fetishistic relation to the feminine body and to language. As so often in medieval literature and criticism, the problem of origins is bound up with that of sexual difference: woman stands in both for the lost pre-linguistic object and for what Julia Kristeva has theorized as the abject.[5] The abject corresponds to the vanishing point of symbolic and social control over the fragmenting and dissolving impulses of what Kristeva terms "semiotic" drives; through the process of abjection or "casting off," unpleasurable bodily processes become gradually implicated in processes of signification, leading to the binarist scapegoating and quasi-mythic sacrifices that inform all representational systems. For Kristeva, the drama of abjection involves the subject in an unwilling confrontation with the perilous borderline between inside and outside, source and supplement, life and death. Bodily residues, proof that the body itself is not a closed system, must be repulsed, as must any reminders that borders are untenable. Not surprisingly, Kristeva's analysis leads to the image of the "two-faced mother," who is both the "condition of writing" and "the black power who points to the ephemeral nature of sublimation and the unrelenting end of life, the death of man."[6] The mother is both the archaic object, idealized in lyric and elegy, and the despised abject, a reminder of the link between origin and end. D'Ardenne's association of this violent and voyeuristic text with pleasurable flows and archaic feminine enclosures is thus not as incongruous as it might seem. As Kristeva points out, a confrontation with the abject is always a confrontation with "the desirable and terrifying, nourishing and murderous . . . inside of the maternal body."[7] A confrontation, in short, with an origin both repulsive and erotic, which we simultaneously desire to expel and incorporate.

Kristeva's theory of abjection offers a framework for understanding the contradictions and paradoxes of the *Juliana*, a text at once nostalgic, reverent, and violent, linking courtly romance, originary fantasy, and hagiographic sacrifice in disturbing and fascinating ways. One way of approaching these points of conflict in the text, it seems to me, is through its invocation and manipulation of abjection's putative opposite: courtly idealization.[8] Significantly, the idealizing tropes of romance are allied with the heathen in the *Juliana*; the only romance vocabulary in the narrative is associated with the pagan oppressor Eleusius. This vocabulary serves to invoke the entire cultural system of courtly romance, a system which, in this early period, was still foreign in (Anglo-Saxon) England. When Eleusius first sees Juliana, his reaction is that of a conventional romance hero:

> As he hefde en-chere bihalden swiðe ӡeorne hire utnume feire ant freoliche ӡuheðe, felde him iwundet inwið in his heorte wið þe flan þe of luue fleoð. . . . (33–35)

> (When he had beheld very eagerly her exceptionally fair and noble youthfulness, he felt himself wounded within his heart with the arrow that flies from (i.e., on account of) love. . . . )

Similarly, he sets out to woo her in an opulent carriage, the description of which seems more in keeping with French romance than English hagiography:

> Al þe *cure* wes ouertild þet he wes itohen on wið *purpres* and *pelles*, wið *ciclatuns* ant *cendals* ant deorewurðe claðes. . . . (66–68)

> (The whole carriage that he was pulled on was canopied with purple cloths and other costly stuff, with scarlet cloth and fine silks and precious materials. . . . )

In this self-consciously Germanic English narrative, these Latin and French words cannot but be conspicuous. Eleusius is cast in the role of romance hero, and Juliana becomes yet another reluctant damsel to be wooed away from her father. The hagiographic system subsumes that of romance, however, and we are forced to read courtly convention through the Christian code of the saint's legend. The romance hero is metamorphosed into mere sadist, the would-be courtly heroine becomes the victim of his unbridled passion: lust passes easily into torture, romance into violence.

Love and romance are, moreover, allied with torture and fragmentation in an explicitly visual way. Upon seeing Juliana, Eleusius suffers love-pangs that transgress the limits of conventional figuration:

As he biseh ant biheold hire lufsume leor, lilies ilicnesse ant redi ase rose, . . .
his heorte feng to heaten, ant his meari mealten; þe rawen rahten of luue
þurh euch lið of his limes. . . . (195–201)

(As he saw and beheld her lovely complexion, in likeness of a lily and red as
a rose, his heart began to heat, and his marrow to melt; the rays of love made
their way through every joint of his limbs. . . . )

Later, *Juliana*'s body will be pierced through the joints, and her bone
marrow will "burst out" as she undergoes repeated tortures at the hands
of her father and her would-be lover. Eleusius's courtly discourse conceals
an aggressive and sadistic subtext that is, in the legend, allied with both
pagan and Norman political hegemony. The text sets up an analogy between early Christians and Anglo-Saxon aristocrats, marginalized under
pagan and Norman domination respectively. This analogy only works if
the English language is thought to have had an originary integrity that
corresponds to that of the Word itself. In the beginning, we are implicitly
told, there was Anglo-Saxon English, uncorrupted and undivided by any
conquering tongue. This mythic integrity is given further support by the
text's "ornamental" use of alliteration, the Anglo-Saxon compositional
meter. The linguistic non-differentiation that the hagiographer seeks to
(re-)create finds acoustic confirmation in the non-differentiation of pho-
nemes, the incantatory unities of alliteration, itself a marginalized mode in
thirteenth-century England.[9] This artificial reassertion of an archaic meter
enables the hagiographer to articulate the fantasy of origins rhythmically,
as it were, and to deny the difference that inheres not only in the English
language, but in language per se.

Not surprisingly, Juliana's speech is more consistently alliterative than
that of the other characters. What is more, only she indulges in word-play,
which, as Freud has shown in his work on jokes, is a kind of rhetorical
violence.[10] Her metrically integrated speeches often follow some of the
most violent moments in the narrative. For example, she answers her father's threats of dismemberment with a threat of rhetorical destruction:

"Beaten se ȝe beaten, ȝe Beliales budeles, ne mahe ȝe nowðer mi luue ne mi
beleaue lutlin towart te liuiende godd, mi leofsume leofmon þe luuwurðe
lauerd; ne nulle ich leuen *ower read þe forreadeð ow seolf*. . . ." (159–64)

("Beat howevermuch you will, you ministers of Belial, you may diminish
neither my love for nor my belief in the living God, my loveable lover, the
love-worthy lord; nor will I believe *your counsel that counsels you to your own
destruction*. . . .")

Later, her command of the poetic law of alliteration works to destabilize the entire signifying system of her pagan oppressor:

> ". . . 3ef þu cneowe ant were cuð wið þe king þet is ouer alle kinges icrunet in heouene, lutel waldest tu leoten of *ower lahelase lahen*, þe leareð ow to luken deadliche schaftes. . . ." (Roy. 17a, 158–61)

> (". . . if you knew and were familiar with the king who is crowned over all kings in heaven, little would you esteem *your lawless laws*, which teach you to worship deadly creations. . . .")

When law can be likened to anarchy, signification, based as it is on cultural agreement, becomes an impossibility. The subject of such a discourse ("read") would indeed rhetorically self-destruct ("forreadeð" himself).

Ultimately, the destruction of the saint's body guarantees the integrity of her discourse and the dismantling of her oppressors', just as in the Christian scheme the discursive integrity of the faith depends upon the abjection of the feminine (or feminized) body.[11] The contiguous relationship between the scenes of dismemberment and the saint's metrically integrated speech compels us to see these two aspects of the text as linked. At one point, the hagiographer even suggests that Juliana's rhetorical assurance is predicated on her physical pain:

> Ah heo hit al þuldeliche þolede for drihten, *ant hwen ha felde meast sar, sikerlukest seide*: "Halde on longe, ne leaue 3e neauer! for nulle ich leauen his luue þet ich on leue, ne for luue now er ne for luðer eie." (228–34)

> (But she suffered it all patiently for the lord, *and when she felt the most pain, said with most assurance*: "Hold on long, and never leave off! For I will not abandon his love, neither for love nor for wickedness.")

The emphasis on the saint's rhetorical power is, of course, a generic commonplace. What distinguishes this text from most others, however, is its fascination with the body and with the look. Obsessed with physical violence, the *Juliana* uncovers the latent violence of Christian dualism: the body is sacrificed/sublimated to ensure the continuity of the Word.[12] At the same time, however, the narrative's prurient excesses work to preserve the traces of the drives, thus enabling the eroticization of the abject so necessary to mystical theology.[13] In short, because of its excessively specular relation to violence and to the female body, the *Juliana* works at cross purposes. On the one hand, it allegorizes and justifies the dualism of Christian ideology. On the other, it unveils the libidinal substructure of the Christian signifying system, the visual/erotic subtext of the Christian story that effaces the border between body and spirit, and makes possible the metaphoric excesses of mystics and poets.

## The Body and the Look

Even within a genre fascinated by the political and epistemological power of the visual, the *Juliana* seems excessive in its fetishistic relation to the act of looking. In fact, the narrative is set in motion by the look: Eleusius becomes obsessed with Juliana after seeing her in her father's house, and later, as her body is broken, fragmented, and exposed, we are called upon to watch:

> þe reue feng to rudnin i grome of great heorte, ant het his heaðene men strupen hire steort-naket, ant strecchen o þer eorðe, ant hwil þet eauer six men mahten idrehen, beaten hire bodi, þet ha al were bigoten of þe blode.
>
>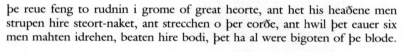
>
> þer wes sorhe to seon on hire freoliche flesch hu ha ferden þer-wið. (210–15; 228–29)

> (The reeve began to redden in great anger, and had his heathen men strip her stark naked, and stretch her out upon the earth, and for as long as the six men might hold out, beat her body until it was all drenched in blood.
>
> It was sorrow to see how they dealt with her noble body.)

The reader/hearer is implicated in these torture scenes; like Eleusius himself, we gaze with prurient interest at the spectacle of the broken female body:

> . . . ha bigon to breoken al as þet istelede irn strac hire in oueral, from þe top to þe tan, aa as hit turnde, tolimede hire ant leac lið ba ant lire; bursten hire banes ant þet meari bearst ut, imenget wið blode. þer me mahte iseon alre sorhene meast, þe i þet stude stode. (560–65)

> ( . . . they began to break her into pieces as that steeled iron pierced her everywhere, from head to toe, all over. Ever as it turned, it tore her limb from limb, and broke her bones so that the marrow burst out, mingled with blood. There one might see the greatest of all sorrows, who stood in that place.)

The power of the gaze eclipses that of the word; on two occasions, when Juliana refuses to renounce her faith, Eleusius commands not that she be silenced, but that she be taken "ut of his eh-sihðe" ("out of his eyesight"). Similarly, Juliana prays to Christ that he not cast her out of his eyesight (654–55).

It is the spectacle of dismemberment that fuels this scopophilic fantasy; the text is, in fact, framed by the image of mutilated flesh. Early in the story, Juliana's father urges her to take Eleusius for her husband, threatening her with a horrible death:

> ". . . 3ef þu haldest her-on, ich schal leote wilde deor toluken ant toteore þe ant 3eoue þi flesch fode to fuheles of þe lufte." (109–11)

> (". . . if you keep this up, I will let wild animals tear you limb from limb, and give your flesh as food to birds of the air.")

After her martyrdom, and just prior to the end of the narrative, it is Eleusius and his men who suffer this fate:

> . . . wilde deor limmel to-luken ham ant to-limeden eauer-euch lið from þe lire. . . . (763–65)

> ( . . . wild animals tore them limb from limb and ripped every joint from the flesh. . . . )

We also learn that spiritual degeneration plays itself out on the body rather than the soul of the sinner. The devil whom Juliana captures boasts of his evil deeds against humankind in physical rather than spiritual terms:

> "Ich habbe iblend men ant ibroken ham þe schuldren ant te schonken . . . ant hare ahne blod ich habbe ofte imaket ham to spitten ant to speowen. . . ." (465–68)

> ("I have blinded men, and broken their legs and shoulders . . . and I have often made them spit and spew out their own blood. . . .")

Emphasizing corporeal fragmentation, abjection, and blinding, the devil's boast confirms what the strategies of the voyeur and the fetishist work to deny: that the look itself originates in the body, and is thus capable of being interiorized by a gaze that originates elsewhere. Blindness, in short, is but another form of dismemberment; the eye partakes of the body's vulnerability and lack.

The problematic relation between the body and the look has been most thoroughly explored by psychoanalytic theory. Film theorists, in particular, have made much of the epistemological significance of the visual within Freud's texts.[14] Feminist film theory has carried this question a step further, stressing Freud's ambivalence with respect to the correspondence of looking and knowing. The feminist discussion of spectatorship in cinema has consistently focused on two related Freudian scenarios, both of which turn on the question of sexual differentiation: castration and fetishism.[15] In the first of these scenarios, a traumatic moment of looking confirms the anatomical lack of woman; in the second, this lack is at once acknowledged and denied in yet another specular moment, wherein the fetish stands in for the mother's missing penis.[16] The fetishistic scenario effectively re-stages the castration scene, with the addition of the all-important object that the first look failed to see.

The privilege accorded the look within Freudian theory corresponds to the privilege accorded the penis within patriarchal culture: masculine hegemony depends on this perception of absence, on the look that reveals the difference between having and not having. In his re-reading of Freud, Lacan understands the castration myth as a decisive metaphor for all the losses and divisions which attend the subject's entry into the symbolic order. Foremost among these is the loss of an immediate relation to the maternal object: a loss that both film and narrative theory have associated with the loss of the pre-linguistic or extradiegetic real.[17] To the extent that they constitute a denial of this loss, voyeuristic and fetishistic moments in literature and cinema rely on sexual difference as a means of establishing an opposition between presence and absence, an opposition that invariably places the male spectator on the outside vis à vis the interiorized feminine object of the look.[18]

Thus, in the *Juliana*, the inscribed spectator, Eleusius, and Christ are all associated with visual exteriority, possessing, so it would seem, a gaze that transcends the vulnerability of the feminine body. In the case of the pagan Eleusius, however, this visual dominance cannot be sustained. As Juliana continues to triumph rhetorically, he finds himself increasingly unable to look at her. Ultimately, his look is incapable of asserting its distance from the body: his inability to master the scopic regime is but a prelude to his final dismemberment. The saint's metaphoric assertion that Eleusius and his men are part-objects—"deofles limen"—is literalized in the scattering of their body parts at the end of the narrative.

Juliana's discursive mastery, on the other hand, works against the fragmenting tortures of her oppressors. Her words, metaphorically allied with the divine *logos*, make possible the miracle of re-integration. In a manner not unlike that of a film running backwards—or so we imagine—her body is made whole once more. Unable to reduce Juliana's body to fragments, and thus unable to rid himself of his own symbolic lack, Eleusius finds no pleasure in the spectacle.[19] Since his sense of phallic exteriority depends upon his ability to associate his feminine victim with castration and interiority, it is not surprising that he eventually vents his frustration by ordering that she be removed from his field of vision until she can be finally silenced by means of decapitation:

> "Swiðe," quod he, "wið hire ut of min ehsihðe! þet ich ne seo hire nawt heonne forð mare, ear þe buc of hire bodi ant tet heauet liflese liggen isundret." (685–87)

> ("Quickly," he said, "Get her out of my sight, so that I may see her henceforth no more, till the trunk of her body lie lifeless, sundered from her head.")

Ultimately, it is Juliana herself who has the last look. Just prior to her martyrdom, she metaphorically pierces the devil with her gaze, as if to retaliate for the literal penetration of her own flesh during the numerous torture scenes:

> Iuliene þe eadie openede hire ehnen ant biheold towart him, . . . ant tet Belial blencte, ant breid him aӡeinwart bihinden hare schuldren, as for a shoten arewe. (697–701)

> (The blessed Juliana opened her eyes and cast a look toward him, . . . and Belial cringed, and started backwards behind their shoulders, as from a shot arrow.)

Juliana's gaze, which marks the transformation of spectacle into spectator, has the effect of surprising the reader/voyeur in the act of looking. Like her metrically integrated discourse, the saint's look would seem to stand outside the specular/libidinal economy of the narrative, and thus outside desire. Both her gaze and her speech are, moreover, irreparably cut off from her body: her final decapitation can be seen as a somewhat paradoxical attempt to literalize the hagiographer's dualist agenda. As Juliana's rhetorical transcendence of the body allies her with the divine Word, her putatively extrasemiotic gaze mirrors the ubiquitous "eh-sihðe" of Christ himself.

There are thus two kinds of looking in the *Juliana*: the prurient, fetishistic looking of Eleusius and his men, and the seemingly extradiegetic gaze of Christ, metaphorically linked to that of his saintly likeness, Juliana. In his *Seminar XI*, Lacan discusses this phenomenon in terms of what he calls "the split between the eye and the gaze."[20] According to Lacan, the gaze issues from all sides, while the eye sees "only from one point."[21] The gaze is situated outside the voyeuristic exchange, an exchange within which the eye would seem to aspire to transcendent exteriority. It is precisely at this moment—the moment when the eye is placed at the keyhole—that the gaze "surprises [the subject] in the function of voyeur, disturbs him, overwhelms him, and reduces him to shame."[22] Lacan adds that the surprised voyeur can be understood as a subject who is "sustaining himself in a function of desire."[23] The gaze, like the extrasemiotic realm of the real, is elusive, finally unapprehensible:

> In our relation to things, in so far as this relation is constituted by way of vision, and ordered in figures of representation, something slips, passes, is transmitted, from stage to stage, and is always to some degree eluded in it—that is what we call the gaze.[24]

The gaze is the absent first cause, the Other through and in which the subject is constituted. Given the elusiveness of the gaze-as-origin, what we are left with is the eye: the eye which can confer identity, as in the "mirror stage," or uncover lack, as in the Freudian castration scenario, or in the situation of the "surprised voyeur." Although the eye is, according to Lacan, always subordinated to the gaze, there is a sense in which the eye as embodied look exceeds the gaze as well. In her reading of *Seminar XI*, Kaja Silverman suggests that although the gaze

> always exceeds the look, the look might also be said to exceed the gaze, to carry a libidinal supplement which subordinates it, in turn, to a scopic subordination. The gaze, in other words, remains outside desire, the look stubbornly within.[25]

The paradoxical excesses of the eye or look vis à vis the gaze are also those of the hagiographical text, which elicits specular desire in the service of theology and transcendence. The binarist agenda of the legend depends upon the "libidinal supplement" generated by the desiring eye; in this text at least, the gaze is propped upon the embodied look.

Interestingly, Lacan's distinction between the elusive gaze and the insufficient-but-excessive look exactly parallels his distinction between metaphor and metonymy. Since theological representations are always intimately allied with the question of "likeness" or metaphor (a question that is itself bound up with the visual), I would like to turn, in this next section of my study, to the role of figuration in the *Juliana*. It is my hope that this discussion will begin to clarify the problematic conceptual nexus of the body, the look, and figural substitution in this difficult and fascinating text.

## The Paternal Metaphor

Given the text's obsession with bodies and words, it is not surprising that the word/suffix "lich[e]," denoting both body and likeness, appears throughout. On numerous occasions, we are told that Juliana has a "leofliche lich," and that she is, moreover, "patriarchen ilich." God, however, is "unlich . . . al worltliche men"; that is to say, God has no body, and is therefore "unmetaphorizable" or untranslatable. In poetic discourse, it is most often the body of woman that generates the tropes which *represent* the unity of the One, the Father who is unlike any other, and yet is the apotheosis of Otherness. The text's continual punning on the body ("lich") and the ability of words to represent something beyond themselves ("_____ liche") etymologically unveils the forgotten relationship between metaphor and the body, between the Word and the Flesh, thereby returning to the material/maternal origins of poetic speaking.

Although the *Juliana* is not a poetic text, its theological commitment to dialectical resolution uncovers certain similarities between hagiography and lyric poetry, similarities having specifically to do with the mutual dependence of sublimation and substitution. Sublimation, as Hegel pointed out, is predicated upon negativity, upon a denial of difference. In this it mirrors fetishism, wherein difference is denied specifically through substitution: in place of the mother's missing penis, an object or body-part. As the trope of substitution and similarity, metaphor, too, can be understood as a negation of difference; as Paul Ricoeur argues, metaphor unites mutually impertinent terms in a relation of "new pertinence."[26] The difference between terms is annulled or effaced, the epistemological gap is closed, or at least covered over.[27] This link between substitution and sublimation helps explain the centrality of both metaphor and fetishism in theological discourse: like courtly idealization and abjection, they are two sides of the same coin.

To the extent that it is concerned with continuity, with "living on" through patrilineal descent, lyric poetry is similarly theological: canonical lyrics since the Song of Songs have gestured metaphorically toward eternity. If God, or immortality, is that which is irremediably "other" or "unlich," then the task of both mystic and poet must be to affirm likeness by negating difference; in the *Juliana*, as so often in medieval Christian literature, metaphysical or ontological difference is figured as sexual difference. Juliana herself makes this conventional association in one of her final prayers:

> "Drihtin undeaðiich, an godd, almihti, alle oþre unlich, heouene wruhte ant eorðes ant alle iwrahte þinges, þe ich þonki to-dei alle þine deden. þu makedest mon of lame ant 3eue him liuiende gast ilich to þe seoluen, ant settest for his sake al þet i þe worlt is. Ah he forgulte him anan þurh þe eggunge of Eue ant wes iput sone ut of paraise selhðen." (572–78)

> ("Lord immortal, one God, Almighty, unlike all others, maker of heaven and earth and of all created things, I thank you today for all your works. You made man of clay and gave him a living spirit like to yourself, and placed, for his sake, everything that is in the world. But soon he ruined himself by guilt, through the urging of Eve, and was cast out of the joys of paradise.")

Through Eve, likeness became unlikeness; the gap between signifier and signified, man and God, could no longer be bridged, except through metaphor.[28] It is a philological paradox that Eve's unlikeness or dissimilarity to God bound her forever to the body: no longer "ilich" to God, she is incapable of transcending "lich."

What this paradox reveals, however, is that that figural substitution based on likeness can only succeed by negating its own origins: only by effacing or abjecting the mother's body can "lich" become "lichnesse." Both theological and poetic texts base their claim to patrilineal heritage upon a repudiation of the mother-as-matter. The feminine body, so often the object of and occasion for poetic and figurative expression, stands in for the lost origin that poetry evokes, contains, and ultimately denies. As object of the look, Juliana's body captures the libidinal energy of the reader/spectator; thus cathected, her body is then discarded as that energy is given over to political and theological "truths" based on patriarchy. Through this "casting off" of Juliana's "leofliche lich," the "lichnesse" of man and God, of Anglo-Saxon and early Christian, is affirmed.

In the hagiographic text as in the love lyrics we will consider presently, the fetishized feminine body bespeaks a negation or denial of the difference that is the condition of being-in-language. The discursive integrity of the Faith, linked to the integrity of the "original" English language, is shown to depend on the specular and spectacular dis-integration of woman as body. This strategy is only partially successful, however; there is a sense in which the text undermines its own ideological and religious agenda. The alliterative word-play that links body and likeness, or body and metaphor, constitutes a return of the repressed relation of figure to figure of speech; like Margery Kempe's *Book*, the *Juliana* can be said to turn figural language "up-so-down." The word "lich" mirrors Juliana's own broken body in refusing to surrender to the metaphors or similes it generates; we are not allowed to forget that rhetorical likeness is also "lich"-ness, that the Word originates in the Flesh.

In psychoanalytic terms, the *Juliana* helps explain why the body of the other—woman—is most often the poetic means to the transcendent Other; through woman, the poetic voice may claim the authority of the disembodied *logos*, or, in theological terms, the unrepresentable Father. In this final section of my analysis, I would like to turn once again to the work of Lacan in exploring what I take to be the most salient feminist issue in the *Juliana*: the relationship between the fetishized feminine body and the "paternal mystery" which is the structuring mythology of this, as of any hagiographic text. At the center of this theoretical crux is the question of metaphor.

Lacanian theory, proposing a "return to Freud" through structural linguistics, would seem to have much to say about the relation of metaphor to the question of sexual difference, and thus much to offer to our reading of *Juliana*. Indeed, both Lacan and his exegetes have written extensively on both feminine sexuality and the metaphor/metonymy opposition. For the most part, however, these two concerns remain parallel yet separate in Lacan's work, although Jane Gallop effects a momentary intersection of these two strands of Lacanian thought in her suggestion that Lacan has in fact "metaphorized" the metaphor/metonymy dyad in sexual terms, metaphor being the privileged term, denoting presence and plenitude, while metonymy bears the burden of lack or insufficiency.[29]

Three of Lacan's essays seem particularly relevant to the problematics of figural language as revealed in the *Juliana*, these being "The Agency of the Letter in the Unconscious," which dates from 1957,[30] and the two central chapters of Lacan's seminar XX, *Encore*, which he gave much later, in 1972–1973.[31] The essays represent two distinct periods in Lacan's career, and my analysis admittedly de-historicizes them. Nevertheless, I believe that the essays explore the same dynamic in different terms. Lacan's analysis of metaphor and metonymy prefigures his later observations about the relation between God as Other and woman as *objet petit a*,[32] or "diminished" other. As metaphor depends upon the rhetorical "excess" generated by metonymy—the trope of displacement and deferral—so the idea of God hinges upon what Lacan calls the "supplementary *jouissance*" of woman. The metaphor/metonymy distinction also qualifies the Oedipal configuration such that the "paternal metaphor," the Name of the Father, ensures the metonymic structure of the "desire to have" which results from the alienation (through language) of the need for union with the mother. As metonymy, desire looks both backward and forward, representing a nostalgia for the lost object relation as well as the impossibility of satisfaction and closure.

In "The Agency of the Letter," Lacan distinguishes metaphor and metonymy by means of two algorithms, in which metonymy is identified with the horizontal line, the minus sign, while metaphor is presented as a vertical line which "crosses the bar" of metonymy, resulting in the sign of surplus ( + ).[33] The distinction between horizontal and vertical becomes a distinction between lack and surplus, as Lacan reads the Jakobsonian axes in terms of the cultural value of these two tropes. Metonymy is "necessary" but "not sufficient," manifesting "a certain servitude."[34] Metaphor, founded on difference, depends upon metonymy's insufficiency, but also, paradoxically, upon the rhetorical excess generated by its tendency to defer meaning and closure. In "crossing the bar," metaphor constitutes itself as supplement as against the lack or want-of-being (*manque à être*) that characterizes metonymy.

Lacan suggests, moreover, a connection between the plus sign and the cross as sacred symbol; as the trope of surplus, metaphor may be said to claim for itself a theological value.[35] Reading metaphor in Victor Hugo's *Booz endormi*, he uncovers a dynamic very similar to that which we have claimed for *Juliana*. The annihilation of the primary signifier, in this case a man's name, is linked to a specifically male ideal of fecundity:

> . . . it is between the signifier in the form of the proper name of a man and the signifier that metaphorically abolishes him that the poetic spark is produced, and it is in this case all the more effective in realizing the signification of paternity in that it reproduces the mythical event in terms of which Freud reconstructed the progress, in the unconscious of all men, of the paternal mystery.[36]

It is through metaphor's effacement of its own origins that it serves the myth of paternal productivity: the myth, in short, of writing. The "poetic spark" is produced at the cost of the primary term, the term which is bound within the linear or temporal narrative. Metaphor depends upon, yet transcends the narrative proper; it gestures beyond the ephemeral, holding out the promise of eternal continuity. In the literary as well as in the material realm, the fulfillment of this promise is denied man, except through the body of woman.

Lacan's own debt to the material or biological is here apparent. As man moves through the body of woman in his quest for immortality (he cannot get sons without her), so metaphor is said to "cross the bar," or transgress the linearity of metonymy in asserting its transcendent value. In his later work on feminine sexuality, Lacan carries this argument to its logical conclusion in associating woman and (the idea of) God. Within representation, God as transcendent Other depends upon woman as *objet petit a* (as symptom, or as cause of male desire). It is significant for our purposes that his discussion of this relationship should recall his earlier work on Jakobson's two axes of language. Like metonymy, woman represents a paradox: she is insufficient (*pas tout*), but also endowed with "a supplementary *jouissance*."[37] In the case of metonymy, rhetorical surplus is said to derive from deferral, while woman is associated with supplement precisely because she is "excluded from the nature of things which is the nature of words." That is to say, because the *jouissance* of woman is excentric, outside the (re-) productive circuit, it (and thus she), is identified with excess, and thus with figuration itself. Metaphor, like mystical theology, claims this imaginary excess for the Symbolic Order, for the Law. On this point, Lacan speaks with uncharacteristic clarity:

> It is insofar as her *jouissance* is radically Other that the woman has a relation to God greater than all that has been stated in ancient speculation according to a path which has manifestly been articulated only as the good of mankind. The objective of my teaching, inasmuch as it aims at that part of analytic discourse which can be formulated, or put down, is to dissociate the *a* and the *O*, by reducing the former to what belongs to the Imaginary, and the latter to what belongs to the Symbolic. That the Symbolic is the support of that which was made into God, is beyond doubt. That the Imaginary is supported by the reflection of like to like, is certain.[38]

Paradoxically, it is only by exposing the link between *a* (woman as symptom) and *O* (God as unspeakable Other) that Lacan is able to "dissociate" them. This link, hitherto veiled, locates woman at the center of the "double business" of representation. Duplicitously, the feminine body elicits desire in the service of morality: woman provides the mystical means to the Other, and then is sacrificed in order to safeguard the imaginary link between man and God, or, more precisely, between the text and the Law of the Father.

Given the theological implications of feminine *jouissance*, we should not be surprised to find that Lacan associates woman with metaphor rather than with metonymy, in spite of his undeniable "feminization" of the latter. This assertion would seem to be a theoretical non sequitur, or at the very least yet another inscrutable Lacanian paradox. *Juliana* offers a way of understanding the issue, however, which takes into account the question of sexual difference as it relates to *both* narrative axes. It is clear that Juliana's femininity is bound by the linear narrative: she is, in material/temporal terms, given over to the power of men against whom she alone can do nothing. Her metaphoric value as a Christ-figure, a woman who is "patriarchen ilich," enables her to transcend the temporality of the narrative situation and ascend to the realm of the poetic and eternal. Her body, irreducibly material and feminine, is cut off from the immateriality of her patriarchal discourse. Our look at Juliana's tortured body bridges the gap or disjunction between body and word in the text. What emerges from this structural assessment of the legend qualifies the work of both Lacan and Gallop: in medieval hagiography at least, woman is not merely bound to the material and metonymic, nor is she located on the vertical axis of metaphor. My reading of *Juliana* suggests that the feminine body is placed at the point where the two axes intersect, where the linear narrative gives way to the figural and transcendent. The look at the body covers over the point at which the representational system, and the ideological agenda it enforces, is weakest: the moment when the narrative attempts to move beyond its own mimetic circuit, and thereby to lay claim to an Other truth, a "figurative" or typological meaning.

Lacan's work on metaphor and metonymy parallels his analysis of the eye and the gaze in revealing the sense in which the privileged term is propped upon its "insufficient" opposite: as metaphor depends upon metonymy in creating its illusion of plenitude, so is the gaze exceeded by the desiring look. Together, these paradigms provide a theoretical way into the problematic juxtaposition of specular eroticism and Christian theology in the *Juliana*. Within the hagiographic text, the simultaneous gesture toward transcendent truth and lost linguistic plenitude is predicated upon the eroticization of the abject; if women "can wreck the infinite," as Julia Kristeva points out, they can also provide the means to its figural attainment.

Because *Juliana* trades on exposure, its readers have, in effect, nowhere to hide; the unveiling of the feminine body here discloses the violence of interpretation as well. As object of the look, Juliana's body "causes" a mystical desire for the Other as God. Her body is then broken and cast aside so that the text may place that desire in the service of ethnic, and finally Christian, ideology. Metaphor, as I have attempted to show here, operates in much the same fashion. The primary term is "sacrificed" to ensure the poetic/transcendent value of the trope itself, the figure of speech. Having elicited the reader's (or hearer's) desire, the "body" of the trope is discarded; finally disembodied, metaphor evokes nothing so much as what Lacan has called the Name of the Father—he who is "unlich," or bodyless. For the theorist, no less than for any other "on-looker" ("theory" being derived from the Greek verb meaning to look on, or contemplate), the textualized feminine body stands in for the problematics of figural language.

Intended as an ideological affirmation of Christianity and the English language, *Juliana* inadvertently unmasks the figural likenesses it seeks to create. Its exclusion from the Middle English canon can perhaps be traced to its failure to repress the ideological agenda of figuration, the sexual and theological politics of metaphor-making. Through metaphor, the subject of poetic discourse is seduced into an imaginary relationship with language, a relationship which holds out the promise of excess, of surplus value. Jakobson has claimed that metaphor is based on a process of selection and substitution.[39] Both Lacan and Derrida have pointed out that this is but another way of saying that metaphor is founded on negativity, that, in Lacan's words, it "occurs at the precise point at which sense emerges from non-sense."[40]

In metaphor, the figure of speech ob*liter*ates the figure or body from which it is generated. This originary violence is reenacted in *Juliana*: the Flesh is here sacrificed to the Word, in a repetition of the sacred myth of writing, the Holy Scripture itself. It is possible to say, then, that insofar as hagiographic literature bases its claim to transcendent value on the metaphoric sacrifice of the body, it constitutes a re-casting of this myth.

Again, it is not only the double-ness of representation that is exposed here. *Juliana* confronts us with the duplicity of the critical enterprise as well. The critic of canonical literature acts as a sacerdotal mediator between the (presumably innocent) reader and the transcendent truth of which the text is merely a symptom. Popular hagiography, with its emphasis on the text-as-body and the (religious) meaning-as-spirit, literalizes the priestly role of the critic as analyst. It also forces us to confront an aspect of reading, and thus of criticism, that remains veiled in canonical texts. Compelled to acknowledge the symbiosis of abject and transcendent Other, the reader of *Juliana* cannot fulfill a sacerdotal role, cannot analyze the text without acting first as voyeur, as on-looker. In bearing the Word, the critical reader becomes complicit in the abjection of the Flesh; she or he acquiesces perforce in the casting off of the body as the price of a phallocentric, authoritative discourse. Clearly, what is at stake in the literary canon is not merely the preservation of "great" literature. As I hope to have shown here, the Katherine legends remain marginal and largely unread because they threaten to disclose the dynamics of representation, the working of sexual difference and political ideologies in the "sacred" business of writing.

# 3. Women and Riot in the Harley Lyrics

In the previous chapter, I identified the hagiographic text with a lyrical movement whereby the feminine body is sacrificed to the theological metaphor. The Middle English *Juliana*, like so many medieval saints' legends, can be understood as a purification ritual: man is like God only to the extent that he can dissociate himself from body by linking femininity to the notion of an intractable and irreducible materiality. I also made the rather bold claim that many secular texts are similarly bound to the theological aspect of metaphor, and thus to an essentialist notion of sexual difference that allows woman to stand in for the problematics of origin. In the chapters that follow, I will be exploring this idea further, paying particular attention to courtly discourse, and the extent to which it succeeds in repressing the primal violence of tropological substitution, a violence whereby the feminine body is ob*liter*ated ("written out") in a poetic struggle for dialectical resolution or transcendence, a struggle that I am calling lyrical.

A logical point of departure for this interrogation of courtly language is the love lyric itself. Lyric poetry, like autobiography, problematizes the relation between form and affect, figure and voice, or, more generally, inside and outside.[1] While traditional readers of the lyric have tended to privilege one of these constituents at the expense of the other, post-structuralist critics such as Paul de Man have emphasized the sense in which the lyrical voice is itself a figure or a trope which ultimately effaces the boundaries upon which hermeneutic closure depends. De Man argues that the figure of prosopopoeia, the lyrical trope par excellence, "gives a face" to inanimate and imperceptible entities, but not without exacting a price. According to de Man, there is a "latent threat that inhabits prosopopoeia, namely that by making the dead speak, the symmetrical structure of the trope implies, by the same token, that the living are struck dumb, frozen in their own death."[2] In other words, the effacement of the border between life and death which lyric—and particularly elegiac lyric—promises carries with it a potential return to inanimacy and silence.

Psychoanalytic discourse has explored this dilemma in ontological and epistemological terms in conjunction with a theorization of mourning and its pathological sibling, melancholia. Freud notes that the melancholic subject, faced with an irremediable loss, withdraws almost completely from the outside world, becoming, in a sense, "frozen," paralyzed and circumscribed by the specter of loss iself. Following the loss of the object, the free libido is "withdrawn into the ego," resulting in "an identification of the ego with the abandoned object." Thus object-loss becomes ego-loss, and, as Freud puts it, "the conflict between the ego and the loved object [is transformed] into a cleavage between the critical activity of the ego and the ego as altered by identification."[3] As the lyrical trope that "gives a face" to melancholia, prosopopoeia partakes of its pathological tendency to efface the boundaries between presence and absence, or, in de Man's terms, between the living and the dead.[4]

An exploration of the problem of loss is vital to any understanding of the lyric voice and the lyric event in the Middle Ages, since most medieval lyric poems are staged as an attempt to come to terms with absence or privation. This is particularly true of courtly lyrics, in which figural language circulates around an empty center, the place of the absent love-object. Within the courtly lyric, women are celebrated, entreated, mourned and blamed; with the generic exception of *Frauenlieder* and *Wechsel*, they remain fixedly absent within the poems themselves. The absent feminine body becomes the "excuse" for the tropological substitutions that enable the construction of a culturally-specific poetic subjectivity. Like the hagiographical text, the courtly lyric promises a final sublimation or *Aufhebung* of its dialectical terms: the sensual and the spiritual, the particular and the universal seem to move toward synthesis and finally transcendence as the lyric poem draws to a close. As in the saint's legend, this synthesis depends upon the dis-integration of the feminine body through the figural substitutions that appropriate feminine "excess" or *jouissance* in creating an illusion of discursive plenitude. This strategy, this giving of face or figure at the expense of an always absent other is, as both post-structuralist and psychoanalytic theory have suggested, beset with contradictions and fraught with danger. In the pages that follow, I will continue my exploration of the relation between the feminine body and the poetic/authorial voice, this time in the context of an analysis of several of the Harleian love-lyrics. As in previous chapters, my readings will focus on the points of resistance in the semiotic system, and the sense in which these texts fail in their efforts to substitute feminine lack for discursive inadequacy, or, in

Lacanian terms, for the symbolic castration that attends the entry into language and culture.

## Poetic Art Running Riot

The lyrics contained in MS Harley 2253 mirror the Middle English *Juliana* (and, until recently, the *Book of Margery Kempe*) in the dearth of critical responses they have evoked. What little secondary literature there is on the Middle English lyric has been devoted almost exclusively to the religious poems; work on the secular lyrics has for the most part been marred by critical prejudice and aesthetic qualification. In his valuable reference work on Old and Middle English poetry, Derek Pearsall notes that "MS Harley 2253 is one MS which needs no preamble, which demands consideration in its own right, as a unique record of the state of English poetry during the early years of the fourteenth century." Nevertheless, his discussion of the secular love lyrics in the collection focuses on lack. The love poems, we are told, "lack the theorising, abstraction, analysis and paradox of courtly Provençal and French lyric," they are "fundamentally simple," "a little *passé*," and ultimately "lack real sophistication."[5] It is a testament to how little the field has changed its view of the lyric that some three decades ago, in one of the few books devoted exclusively to a study of the secular lyric, Arthur K. Moore lamented the "conceited style and wooden formulas," the "patchwork of redundant phrases and hackneyed images" in many of the Harley texts.[6] For Moore, the most salient issue was that of thematic and rhetorical unity; the chief "flaw" in the Harleian poems is their inability (or refusal) to maintain a boundary between a courtly aristocratic discourse and a fundamentally irreverent popularization of that discourse. They are, as Moore and others have noted, "overdone" and "excessive" in their manipulation of courtly codes, alliteration, and figural language in general.[7]

It is because these texts are—like Margery's *Book* and the *Juliana*—fundamentally transgressive that I have chosen to discuss them here. In their violations of tone and register, their dismantling of courtly commonplaces, we may read more clearly the points of contradiction and resistance in the courtly system itself, and thus pave the way for a reconsideration of Chaucer's own manipulation of courtly conventions, his affirmation and violation of the sexual and cultural laws which those conventions inscribe and sustain. I have chosen to limit my analysis to five poems, to which I will refer using G. L. Brook's editorial titles: "Annot and John," "The Fair

Maid of Ribbesdale," "The Meeting in the Wood," "De Clerico et Puella," and "The Poet's Repentance."[8] (The full texts of these poems, with translations, are collected in an appendix). Obviously this study cannot be exhaustive; in these five poems alone there are sufficient theoretical, historical and philological problems to keep adventurous scholars busy for some time. What I would like to do here is to begin to open up a critical discourse on the secular lyrics by focusing on the relationship between sexual difference and figural language in five of the poems that seem to have presented the most difficulty for canonical readers. While this extra-canonical reading cannot redress the decades of silence and seeming indifference to the secular lyrics on the part of the critical community, it will, I hope, chart some possible directions for future inquiry.

In a translation of the Harley lyrics published in the early 1960s, Brian Stone labeled "Annot and John" as a case of "medieval poetic art running riot."[9] In the pages that follow, I will be exploring the extent to which this "riotousness" can be understood in terms of an illusory boundary between sexual and rhetorical excess. In all these poems, the question of femininity is the question of language; sexual difference stands in for a prior division within the speaking subject, a division that psychoanalysis understands as the effect of an originary loss. In poems such as "Annot and John" and "The Fair Maid of Ribbesdale," the instability of language is inscribed across the body of woman. Because the feminine body remains a blank place which nonetheless solicits an explicitly specular desire, however, the love lyric presents us with an epistemological dilemma which mirrors that of the Freudian castration scene. If the origin of linguistic instability is sexual difference, as these lyrics seem to suggest, the "proof" can only be found in absence, or, more precisely, in looking at what isn't there. By structuring woman as lack and absence in this decidedly specular way, the lyric poet effectively rationalizes his own fetishistic pleasure in a poetic language irreparably cut off from the realm of the real.

This illicit pleasure in the signifier is perhaps most explicit in "Annot and John," so named by G. L. Brook because it is one of the few lyrics which seems to reveal the name of the love-object. It is a poem that unsettles; the abundance and opacity of its figures of speech and its parodic evocation of the imagery of the Song of Songs have made it distasteful to most of its would-be exegetes. Here, as in many of the Harleian love poems, all senses are subsumed under the visual. In the first stanza, the lady is likened to precious stones, valued because they are "semly on sight"; in the second, she is associated with various herbs and flowers which are normally prized for their fragrance, but here for their appearance:

> He is blosme opon bleo, brightest under bis,
> With celydoine and sauge, as thou thyself sis.
> That sight upon that semly, to blis he is
> broght. . . .

> (She is a blossom with regard to her face, brightest under fine linen, /
> With celandine and sage, as you yourself see. / He who looks on that
> fair one, to bliss he is brought. . . . )

After the second stanza, the catalogue of metaphors and similes strays be-yond the boundary of conventional figuration; the link between percep-tion and cognition which metaphor sustains so tenuously is broken as the woman becomes a thrush "thriven in thro" (doughty in contention), a "wolc" (hawk), various spices and herbal medicines, and several Celtic, Scandinavian and romance literary figures of both sexes.[10] The poem closes with a theological allusion, a gesture toward transcendence that is typical of lyric texts; in light of the figural excesses of the preceding lines, how-ever, the reference to the biblical Jonas can only be seen as yet another non sequitur.[11] The closing gesture toward an other, extraliterary truth is finally undercut by an image that defies closure; by concluding this gratuitous catalogue with the image of a woman who "ioyeth," the poet links rhe-torical excess and feminine *jouissance*, masculine poetic pleasure and femi-nine sexual pleasure:

> He is medicine of miht, mercie of mede,
> Rekene ase Regnas resoun to rede,
> Trewe ase Tegeu in tour, ase Wyrwein in wede,
> Baldore then Byrne that oft the bor bede;
> Ase Wylcadoun he is wys, doghty of dede,
> Feyrore then Floyres folkes to fede,
> Cud ase Cradoc in court carf the brede,
> Hendore then Hilde, that haveth me to hede.
> He haueth me to hede, this hendy, anon;
> Gentil ase Jonas, heo joyeth with Jon.

> (She is a mighty medicine, a compassionate reward, / Ready as
> Regnas to advise reason, / True as Tegeu in a tower, as Wyrwein in

clothing, / Bolder than Byrne, who often challenged the boar, / She is as wise as Wylcadoun, doughty in deeds, / Fairer than Flores to please people, / As famous as Cradoc in court, who carved the roast meat, / More gracious than Hilde, who has me to care for. / She cares for me, this fair one, at once; / As gracious as Jonas, she enjoys herself with John.)

Most of these literary references remain opaque to us; probably at least some of them were unknown to the poem's audience as well. As the poem moves away from its highly conventional opening it becomes progressively more uncanny: the catalogue of conventional tropes continually slips into the improbable. We are told that the lady surpasses "the primerole . . . the perwenke of pris"; the poet then counters this conventional praise with a line that makes sense metrically, but non-sense thematically: "with alisaundre thareto, ache and anis." Similarly, in the fourth stanza, the lady is lost entirely as the poet seems to forget the celebratory purpose of his song:

Muge he is and mondrake thourgh might of the
        mone,
Trewe triacle itold with tonges in trone;
Such licoris may leche from Lyne to Lone;
Such sucre mon secheth that saneth men sone;
Blithe iblessed of Crist, that baytheth me my
        bone,
When derne deeds in day derne are done.
Ase gromil in greve grene is the grone,
Ase quibibe and comyn cud is in crone,
Cud comyn in court, canel in cofre,
With gingiure and sedewale and the gilofre.

(Nutmeg she is, and mandrake, through might of the moon, / True remedy, esteemed in speech in heaven; / Such licorice can heal from Lyn to Lune; / One seeks such sugar, that heals men quickly; / Happy one, blessed by Christ, who grants me my prayer / When secret deeds are done secretly in daylight. / As gromwell in a thicket, green is the seed, / As cubeb and cumin, known by its crown, / Cumin famous in court, cinnamon in a coffer, / With ginger and setwall and clove.)

Here, again, the theological gesture is neutralized by the line that follows: the poet's prayer is at once sexual and spiritual, and the reference to "derne deeds" points once again to the troubling connection between divine and feminine "privitee," between spiritual and sexual mysteries. The sublimation of matter that lyric generically promises is undone by the poem's continual appeal to specular desire, and by its inability to overcome or annul its pleasure in the signifier. Behind this profligacy of language, we are afforded a glimpse of another kind of excess, of "derne deeds in day," and of what may lie "under gore." Although woman herself is reduced to a "note of the nightegale," that is, to a pun, the poem itself holds out the promise of something more: the satisfaction of a desire to see both the feminine body and the "derne deeds" themselves. The rhetorical extravagance of "Annot and John" thus has a veiling effect; the veil serves as a lure for the reader/hearer.[12]

A similar veiling strategy can be discerned in another of the Harleian lyrics, "The Fair Maid of Ribbesdale." Here, too, the poet links tropological substitution to voyeuristic pleasure:

> When I biholde upon hire hond,
> The lilie-white lef in lond,
> Best heo mighte beo;
> Either arm an elne long,
> Baloigne mengeth all bimong;
> Ase baum is hire bleo;
> Fingres heo hath feir to folde;
> Mighte ich hire have and holde,
> In world well were me.
> Hire tittes aren anunder bis,
> As apples two of parays
> Youself ye mowen seo.

> (When I look upon her hand, / The lily-white dear one on land, / The best she may be; / Either arm an ell long / Whalebone mingles all among; / Her complexion is like balsam; / She has fingers fair to folde; / If I might have her to hold, / I would be doing well in the world. / Her breasts are under fine linen / As two apples of paradise — / You yourselves may see.)

Again, the poet offers his readers a glimpse of what lies "under bis." The metaphor enables a gaze that would otherwise be blocked; despite the veil of linen—itself a metaphor for metaphor—we may indulge our prurience, our desire to see the body exposed. In the stanza that follows, the specular moment is likewise both facilitated and veiled by fetishistic displacement:

> Hire gurdel of bete gold is all,
> Umben hire middel small,
> That triketh to the to;
> All with rubies on a rowe,
> Withinne corven, craft to knowe,
> And emeraudes mo;
> The bocle is all of whalles bon;
> Ther withinne stont a ston
> That warneth men from wo;
> The water that it wetes in
> Iwis it wortheth all to win;
> That seyen, seyden so.

(Her girdle is all of beaten gold, / Around her small waist, / That hangs down to the toe, / All with rubies in a row, / Carved within, to reveal craft, / And more emeralds; / The buckle is all of whalebone; / There within stands a stone / That protects men from woe; / The water in which it is dipped / Indeed it turns all to wine; / Those who saw it said so.)

By focusing on the belt buckle as a fetishistic substitute for the female genitalia, the poet exposes the body behind the tropological and material veils. Moreover, by resorting to metonymy rather than metaphor at this point in the *effictio*, he hints at what the fetishist already knows: that the fetish itself stands in for the absence or lack wherein sexual difference is thought to originate. In other words, the disconcerting move from breasts to girdle suggests that what lies beneath the fetishized article is precisely nothing. The gaze at the fetish—the belt buckle—reiterates the association of femininity and absence, an association upon which the love lyric depends. The switch from metaphor to metonymy at this point in the text suggests that the fixed absence of woman in the love lyric is founded on the assumption of a prior anatomical lack, a lack that is continually reaffirmed in the scopophilic enterprise of representation.

The appeal to scopophilia in these lyrics can be understood in another way as well. In his essay *Jokes and Their Relation to the Unconscious*, Freud distinguishes between "innocent" and "tendentious" jokes, and in his discussion of the latter, between those jokes motivated by hostility and those motivated by the "desire to see what is sexual exposed."[13] In this next section of my study, I will be exploring the relevance of Freud's analysis to a feminist reading of these lyrics. Ultimately, I will argue that Freud's work on jokes provides a way into an analysis of Chaucer's own problematic relation to the violence and scopophilia that subtends and sustains the semiotic system of courtly romance. It is my contention that the exclusion of the lyrics from the canon is mirrored in the critical exclusion of these troubling issues from the field of Chaucer Studies, and that a rethinking of these problematic texts can open up new possibilities for reading "extracanonically."

## Between Men: Lyrics, Tropes, and Dirty Jokes

According to Freud, obscene jokes uncover the mutually dependent relation between wooing or seduction and sexually-based aggression. In his analysis of obscene or "smutty" jokes, he notes the connection between voyeurism, violence and word-play:

> Smut (*die Zote*) is . . . originally directed towards women and may be equated with attempts at seduction. If a man in the company of men enjoys telling or listening to smut, the original situation, which owing to social inhibitions cannot be realized, is at the same time imagined. A person who laughs at the smut he hears is laughing as though he were the spectator of an act of aggression. . . . Smut is like the exposure of the sexually different person to whom it is directed. By the utterance of the obscene words it compels the person who is assailed to imagine the part of the body or the procedure in question, and shows her that the assailant is himself imagining it. It cannot be doubted that the desire to see what is sexual exposed is the original motive of smut.[14]

The goal of this smutty talk, like that of the "wooing speech" from which it derives, is to provide a rhetorical framework for the "assailant's" sexual excitement, and to "induce a corresponding excitement in the woman herself."[15] It is when the assailant meets with resistance, however, that the wooing speech degenerates into smut; it is also at this point that the smutty talk is redirected toward a third party, before whom the woman is now exposed as object of the dirty joke. The sexual excitement now passes between two men; the woman herself becomes merely the excuse for this erotically charged exchange. Freud argues that this shift occurs because of social and cultural interdicts that block the woman's surrender to and acquiescence in the proposed sexual act. It seems clear, however, that the dirty joke allows for a transgression of an even greater kind, in that it provides a socially acceptable context for the release of the libidinal tension that grounds homosocial relations between men. This explains why dirty jokes are most effective, as Freud points out, when the woman is *not* present.[16]

The appeal to a third party as on-looker in the Harleian love lyrics can be understood similarly. The wooing-song slips easily into a narrative of exposure directed not toward the absent woman, but rather toward the implicitly present voyeur, whose prurience and pleasure mirror and sustain that of the poet/speaker. As in the obscene or exposing joke, looking replaces touching; the desire to see one's pleasure reflected in the eyes of another supersedes any desire to possess the woman sexually, to perform "the procedure in question." The result of this displacement, Freud tells us, is "a generation of pleasure far greater than that offered by the supervening possibility."[17] In short, the pleasure in the signifier, here linked to the scopic drive, replaces and potentially exceeds the pleasure in the act itself. By channeling all desire's satisfaction into the word, the lyric/joke offers a yield of pleasure without social consequences, without danger.

As the absent other, woman legitimizes the narcissistic moment in courtly discourse. Her presence-as-absence facilitates the equation of femininity and psychic danger; she is, within the courtly lyric, both desired object and jettisoned abject. This ostensible paradox provides the epistemological basis for the metaphoric condensation of feminine instability and linguistic indeterminacy. Elusive or perfidious women stand in for slippery signifiers, and for the sexual undecidability that is a condition of psychic life. It is thus through the representation of women that the explicitly homosocial and implicitly homoerotic exchange that marks the lyric event becomes an affirmation of patriarchy rather than a threat to it; the sexual and metaphysical undecidability that haunts the borders of this pleasurable moment between men is neutralized, as so often, by an appeal to sexual difference.[18]

The correspondence between feminine and linguistic instability constitutes the ideological and, to some extent, thematic basis for one of the most difficult poems in the Harley collection: "The Poet's Repentance." Not surprisingly, the poem's discussion of the vices and virtues of women provides the setting for a confrontation between two men: the poet and "Richard, riht of reson rote," who emerges as the addressee in the final stanza. The difficulty of the lyric lies in its obsession with images of inversion and indeterminacy; chiastic syntactic structures and semantic instability at the level of the signifier combine with conventional binaries to create a mirroring effect, with the disconcerting result that most of the poet's assertions seem to collapse, uncannily, into their opposites. The poem begins with the speaker's promise to right the wrongs he has committed in writing about women, that is, to invert his former misogynistic stance:

> Weping haueth min wonges wet
> For wikked werk and wone of wit;
> Unblithe I be til I ha bet
> Bruches broken, ase bok bit,
> Of levedis loue, that I ha let,
> That lemeth all with luevly lit;
> Oft in song I have hem set,
> That is unsemly ther it sit.
> It sit and semeth noght
> Ther it is seid in song;
> That I have of hem wroght
> Iwis it is all wrong.

(Weeping has wet my cheeks / On account of wicked deeds and lack of wit; / I will be unhappy until I have atoned for / Broken breaches, as the book bids / Of ladies' love, that I have abandoned, / Who all gleam with a beautiful hue; / Often I have set them in song, / That is unsuitable where it suits [or, that is unsuitable where it is placed]. / It is placed, and is not suitable / There where it is said in song; / What I have written about them, / Indeed it is all wrong.)

Here, as throughout the poem, semantic and syntactic ambiguity indicate a profound ambivalence about the relationship between aesthetic perception, which traditionally lays claim to a certain immediacy, and cultural convention. In particular, the semantic slippage that adheres to the word "seme" (and its variants) throughout foregrounds a fundamentally problematic juxtaposition of difference and sameness ("seme" being the etymological cousin of "same"), or loss and recuperation.

In the second stanza, this tension is figured, as so often in medieval literature, in the typological antithesis of Eve and Mary. The figure of Eve gives a wider context to the poet's "weping"; his sins against women are placed within a larger theological drama of signification, of meaning lost through the Fall into a language based on substitution:

> All wrong I wroghte for a wif
> That made us wo in world full wide;
> Heo rafte us alle richesse rif,
> That durfte us nout in reines ride.
> A stithie stunte hire sturne strif,
> That is in heovene hert in hide.
> In hire light on ledeth lif,
> And shon thourgh hire semly side.
> Though hire side he shon
> Ase sonne doth thourgh the glass;
> Wommen nes wicked non
> Sethe he ibore was.

(All wrong I wrought concerning a woman / Who made woe for us in the world full wide; / She robbed us of all abundant riches / She, who shouldn't have dared to ride us in reins. / A strong and excellent person put an end to her violent strife, / That one is hidden in heaven's heart. / [Having] alighted in her, one leads life [i.e., lives] / And he shone through her excellent side [i.e., body]. / Through her side he shone / As sun does through glass; / There was never a [single] wicked woman / Since he was born.)

Eve's usurpation of male prerogatives is here given a sexual resonance. Her sin is excessive, even exhibitionist, encompassing as it does the "world full wide." Moreover, the conceptual link between feminine usurpation of masculine privilege and the usurpation that characterizes tropological substitution in language has a long history in misogynist literature.[19] Within medieval and renaissance rhetorical theory, the inversion of the right and proper in the making of tropes was often allied with Eve's initial subversion of moral and spiritual hierarchies. If Eve was the origin of the alienation of meaning, however, she was also the material origin of human life itself. The fear of rhetorical excess therefore carries with it the fear of the origin, of the mother as the absent first cause.

It is thus not surprising that the poet of the "Repentance" sets Eve's boundless public transgression against the virgin mother's containment and concealment "in heovene hert." If Eve exceeds and transgresses the boundaries of sexual difference, Mary transcends them: she is described as a "stithie," a term usually reserved for warriors, and her triumph over Eve is figured in martial terms. Perhaps most unusual is the poet's reversal of one of the traditional images of the incarnation. While exegetical writers and religious poets speak of Christ's conception as "sun passing through glass,"[20] our poet inverts the image so as to emphasize the transparency of the maternal body. Mary is here both contained (in heaven's heart) and container; the male child is enclosed but not bound, secure but not suffocated.[21] The transparency of the maternal body provides what I take to be a deliberate contrast to the opacity of the poet's "fallen" language. Effacing yet preserving the body of the mother, the poem represents the lost origin as a fantasy of a specifically discursive kind. The transparent maternal body is a figure for a transparent, neutral language, untainted by the lapse into difference that was Eve's legacy to man-kind.[22]

"The Poet's Repentance" encrypts a nostalgic yearning for non-differentiation, a desire to return to a state of unity and plenitude—a state which psychoanalysis understands as an archaic unity or fusion with the maternal object. At the same time, the poem evinces a certain paranoia about the maternal body, a fear of interiority that grounds the fantasy of a transparent and permeable womb, wherein security and unity do not also entail suffocation and silence. This ambivalence has as its consequence the transformation of object into abject, and accounts—at least partially—for the sadistic and aggressive subtext of this as well as many other secular lyrics of the period. Aggression, Freud tells us, is a fundamental component of the tendentious joke: the "inflexibility" of the desired object elicits both sexual excitement and hostility from the speaking subject.

Within the courtly fantasy, the "inflexible" woman is thus both central and marginal, both the condition and the conduit for a poetic exchange between men. Because the lyric voice is a tropological substitute for the empty center of the lyric event, it remains parasitically dependent on the absent presence of the object/abject. What makes "The Poet's Repentence" such a fascinating poem is its seeming awareness of the poet's essentially negative speaking position, and of the problematic of negativity within courtly discourse in general. Perhaps the most striking instance of this uncanny awareness occurs in the penultimate stanza, in which the poet

states his relation to femininity and poetry in terms so weighted in nega-
tives as to be comical:

> Ever wimmen ich herie ay,
> And ever in hyrd with hem ich holde,
> And ever at neode I nickenay
> That I ner nemnede that heo nolde.
> I nolde and nullit noght,
> For nothing now a nede,
> Soth is that I of hem wroght,
> As Richard erst con rede.

(I always praise women, / And I always defend them in a crowd, /
And always, when necessary, I deny / Having said anything they did
not wish. / I did not and will not [say] anything / For nothing now
of necessity, / What I have written of them is true, / As Richard first
did say.)

Representing the negativity at the heart of language, woman is the vanishing point of the poet's repentance: in negating his prior negation of an
essential negativity, the lyricist exposes the fragility of a courtly poetic
system grounded in absence and symptomatically characterized by denial—denial, that is, of its own inherent aggressivity toward the women
it purports to celebrate. Significantly, all this negativity leads us to the
poem's true addressee: the rhetorically and sexually masterful "Richard" of
the final stanza.

The correspondence between the unruliness of women and the unruliness of language—between sexual and rhetorical usurpation—conceals
the possibility of another interdicted usurpation whereby the male addressee might be substituted for the woman as the eroticized object of
poetic discourse. The yearning for non-differentiation and unity in "Repentance" carries with it an equally narcissistic desire for the image in the
chiastic mirror: the image represented by the rival poet with whom the
speaker shares this tendentious joke about women and language.

## The Violence of the Letter

Before moving on to my discussion of Chaucer's own courtly poetry, I
would like to explore in more detail the question of aggressivity as it

relates to the problem of voice and origin in the love lyric. I have already discussed the hagiographer's manipulation of the violence that subtends the language of courtly romance. In this final section of my study, I would like to look briefly at the lyric sub-genre that explores most explicitly the connection between courtly language, sexual difference and violence: the medieval *pastourelle*. Traditionally, the pastourelle is narrated in the past tense; the speaker assumes the persona of an aristocratic male who, while riding through the countryside "the other day," chanced upon a beautiful rustic or *bergère* whom he entreated for sexual favors.[23] The outcome of this encounter varies. In some cases, the woman outmaneuvers her assailant rhetorically; in others, she objects and then yields suddenly and inexplicably at the poem's end; more rarely, there is an attempted rape from which the woman's family rescues her at the last minute.[24]

Despite these superficial differences, it seems clear that the tension within the pastourelle centers around the issue of feminine speaking.[25] The object of the game or confrontation which the pastourelle stages is, in some sense, to deprive the woman of voice by reducing her to body. As in the lyrics discussed above, sexual difference is put in place as a defense against the dissolution of other hierarchical oppositions such as class difference, and, perhaps most significant, the metaphysical opposition of nature and culture. The male speaker of the pastourelle is frequently represented as a clerk, while the woman is portrayed as a rustic whose use of language is rough and to the point, as in this exchange from "De Clerico et Puella":

(He:)    Sorewe and sike and drery mod  
         Bindeth me so faste  
         That I wene to walke wod  
         If it me lengore laste;  
         My serewe, my care, all with a word  
         He mighte awey caste.  
         What helpeth the, my swete lemmon,  
         My lif thus for to gaste?  
(She:)   Do wey, thou clerk, thou art a fol!  
         With thee bidde I noght chide.  
         Shalt thou never live that day  
         My love that thou shalt bide.  
         If thou in my bour art take,  
         Sham thee may bitide;

> Thee is bettere on fote gon
> The wicked hors to ride.

(Sorrow and sighing and melancholy spirits / Bind me so tightly /
That I think I'll go crazy / If it lasts any longer for me; / My sorrow,
my care, all with a word / She might cast away. / What good does it
do you, my sweet lover, / Thus to cast my life away?
Get away, you clerk, you are a fool! / I don't wish to wrangle with
you. / You'll never see the day / That you'll get my love. / If you are
caught in my bedroom, / Shame may befall you; / It is better for you
to go on foot / Than to ride a wicked horse.)

The clerk's highly conventional entreaty is here set against a rebuke that
goes to the heart of the class issue. In asserting that it is better to walk
than to ride with ill intent, the woman casts doubt on the ethical basis of
class distinctions, thereby undermining the myth of aristocratic virtue that
is the ideological foundation of courtly romance. This threat is neutralized
in the poem's last stanza, however, when the woman suddenly yields; the
clerk wins her over with his courtly language, and she vows "to do all
his will."

The specter of rape haunts the pastourelle; the woman is always alone
in her idyllic setting, the man nearly always mounted and ready to abandon
his courtly/chivalric veneer should words fail to convince. The threat of rape
is balanced against the threat of feminine rhetoric. The inability of the man
to win the verbal battle carries with it a reversal of the hierarchical binaries
upon which patriarchy depends: man/woman, aristocrat/peasant and cul-
ture/nature. Through rape or "coerced" sexual intercourse, the female
voice is submerged in the female body; this corporealization of woman
enables the male narrator of the pastourelle to speak from a position of
discursive potency vis à vis the physically vulnerable and rhetorically inca-
pacitated female. The silencing or "absenting" of woman is a prerequisite
for the nostalgic yearning that characterizes the pastourelle's more sophis-
ticated literary descendants. If she is to represent the lost object for the elegiac poet, woman must first be reduced to body, that she may be written
out of the lyrical drama. To the extent that it dramatizes the corporealization and silencing of woman that sustains a paternalist poetics, the pastourelle reveals the violent origins of the elegiac lyrical voice. The drama
of abjection is by no means a closed system, however. Because the threat
of feminine rhetoric corresponds to the latent instability that inhabits

language itself, the poetic voice is always caught between desire and identification, between a masculine recuperative impulse and a pleasurable
identification with the position of lack. This ambivalence is apparent in the
undecidability of the pastourelle; for every poem that succeeds in silencing
the feminine voice, there is another in which the woman triumphs rhetorically, putting her would-be assailant in his place.

This indeterminacy is particularly evident in the Harleian pastourelle,
"The Meeting in the Wood." The poem places far more emphasis on the
woman's position than on that of the speaker; so much so, in fact, that the
reader is compelled to identify with the feminine position, rather than that
of the would-be lover/assailant. The speaker is uncharacteristically on foot
when he encounters the "burde bright" in the woods. Nevertheless, his
superior class status is made clear in his offer of beautiful clothes—a detail
typical of the pastourelle. Equally typical is the woman's superior moral
position in refusing his offer:

> Clothes I have on for to caste,
> Such as I may weore with winne;
> Betere is were thunne bote laste,
> Then side robes and sinke into sinne.
> Have ye yor will, ye waxeth unwraste;
> Afterward yor thonk be thinne;
> Betre is make forewardes faste
> Then afterward to mene and minne.

> (I have clothes to put on, / Such as I may wear with pleasure; / It
> is better to wear thin clothing without vice / Than ample robes
> and sink into sin. / If you have your will, you will become evil; /
> Afterward your pleasure will be slight; / It is better to secure
> promises / Than afterward to lament and remember.)

The emphasis on clothing as a wooing-gift is a generic commonplace.
Clothing is, of course, one of the oldest and most common figures for
figuration; an offer of clothing or other ornamentation can thus be read as
an offer to adorn the woman rhetorically, that is, to make her the object
of poetic speech. At the metadiscursive level, her refusal to be thus
adorned represents a refusal to allow herself to be interiorized within the
poetic fantasy.

One of the most interesting and generically atypical aspects of "The

Meeting in the Wood" is its emphasis on context, an emphasis that is linked to the privilege accorded the female voice in the poem. After listening to the poet's plea, the woman justifies her reluctance to acquiesce in social and political terms:

> Such reed me might spacliche reowe
> When all my ro were me atraght;
> Sone thou woldest vachen an newe,
> And take another withinne nye naght.
> Thenne might I hongren on heowe,
> In uch an hyrd ben hated and forhaght,
> And ben icaired from all that I kneowe,
> And bede clevian ther I hade claght.

(Such advice might I quickly rue / When all my peace is taken from me. / Soon you would fetch a new one, / And take another within nine nights; / Then might I lack a family / In each household be hated and despised, / And be separated from all that I know, / And bid cling where I had embraced [i.e., beg my lover to remain faithful to me].)

The next two stanzas, however, are characterized by a reversal that is a generic trademark of the pastourelle:

> Betere is taken a comeliche i'clothe,
> In armes to cusse and to cluppe,
> Then a wrecche iwedded so wrothe
> Thagh he me slowe, ne might I him asluppe.
> The beste red that I con to us bothe:
> That thou me take and I thee toward huppe;
> Thagh I swore by treuthe and othe,
> That God hath shaped mey non atluppe.

> Mid shupping ne mey it me ashunche;
> Nes I never wicche ne wile;
> Ich am a maide, that me ofthunche;
> Luef me were gome boute gile.

(It is better to take a person comely in clothes / To embrace in my arms and kiss / Than to be wedded to a wretch so bad, / That though he beat me, I might not escape him. / the best advice that I know for both of us [is]: / That you take me and I leap toward you; / Though I swore by oath, / What God has decreed, one may not escape.

(With shape-shifting I may not escape him; / I was never a sorceress. / I am a maid, and that displeases me; / Dear to me would be a man without guile.)

The last stanza of the poem is ambiguous, owing partly to unresolvable philological problems,[26] and partly to the signifying indeterminacy of the word "maide," which can mean either "virgin" or simply "girl." The speaker may be displeased with her lot in life as a woman, or she may be (as is more usual in the pastourelle) eager to cast off her virginity. As in the lyrics discussed above, the unruliness or profligacy of woman is intimately allied with the question of language; the woman who turns from chastity embodies the errancy of troping or "turning" itself. Rejecting the real as a realm of social oppression and violence against womankind, the speaker embraces the more ephemeral poetic fantasy offered by her suitor, despite the social consequences of unchastity, and despite the fact that she is not—as literature would often have it—a witch or a sorceress. Turning away from reference or context, the female voice mimics the turning of lyricism itself; the speaker's refusal to accept her historical fate as woman mirrors at the thematic level the foreclosure of the real that accompanies the figural turn.[27]

The poem does not end here, however. In the final line, the speaker expresses her somewhat resigned longing for a "gome boute gile": a man who means what he says. Wishing that the poetic fantasy might become a reality, the woman of "The Meeting in the Wood" prefigures Chaucer's Wife of Bath, whose tale is closely related to the pastourelle tradition. The fantasy of a "gome boute gile" corresponds to a desire to strip away the difference in language; like the poet of the "Repentance" and, to some extent, the Wife herself, the speaker longs for non-differentiation, for a transparent language that bears an immediate relation to experience. The turn to poetry bears the shadow of loss, loss of the archaic object that is also a loss of the world of objects, of the extrasemiotic real from which language has alienated humankind. Here, as in Chaucer's tale, the poetic voice allies itself with the feminine, with a position of lack that is simultaneously a position of rhetorical and sexual excess. Seduced by language yet aware of its fundamental negativity/duplicity, the feminine speaker of the pastourelle stands at the borderline, the place of the mother, the abject, and the poet.

In the three chapters that follow, I will be exploring this paradox further in conjunction with an analysis of the work of Chaucer and the Gawain-poet. I will be paying particular attention to the question of loss as it informs the poetics of the *Book of the Duchess* and the *Troilus*; I will argue that, in these Chaucerian texts as in the extracanonical works I have discussed thus far, the problematic of loss circulates around the allied epistemological categories of woman and body. The final chapter, on *Sir Gawain and the Green Knight*, will take us back to the issue with which the book began: that is, to the problematic relation between the maternal body and the paternal word. Throughout this second half of the book, I will explore the extent to which this theoretical matrix linking woman, body, and loss has also informed recent debates on the role of historicism in the field of medieval studies. Ultimately, I hope that the methodological and theoretical construct that I have been calling extracanonical reading will provide a useful foundation, a basis from which medievalists can begin to address the related issues of historicity and corporeality in feminist terms.

# 4. Originary Fantasies and Chaucer's *Book of the Duchess*

With this chapter, I begin a discussion of canonical texts in Middle English, a discussion that seeks ultimately to undermine the binarism it seems to establish. To the extent that this project structurally re-enacts or allegorizes the opposition between "great" works and those deemed to be aesthetically inferior, it stages a confrontation that is admittedly "no contest." As I stated at the outset, however, my intention is neither to redeem extra-canonical works nor to diminish the stature of canonical ones; I intend rather to pose the question of canonicity from a feminist theoretical perspective, in an effort to uncover the specific textual conditions that *exclude The Book of the Duchess, Troilus and Criseyde*, and *Sir Gawain and the Green Knight* from the ranks of the marginal works I discussed in part one. Basing my reading upon negativity, I follow the example of Margery Kempe: my stategy turns the canon "up-so-down" in an attempt to efface the boundary between inside and outside, and thereby to open up a space wherein we might begin to rethink the ideological and institutional assumptions that have hitherto informed and structured medieval literary studies.

One way of "posing the question" of canonicity is to interrogate the oppositions whereby it is constituted. Early in our education we learn to separate "great" artifacts from lesser ones: aesthetics is the foundation of humanism, as well as its most formidable weapon against its detractors. Because aesthetic judgments are based on distinctions of a specifically moral kind, however, they leave behind traces of their own violent engendering.[1] The differences between "good" and "bad" poems, for example, are made possible only by repressing the differences within each category, differences that often work to efface the opposition itself.[2] One of the aims of this second part of the study will be to explore these internal differences within canonical texts, and to discuss the extent to which they undermine the aesthetic opposition implicit in canonicity itself.

The larger concern of this second part, however, is specific to the historical context of these three texts, and to the institution of medievalism in general. It is my contention that the issue of canonicity leads us back, inexorably, to the question of origins. I will argue that Chaucer and the Gawain-poet share a productive anxiety about origins, and that this anxiety is mirrored in the critical history of medieval canonical texts.[3] These next three chapters represent an attempt to rupture this imaginary stasis; by inserting the question of difference into the narcissistic illusion of sameness, I will endeavor to subvert the dualist assumptions that enable the formation of canons, and thereby to disrupt the imaginary dyad that binds medieval poetry and medievalist criticism within a patriarchal ideological framework. This agenda necessitates first of all a return to history, or more precisely, a return to the questionable nature of historical truth. The urgency of this question for the poets themselves is inextricable from certain material—that is, political and linguistic—conditions specific to late medieval England. In brief, the originary anxieties of these poets derive in part from the fact that the establishment of national literatures (and thus literary canons) depends upon the institutionalization of a patrilineal system of inheritance. Both biological and textual fatherhood depend upon the accurate location of origins; nevertheless, one can never be certain about fathers.

As I hope to have shown in the first three chapters, the question of historical or textual origins can never be answered without invoking a false closure predicated on sexual difference, on the sacrifice/foreclosure of ma(t)ter. The marginal author's unwillingness or inability to master the realm of matter, or, in psychoanalytic terms, to effect the foreclosure of maternal desire, results in texts that are both subversive and pathologically ambivalent. Margery Kempe's insistence on the materiality of figural language, the hagiographer's failure to separate "lich" from "lichnesse," or body from metaphor, and the lyricist's inability to transcend the prurience of his own tropes all point to a larger failure to embrace the metaphysical dualism which canonical texts seem to affirm. I say "seem" because, while the works of Chaucer and the Gawain-poet appear to have contained and transcended the problematics of origin and of materiality, poems such as *The Book of the Duchess*, *Troilus and Criseyde*, and *Sir Gawain and the Green Knight* in fact succeed only in allegorizing their own failure to "master matter."

If this sounds shamelessly reductive, it is because the word "allegorize" carries with it the entire aesthetic universe of tropological substitution, of masterful figuration that distinguishes canonical poets from their "clumsier" contemporaries. These next three chapters thus lead us once more into the rhetorical realm of *différance*, where the making of metaphors and the pleasure of tropological deferral place sexual difference in the service of an illusory plenitude, which in turn masks the lack or absence at the point of textual origin. At issue here is the materiality of language itself, the ma(t)ter which/who continually threatens the stability of the paternal system of poetic production. In the pages that follow, we shall see that, in Chaucer's *Duchess* as in Freudian theory, this potentially pathological dilemma can only be evaded by staging a metaphysical confrontation between fantasy and reality. How this confrontation unfolds, and why it should be so vital to the continuity of a paternalist poetics, will be the subject of this chapter.

## Paternal Fantasies, or, How to Start a Tradition

Throughout English literary history, sleep has been a productive metaphor for the poetic process.[4] In sleep, consciousness is suspended and dreams are generated; dreams re-enact history through condensations and displacements that turn the familiar into the uncanny. Given the poetic nature of dreams, moreover, it is not surprising that poems that invoke the figure of sleep seem to concern themselves with issues of transmission and inheritance. For example, John Keats begins his *Sleep and Poetry* with an epigraph from *The Floure and the Lefe*, a medieval verse allegory that was erroneously attributed to Chaucer in Keats's time. Keats ends his poem with a metaphor linking poetic creation to a parturition that separates father and son: the speaking subject of poetry is generated by and alienated from a father/maker through whose name the immortality of the artifact is insured.[5] The pseudo-Chaucerian epigraph calls this paternal closure—and thus the poem's transcendent value—into question, however. It remains outside the borders of the poem itself, and yet threatens the poet's assertion of primacy, of fatherhood. The poem's "legitimacy" hinges on a resolution of the oedipal conflict, but its last line, which would seem to offer this resolution, takes us back to the epigraph, to the "father" of English poetry, whose presence forces us to acknowledge the legal dilemma of fatherhood, the indeterminacy of poetic origins. The fact that the attribution to Chaucer is erroneous further complicates matters. If poetry is patrilineal, what are the consequences of misremembering one's fathers?[6]

This is a question which seems to have occupied Chaucer throughout his career. In *Anelida and Arcite*, poetic continuity depends on memory, which is always in danger of disappearing. The tale of Anelida and Arcite is an old story

> That elde, which that al can frete and bite,
> As hit hath freten mony a noble storie
> Hath nygh devoured out of oure memorie. (11–13)

Memory is also perilous to the medieval poet, however. There is always the chance that his poetry may remain, like Anelida herself, "thirled with the poynt of remembraunce," that is, paralyzed by an imaginary relationship to the past. In *Troilus and Criseyde*, the paternal figure of Lollius stands in for the narrator's anxieties about literary history. His name is a morphological paradox that represents the poet's own troubled relation to the literary past: its ending evokes the nobility of a lost classical tradition, while its stem brings to mind a contemporary heterodox movement.[7] As a "front" for the poet himself, Lollius at once commemorates the classical fathers of vernacular poetry and heretically violates their legacy.[8]

In Chaucer's earliest narrative poem, *The Book of the Duchess*, the dilemma of memory and its relation to tradition is played out in a rather different and perhaps less explicit way. Critics have long been aware of the poem's indebtedness to French courtly poetry: the *Duchess* is in fact a mélange of conventional moments borrowed from Machaut, Froissart, and Guillaume de Lorris.[9] Surprisingly, however, nearly all the poem's readers have overlooked the political implications of this "borrowing." Its appropriation and "Englishing" of these conventional texts certainly represents an ideological intervention on behalf of a national vernacular that was finally gaining ascendency. The poem speaks to and of the need for a specifically English literary tradition that might rival that of the continent. Given John of Gaunt's probable role in the genesis of the poem, and his well-documented efforts to promote the official use of English, the poem's *political* investment in "originating a tradition" can hardly be ignored.[10] Within the poem itself, this political imperative takes on an aesthetic urgency. As we shall see, the absence of tradition, of literary fathers, is recast as a drama of loss in which sexual difference plays a determining role.

Before turning to the *Duchess* itself, however, it may be useful to see how yet another "founding father"—the Father of Psychoanalysis— worked to paternalize the origins of his own theoretical discourse by associating woman with the category of the lost real. In the first chapter of this book, I discussed Freud's refusal to disassociate the maternal seduction scene from the realm of the real: while paternal seduction is said to be a hysterical fantasy, seduction by the mother "touches the ground of reality." In *Beyond the Pleasure Principle*, the *"fort-da* game" becomes a story of loss in which the mother's absence is mastered through representation. Through the child's "artistic play," the pleasure of representation alleviates the unpleasure of the mother's disappearance.[11] Again, the mother remains outside the game itself; she is bound to the realm of reference and thus lost with the entry into language and signification. With the mother exiled to the realm of matter, her body can serve as the "ground" for the metaphors that sustain the myth of paternal productivity. This exclusion of woman from the *act* of representation is nonetheless a semiotic gesture that—paradoxically—serves to relegate her to the *interior* of the mimetic circuit, while placing the male artist or analyst at the point of textual origin. In short, women can *represent* loss or lack, but only men can cover over that loss with representation.

In a recent fascinating article, Wayne Koestenbaum shows how Freud metaphorically appropriates the female power of generation in establishing an originary narrative for psychoanalysis.[12] In fact it is Breuer's patient Anna O. who invents the "talking cure," and it is through her hysterical pregnancy that psychoanalytic theory is born.[13] In transforming the hysteric's narrative into "case histories that read like short stories," Freud succeeds in displacing the origins of theory from the body of the mother—Anna O.—to the discursive collaboration between himself and Breuer. Her hysterical pregnancy, which Breuer omits from his own narrative, becomes a gap in the text which Freud fills; the hysteric's material female space (her womb) is translated or metaphorized into the analyst's textual space.[14] The feminine body is written out of the originary drama, only to return in the form of tropes that affirm the generative power of discursive unions between men.[15]

The *Book of the Duchess* is also the story of generative collaborations between men: between Chaucer and Ovid, Chaucer and the French courtly poets, and between the poem's narrator and the Black Knight.[16] The poem enacts its own version of "artistic play": here, too, the body of woman is a priori a lost object that grounds tropological substitutions, metaphors that work to sustain the illusion of paternal productivity and male discursive mastery.[17] Because the success of this illusion depends on the author's ability to displace the origins of discourse from ma(t)ter to father, from the world of objects to that of figures, it finds effective expression in both the elegy and its generic sibling, the dream-vision. Both genres assert that loss can be productive: the elegy proclaims language as death's opposite and adversary, thereby endowing poetry with an illusory plenitude, while the dream-vision establishes the foreclosure of the waking or referential world as the price of a transcendent vision. In Lacanian terms, both the elegy and the dream-vision enable the poet to work through the trauma of loss or castration that accompanies the entry into language, and, as in the case of the *Duchess*, to project that lack onto woman by locating her in the realm of the lost real. Once the realm of mother-as-matter has been foreclosed as the site of textual production, origins can be re-located within language itself: the father's "olde stories" supplant the mother's body, and a literary tradition is born.

Following the Freudian model of the *fort-da* game, then, we may be tempted to conclude that Chaucer's *Book of the Duchess* succeeds in mastering loss through representation, in placing unpleasure in the service of the economic demands of the so-called pleasure principle.[18] The anxiety the poem has aroused within the critical community, however, is one indication that the poem is not the "closed system" its readers would like it to be. There has been a marked tendency among the poem's critics to close off the unpleasurable moments within the text, either by proposing allegorical readings that the work itself ultimately resists, or by attempting to "suture" the poem's various disjunctions ideologically. For the allegorists, the Black Knight is the embodiment of *tristitia*,[19] or of melancholic narcissism;[20] the narrator represents "imagination" as against the Black Knight's "intellect;"[21] and Lady White—if she is discussed at all—is most often associated with "life itself" or with a Boethian false felicity that must be accepted as such.[22] Recently, critical attention has turned to the metapoetics of the text; these readings, in particular, betray an anxiety about closure and unity. Robert Jordan's recent analysis of the poem focuses on its "structural irregularities and violations of tone and scale," but ultimately relies on a conventional panegyric gesture to give the poem an ideologically necessary transcendent value:

> . . . if the *Book of the Duchess* lacks the smoothly integrated texture of an organic unity, it amply compensates with its aggregative brilliance, its rhetorical energy, and its rich variety of tone and nuance.[23]

Having identified the poem with lack, the critic must find a way to "compensate" for it, lest the paternal origins of English poetry be destabilized and thus called into question. For Robert Hanning, this "undeniably idiosyncratic" poem dramatizes a process of externalization or objectivation of affect that finally leads to an affirmation of male bonding as the basis of artistic productivity:

> The narrator-dreamer and the Black Knight establish a human community of
> *routh* and mutual involvement which, by overcoming isolation, seems to
> transform their life-threatening sorrow—both have survived thus far in defi-
> ance of "nature" or "kynde"—into states of personal acceptance and renewed
> creativity.[24]

Male generativity can only take place in the absence or "defiance" of nature, in which category are contained the traditionally feminine subcate-
gories of matter and affect. The externalization, or, in Kristevan terms,
abjection of femininity is essential to the homosocial interests of the male
poetic and critical community, here universalized as "human." Both Jordan's reading and Hanning's say more about the institution of Chaucer
Studies than about Chaucer's poem: for the former, criticism is a mirroring of critical ego and poetic ego-ideal, while the latter envisions an ideal
artistic community where heroic critics join masculinist poets in a productive union.[25]

These readings are particularly interesting to the feminist reader of
Chaucer, in that they foreground the issue upon which the poem's patriarchal ideology founders: the problematic relations between fantasy, desire
and identification. The critical insistence on mirroring unities, on recuper-
ating the poem's "excesses," partakes of the fantasy of coherence that the
*Duchess* both creates and subverts. For both the poem and its critics, femininity—as excess or as "nature"—is the psychic danger that necessitates
and undermines this fantasy. The male critic's identification with a masculinist poet, I will argue, is continually threatened by that poet's own
deviant identification with feminine desire. In the remainder of this chapter, we will not only confront the lack that fuels the fantasy of paternal
generativity; we will also explore the poet's own identification with that
lack. In this way we may begin to rethink our relation to the *Book of the
Duchess*, and perhaps to question our assumptions about the patrilineal
tradition Chaucer is said to have fathered.

## The Poetics of Loss

The *Book of the Duchess* begins by asserting the narrator's melancholic alienation from life. He traces his "defaute of slep" to a "sicknesse" for which
"there is phisicien but oon." But, he says, "that is don." The reference to
a particular physician would seem to indicate that the narrator is suffering
from lovesickness, and that only the return of his lost love can restore him
to health. The efficacy of this conventional sentiment, at least in the lyric

tradition, normally depends on a maintenance of the fiction that such a restoration is at least possible. The narrator's abrupt assertion that "that is don" closes off the possibility of further experience. Life, it would seem, can offer no more to literature. His condition, moreover, is said to be "agaynes kynde"; he is cut off from nature, from the world of objects. These opening lines attempt to evoke a state of absolute negativity, of pure difference made manifest as in-difference. In this fantasy of absence, the narrator's pathological isolation is the antithesis of a distanced objectivity, for it is precisely critical judgment that fails him:

> . . . by my trouthe, I tak no kep
> Of nothyng, how hyt cometh or gooth,
> Ne me nys nothyng leef nor looth.
> Al is ylyche good to me— (6–9)

Needless to say, subjectivity and (thus) poetry are impossible where difference does not exist; the fantasy cannot be sustained. Indeed, indifference yields to *différance* when the narrator tells us "sorwful ymagynacioun" is always "hooly" in his mind: no sooner is imagination linked to lack, than lack is recuperated as wholeness and plenitude. Like the figure of sleep itself, these opening lines tread the borderline between presence and absence, loss and reparation. On the one hand, poetry is said to originate in loss of the real: experience is foreclosed as the source of mimesis. On the other, absence is said to constitute a different sort of wholeness or presence, as "sorwful ymagynacioun" and "fantasies" take the place of pure negativity and absolute alienation from the signifying process.

As in the Freudian paradigm, the unpleasurable tension between presence and absence is here mastered through representation which is seen as "play." The narrator's sleeplessness or lack of poetic inspiration leads him back to "olde stories," in this case Ovid's tale of Ceyx and Alcyone. The Ovidian text is itself endowed with an originary plenitude that compensates for the narrator's own unnatural state; it is found among a book of

> . . . fables
> That clerkes had in olde tyme,
> And other poetes, put in rime
> To rede and for to be in minde,
> While men loved the lawe of kynde. (52–56)

The classical text possesses the connection to nature which the narrator lacks, for it is said to derive from an age of prelapsarian textual innocence,

before the "lawe of kynde" was occluded by the laws of signification.[26]
The narrator's pathological state of alienation from nature or experience,
which initially subverts his desire to generate poetry, is mitigated when
the paternal text becomes naturalized as the true origin of poetic inspiration. The realm of matter or experience, foreclosed with the narrator's
assertion that "that is don," is supplanted as the source of poetic speaking.
In effect, the Ovidian text fetishistically compensates for the lost real, and
sleep—or poetry—follows soon after.

Clearly, the matter is not closed, however. Chaucer's Ovidian tale,
unlike the original, is everywhere obsessed with the gap between what
seems to be and what is, or, more specifically, between representation and
reality. In Chaucer's tale of Ceyx and Alcyone much is made of the fact
that Morpheus appears in Alcyone's dream in the body of Ceyx. In the
poetic world of dreams, we witness the appearance of life, not life itself.
Juno's instructions to Morpheus are explicit:

> Bid hym crepe into the body
> And doo hit goon to Alcione
> The quene, ther she lyeth allone,
> And shewe hir shortly, hit ys no nay,
> How hit was dreynt thys other day;
> And do the body speke ryght soo,
> Ryght as hyt was woned to doo
> The whiles that hit was alyve. (144–51)

Like poetry, dreams can only re-present reality; they have no immediate
relation to experience. In this respect, Alcyone's dream calls the narrator's
own "sweven" into question: if animation is not life, and sleep, however
"dedly," is not death, then perhaps the Black Knight's codified sentiments
are not genuine passion. The Black Knight's elegiac narrative—certainly
the segment of the poem that carries the most ideological weight—is thus
also the site of its deepest anxiety and doubt. The relation of conventional
poetry to reality becomes an ethical issue when placed in the context of
grief and mourning: if elegiac poetry is cut off from genuine affect, then
what possible social function can it serve? More important, what social
role—if any—can a poet have?

This question is less answered than displaced in the poem. The systematic installation of sexual difference as the overriding opposition in
the text works to shift the burden of discursive impotence from male to

female figures. Before the Black Knight even appears in the poem, we learn that elegiac narrative is sexually specific. While he will lament the loss of his lady at length, replacing her lost body with language, Alcyone is incapable of generating a narrative that will similarly stand in for her lost husband.[27] In Chaucer's version of the tale, she is denied both speech and vision:

> With that hir eyen up she casteth
> And saw nought. "Allas!" quod she for sorwe,
> And deyede within the thridde morwe.
> But what she sayede more in that swow
> I may not telle yow as now;
> Hyt were to longe for to dwelle. (213–17)

The Knight's extended conventional lament must be set against Alcyone's failure to elegize Ceyx. Here, as in the Freudian game of loss, women are called upon to represent lack so that men may cover over that lack with language. In this way, sexual difference is set in place as a defense against the trauma of loss/castration. As Alcyone is denied speech, so Lady White remains a pure negativity—the only word she speaks is "nay"—so as to obscure the sense in which the poem itself is merely negation, or "not-life."[28]

Founded in absence or loss of reference, the text must nonetheless affirm its own plenitude and unity by reconstituting the presence/absence dyad within the diegesis proper. The text's authority thus comes to depend on an affirmation of the boundaries separating inside and outside, that is, upon its ability to relegate woman, and thus lack, to the interior of narrative space.[29] It must affirm its *positive* value as against the negativity inscribed as woman. At the same time, however, it must maintain the fiction that representation bears some positive relation to reality, that what seems to be (fiction, or the dream-world) and what is (life) are not forever alienated from one another. The two imperatives constitute an unresolvable paradox for the poet, in that one necessitates an affirmation of boundaries, the other a negation of them. Given this dilemma, literature can do little more than reenact the foreclosure of the real from representation, placing woman at the vortex, the vanishing point of narrative: the place where speaking and reading are alike impossible. This strategy is not without danger, however. Lady White is the "chef myrour of al the feste," reflecting the male subject's castration, specularity, and narcissism, as well as the site of hermeneutic "implosion," if you will. "Hir lokyng" is a barrier, through and beyond which reading is impossible:

> Hir eyen semed anoon she wolde
> Have mercy—fooles wenden soo—
> But hyt was never the rather doo.
> Hyt nas no countrefeted thyng;
> Hyt was hir owne pure lokyng
> That the goddesse, dame Nature,
> Had mad hem opene by mesure
> And close; for, were she never so glad,
> Hyr lokynge was not foly sprad,
> Ne wildely, thogh that she pleyde;
> But ever, me thoght, hir eyen seyde,
> "Be God, my wrathe ys al foryive!" (866–77)

The Knight's inability to read Lady White's look allies her with Fortune, who "baggeth foule and loketh faire," while the destructive power of her gaze ("many oon with hire lok she herte") evokes the Medusa, the "monstres hed" concealed behind Fortune's fair face. Like Lady White's look, however, femininity continually threatens to exceed the limits defined for it within the text. Refusing to remain unproblematic, femininity becomes the site of a radical instability in the poem, an instability which works to subvert the male subject's attempt to distance himself from the spectre of loss and lack.

The reenactment of the trauma of loss, the foreclosure of the real, is made explicit in the dream. The narrator describes his dream-chamber as a kind of poetic "cathedral"; the walls are painted with the text of the *Romance of the Rose*, while the stained-glass windows tell the story of Troy. The Trojan story does not prevent the dreamer from seeing outside, however:

> My wyndowes were shette echon,
> And throgh the glas the sonne shon
> Upon my bed with bryghte bemes,
> With many glade gilde stremes;
> And eke the welken was so fair—
> Blew, bryght, clere was the ayr,
> And ful attempre for sothe hyt was;

For nother to cold nor hoot yt nas,
Ne in al the welken was no clowde. (335–43)

The story of Troy is transparent—beyond it, we may see what lies outside: the "real" world of nature, of objects. The world beyond the chamber is no more "real" than the chamber itself, however. The outside world is a cross between a courtly *locus amoenus* and a *forêt d'aventure*: a place where difference seems not to exist ("nother to cold nor hoot yt nas"), where "hert-huntynge" has meaning only as a pun. It is, in short, the realm of conventional poetry, a fact which the narrator further attempts to disavow by negating the split between the body and the word, between sincere emotion and formalized sentiment.[30] When we first see the Black Knight, he is uttering a "lay," a conventional lament for his lost love (475–86). Immediately after his "song," we are asked to look inside his body, as the narrator affirms the correspondence between conventional expression and clinical fact:

Hys sorwful hert gan faste faynte
And his spirites wexen dede;
The blood was fled for pure drede
Doun to hys herte, to make hym warm—
For wel hyt feled the herte had harm—
To wite eke why hyt was adrad
By kynde, and for to make hyt glad,
For hyt ys membre principal
Of the body; and that made al
Hys hewe chaunge and wexe grene
And pale, for ther noo blood ys sene
In no maner lym of hys. (488–99)

The integrity of the body and the word, inside and outside, is further problematized by the text's obsession with the word "hool" (ll. 15, 115, 326, 553, 554, 746, 751, 756, 766, 991, 1224, 1269). The phallic ideal of wholeness foregrounds the dreamer's own discursive insufficiency, just as, on a larger scale, his initial disavowal of the boundary between the interior and the exterior, clinical fact and codified convention, represents an attempt to compensate for the originary loss of the world of objects which literature must continually reenact.

It is only through the phallic character of the Black Knight that the male subject/dreamer is able to protect himself effectively from the specter of lack, from the knowledge of his own discursive inadequacy. The Knight's mastery of literary conventions allows him to move between inside and outside with ease, to place his other/opposite, Lady White, at the text's vanishing point, thereby securing the illusory wholeness of the poem.[31] In his description of Lady White, the Knight continually crosses the boundary between exterior and interior. He moves from the realm of thought (885) to a description of the Lady's face (895–918), from her voice (919) to her neck (939). Moreover, he equates artificers and physicians (the word and the body) in his assertion that he can be neither healed nor distracted from his "sorwes" (567–71). The dreamer's imaginary transference onto the idealized male figure of the Black Knight constitutes a denial of the originary loss of objects, of history, of the phallus itself. The Knight's fetishization of literary convention effectively permits male desire to masquerade as presence rather than absence.

As Freud pointed out, however, a fetish is always a sign of a split subjectivity.[32] In the *Duchess*, this split manifests itself along the lines of sexual difference: the homosocial identifications in the poem exist alongside heterosocial and heterosexual identifications that are perilous to the poem's masculinist recuperative agenda. If there is a "feminist Chaucer," as has been suggested recently,[33] he can perhaps be found on the borderline where desire slips into identification, where desire for the object becomes identification with the object's desire. One way of approaching this perilous borderline, I would argue, is through the disturbing and fascinating phenomenon of fetishism itself.[34]

## The Desire to Desire

In his essay on fetishism, Freud relates the case of a young man who "had exalted a certain sort of 'shine on the nose' into a fetishistic precondition." We learn very little of the etiology of this particular fetish, except that it had to do with the loss of the mother-tongue (*Muttersprache*):

> . . . the patient had been brought up in an English nursery, but had later come to Germany, where he forgot his mother-tongue almost completely. The fetish, which originated from his earliest childhood, had to be understood in English, not German. The "shine on the nose" [in German, *Glanz auf der Nase*]—was in reality a "*glance* at the nose." The nose was thus the

fetish, which, incidentally, he endowed at will with the luminous shine which was not perceptible to others. [35]

Freud goes on to say that "the fetish is a substitute for the woman's (the mother's) penis that the little boy once believed in and—for reasons familiar to us—does not want to give up." [36] Fetishism is thus presented as added evidence for Freud's theory of the castration complex: it is a symptom of the disavowal (*Verleugnung*) with which the child greets the sight of the female genitalia, and thus his own fear of loss. The fetish, in this case the nose, stands in for the lost object, which Freud identifies with the mother's penis. His narrative reveals something else, however: the fetish is linked to the mother-tongue, the *Sprache* of the mother, as well. What the child disavows through the fetish is not (merely) the mother's lack of a penis, but rather her lack of *Sprache*, of discursive potency. In her perceived inability to generate authoritative narrative, he sees the possibility of his own failure to do so. Speaking becomes linked to looking (the glance); the continuity of narrative is made to depend in large part on the "glance at the nose," that is, the gaze at the fetish.

While fetishism installs sexual difference as a defense against loss, it is perhaps first and foremost an identification with the position of lack: if mother lacks, then so must I. Moreover, the position is a pleasurable one for the fetishist; Freud points out that fetishism provides sexual gratification in a simple and "convenient" way. The externalization of the fetishized object, necessary to the specular disavowal of loss, is thus also the point at which desire for the lost object slips into identification with the lost object, or with the position of lack.

This fetishistic dilemma plays a significant role in the *Book of the Duchess*. As we discussed earlier, the loss of the real, the realm of ma(t)ter, is partially mitigated when the origins of poetic speaking are relocated in the paternal classical text. As in the oedipal myth, the "normative value" of this move depends upon the narrator's identification with the paternal figure. Instead of identifying with Ovid as the maker of the tale, however, the narrator responds empathically to the tale's feminine victim, Alcyone herself:

> Such sorwe this lady to her tok
> That trewly I, that made this book,
> Had such pittee and such rowthe
> To rede hir sorwe that, by my trowthe,

> I ferde the worse al the morwe
> Aftir to thenken on hir sorwe. (95–100)

The narrator here claims the authorial role, while simultaneously affirming his identification with a woman who will come to represent discursive inadequacy in the poem.

Within the dream-vision itself, the narrator's homosocial identification with the Black Knight seems to compensate for his previous deviant identification with Alcyone. Indeed, the dream landscape is presented as a place of natural plenitude, in contrast to the landscape of Alcyone's dream, which is barren and empty. When the narrator first comes upon the Knight in the forest, the Knight is heard lamenting the death of his lady. The narrator is so impressed with the Knight's demeanor and speech, however, that he disavows what he has heard, thereby enabling the Knight to replace his lost lady with a lengthy elegiac narrative. The fetishistic game goes awry when the Knight himself begins to identify with Lady White, the "blank place" on which the entire reparative system depends. The Knight claims the lady's blankness for himself when he tells the story of his amatory education, assuming an explicitly feminine position:

> . . . I was thereto most able,
> As a whit wal or a table,
> For hit ys redy to cacche and take
> Al that men wil theryn make,
> Whethir so men wil portreye or peynte,
> Be the werkes never so queynte. (779–84)

In this fantasmatic moment, the Knight himself moves to the interior of the mimetic or representational space, thereby destabilizing the narrator's own homosocial and compensatory identification, and thus the poem's larger strategy of recuperation. This perilous inversion is explicitly linked to language when the Knight re-lives his lady's initial rejection of his "tale" of love. His sorrow was so great, we are told,

> That trewly Cassandra, that soo
> Bewayled the destruccioun

Of Troye and of Ilyoun,
Had never swich sorwe as I thoo. (1246–49)

By identifying himself with Cassandra, perhaps the most renowned exemplar of feminine discursive impotence, the Knight proclaims the genuineness of his sentiments—the truth of his "tale"—but also the impossibility of ever transcending a state of rhetorical insufficiency.

Perhaps the most dangerous moment in the text, the point at which identification is most unstable, is in the specular description of the lady herself. Here, as in later Chaucerian works such as *Troilus and Criseyde* and the Knight's Tale, specular pleasures become perilous precisely because of the potential slippage of desire into identification. After describing the lady's demeanor and appearance, the Knight moves from her eyes to her look:

And whiche eyen my lady hadde!
Debonaire, goode, glade and sadde,
Symple, of good mochel, noght to wyde.
Therto hir look nas nat asyde
Ne overthwert, but beset so wel
Hyt drew and took up everydel
Al that on hir gan beholde. (859–65)

The parallel between the lady's look, that "drew and took up" everyone who gazed upon her, and the Knight in his youth, ready to "cacche and take" every impression, is striking. The scopophilic moment is also the moment when desire for the object becomes a mirroring identification with the object's own desire. It is the moment when desire becomes "the desire to desire": the desire to be in a position of lack. Lady White's look, associated with a feminine desiring excess, is also a dangerous gap that threatens to overturn the fragile homosocial substructure of the poem itself. There is always the danger that the poet will become trapped by "the myrrour perillous" of Narcissus, as Chaucer calls it in his translation of the *Romance of the Rose*. "Drawn in and taken up" by a fantasy of deviant identification, the poet will be unable to reassert the exteriority necessary to the more normative fantasy of male discursive mastery.

The paradoxical and unstable position of the fetishist is that of a subject compelled by the illusion of plenitude and caught up in the pleasurable drama of lack. Within the *Book of the Duchess*, both the narrator and the Black Knight are constructed by this play of presence and absence, normative and deviant identifications. Although the poem works to contain the trauma of loss by placing the feminine body at the innermost point of narrative space, it ultimately refuses to sustain the illusion of masculine authorial exteriority by failing to "draw the line" between object cathexis and the narcissistic mirroring that structures desire. Moreover, the poem establishes its divisions and losses *prior* to its "discovery" of sexual difference: the narrator's alienation precedes Alcyone's rhetorical failure, and Lady White's fixed absence in the text is only installed after the dream itself unfolds as a foreclosure of reference. The projection of lack onto woman thus constitutes a defensive response to what Lacan has identified as symbolic castration: the loss of the real necessitated by the entry into signification.

The poem disavows this originary loss, but can only defer the acknowledgment of the division that underpins its own illusory wholeness. Between the narrator's "that is don" and the Black Knight's "she is ded," the "artistic play" of *différance* unfolds. On the other side of these statements is the body of the mother, exiled to the lost realm of matter and reference. Ideologically committed to the assertion of the paternal origins of poetic speaking, the poem must repress the maternal desire that both sustains and subverts its patriarchal agenda. Through these fantasmatic moments of deviant identification, however, ma(t)ter returns as something uncanny, something familiar and strange, pleasurable and threatening.

In Chapter Two, I discussed this phenomenon in terms of the two axes of language, metaphor and metonymy. In the hagiographical text, the paternal metaphor whereby Christian discourse is constituted was shown to depend on the metonymic axis of desire, just as the transcendent value of the saint's discourse is predicated on the sacrifice and abjection of her body. The repressed relation between the feminine figure and the implicitly masculine figure of speech returned uncannily in the rhetorical play of "lich" and "_____ liche," or body and metaphor.

In the *Duchess*, as in much of Chaucer's later poetry, this uncanny return finds expression at the thematic level of the text; the poet's speaking subjectivity continually proclaims its sexual undecidability, even as the conventions it enlists persist in installing sexual difference as a defense against the loss wherein they originate. One way in which Chaucerian texts distinguish themselves from works such as the *Juliana* and the Harley Lyrics, then, is in their exploration of what I have called the fetishistic dilemma: the tension between an ideologically necessary recuperative impulse and a fantasmatic identification with the position of lack. This dilemma, and its relation to the construction of a historically-specific subjectivity, is explored most fully in *Troilus and Criseyde*. In the next chapter, we will see how Criseyde inherits the dangerous place of Lady White, becoming the focus of the narrator's—and the poet's—desire to desire.

# 5. Historicity, Femininity, and Chaucer's *Troilus*

Throughout this project, I have argued that, in extracanonical texts as well as in Chaucer's *Book of the Duchess*, the problem of literary origins is bound up with that of sexual difference. To the extent that she becomes associated with an irreducible and intractable materiality, woman embodies the losses and divisions wherein a poetic subjectivity originates. The significance of this assessment for an understanding of medieval poetry lies in its symptomatic reading of Christian dualism, and in its emphasis on the relation between origin and absence. This last has a particular resonance for the contemporary medievalist, whose perspective on the past is to a great extent conditioned by a nostalgic and melancholic critical tradition.[1] The specter of a lost idyllic moment hovers on the border of much of the criticism in the field, resulting in what Nicolas Abraham and Maria Torok have called "endocryptic identification," that is, an identification of the ego (in this case, the critical ego) with the lost object.[2] This narcissistic mirroring accounts for several of the most persistent methodological and ideological obsessions in the field of medieval studies: the "fetishism of the source" that has literally and metaphorically bound Anglo-Saxon studies to archaeology for most of this century,[3] the continuing dispute over anachronism, and, more generally, the widespread critical anxiety about history as a methodological tool and an epistemological category.

Within a field so informed by melancholic/narcissistic identifications, history is credited with enormous reparative and recuperative potential. To invoke history is thus to shore up the myth of critical exteriority and discursive potency, while at the same time fetishistically compensating for the loss that is at the root of any historicist subjectivity. In light of the first three chapters of this study, it may be suggested that the function of history within the field of medieval studies is similar to that of femininity within Christian theology: both are called upon to stand in for the absence at or indeterminacy of the point of textual origin. Psychoanalytic theory makes sense of this parallel through the concept of primary narcissism: the archaic relation to the maternal object which is lost with the entry into signification.[4] In this chapter, I would like to bring this fundamentally ontogenetic theory of origins to bear upon the phylogenetic problematic of historicist thinking, by focusing on the question of history within the field as well as in Chaucer's most historically-minded poem, *Troilus and Criseyde*. I am specifically interested in the ways in which history as a problem of difference becomes entangled with sexuality in Chaucer's text, as well as in the criticism it has generated.

My larger goal in the remainder of this project is to begin a psycho-analytically-inflected dialogue between feminism and historicism, the two most compelling discourses in the field at present. From a feminist point of view, there are several reasons why this dialogue has thus far failed to take place. Because I think that this "conceptual impasse" bears significantly on Chaucer's own historicist dilemma in the *Troilus*, I would like to linger momentarily on the debate over historicism that has been unfolding within medieval studies in recent years.

With the publication of Lee Patterson's influential and controversial book, *Negotiating the Past*, the historicist perspective re-emerged as a force to be reckoned with in the field.[5] Patterson himself has been the most vocal and polemical spokesperson for the new historicist imperative, and at times his rhetoric borders on the coercive. In his introduction to a recent collection of essays entitled *Literary Practice and Social Change in Britain, 1380–1530*, Patterson begins by quoting Fredric Jameson, one of the most compelling proponents of Marxist historicism today:

> "Always historicize!" The motto that Fredric Jameson announced at the beginning of the decade as Marxism's only "transhistorical imperative" has now, at its end, been inscribed on the banner under which literary studies as a whole seems to be marching.[6]

Patterson's invocation of Jameson's *Political Unconscious* here belies his own anti-theoretical critical stance. Where Jameson attempts a neo-scholastic synthesis of contemporary theoretical perspectives within a Marxist framework, Patterson dismisses most poststructuralisms as "merely" formalist, and advocates a rather straightforward return to the privilege of context.[7] More disturbing, however, is the book's inaugural image of "literary studies as a whole" marching under a single banner; the metaphor inadvertently conjures up its own unpleasant historical associations, evoking the enforced uniformity and violent suppression of difference that characterized some of the more potent political ideologies of this century. It is perhaps ironic that here, where no historical reference is intended, the past returns uncannily, revealing the futility of any effort to separate history from the tropes whereby it is constituted. Patterson's metaphor reminds us, moreover, that historiography was engendered on the battlefield: the earliest histories, those of Herodotus and Thucydides, were military chronicles. To the extent that it looks both backward and forward, then, the martial metaphor turns out to be what Freud called a *Fehlleistung* or parapraxis, a "slip of the pen" that reveals the generative relation of violence to historical writing.

What this slip also reveals, I think, is Patterson's own understanding of history as a series of struggles between men—or more precisely, between nations, political factions or classes within which women are not represented as such. Patterson is not alone in this assumption; military conflicts, court politics, and class warfare continue to provide the allegorical basis for the majority of historicist readings in the field. Influenced to varying degrees by Marxist social and economic theory, these critics have read literature in relation to larger public and collective struggles; for example, the Peasants' Revolt and the political fall of Richard II have frequently been offered as interpretive keys to the poetry of Chaucer and his contemporaries, with often fascinating results.[8] Nevertheless, in emphasizing the public and collective sphere as the arena within which history-as-event occurs, this approach gestures toward a dialectical understanding of the past without engaging the philosophical and epistemological difficulties that have adhered to the concept of the dialectic within speculative discourse.

It may seem disingenuous to level such a criticism when a broad philosophical discussion of this kind is beyond the scope of this book as well. My concerns here, however, are quite specific. In its most reductive form, dialectical thinking pits public or collective consciousness against the privatized, transhistorical, and implicitly reactionary values of bourgeois liberalism. Classical Marxism stages a confrontation between public and private, just as Christian theology unfolds as a tension between spirit and body. History replaces faith as a means to transcendence, through which "given being"—that is, nature, or body, or the material conditions of communal existence—is sublimated, annulled, *aufgehoben*.[9] Pressed into the service of dialectical materialism, literature becomes the site of political and social conflict between classes or factions, holding out the promise of "progress" through a Hegelian synthesis of master and slave, fighting and work, and perhaps most important, universal and particular.[10] To the extent that it emphasizes the transformative potential of work—and specifically, creative work—this paradigm allows for the "rescue of the individual" through a seemingly paradoxical focus on the communal, a fact that perhaps explains its appeal for those medievalists who are reacting specifically to the challenge to representation and autonomous subjectivity posed by deconstructive and psychoanalytic theory. Thus Patterson sees the Miller's Tale as Chaucer's dramatization of a lost struggle for peasant recognition (a dramatization that effectively allegorizes the social upheaval of 1381),[11] Paul Strohm depicts Chaucer as a masterful negotiator of the social formations and discourses of Ricardian England,[12] and Stephen Knight argues for a sociohistorical Chaucerian criticism that will ultimately reveal a creative effort that is "much more powerful and admirable" than has been previously thought.[13] These are persuasive and innovative readings; the recent work of Patterson and Strohm, in particular, holds out the possibility of a new dialogue between literature and history, a dialogue which previous historicist work was never able to envision. In all these critical texts, however, we are left with the image of a poet who is, for the most part, in perfect control of his social and political consciousness, a singular mind whose works effectively process or transform collective experience into a powerful affirmation of individual effort.

In light of the fundamentally traditional and recuperative nature of this historicist approach, it seems curious that both Patterson and Knight make a claim for contemporary political relevance, for the material significance of historicist reading.[14] They also make it clear that this relevance can only be preserved by attending to the past in its particularity, that is, by not allowing "presentist" hermeneutic concerns to "infect" the integrity of the reading itself. The assumption that supposedly resolves this paradox is that, to paraphrase Patterson, political action is impossible without a belief in the efficacy and potential significance of the "local and contingent" historical moment.[15] In practice, this privilege accorded the particular is untenable: our understanding of history—indeed, of the "Middle" Ages as an historical category—is implicitly a teleological and allegorical one.

Not surprisingly, this concern for accurate contextualization echoes Robertsonian caveats of earlier decades. Both Christian historicism and its neo-Hegelian successor are epistemologically committed to an allegorical or typological view of the past. Within Marxist thought, this allegorical understanding of history in terms of its "expressive totality" has

constituted a reaction against the privatization of experience and the suppression of collective thinking in general.[16] Although a sensitivity to allegory is essential to any political understanding of events, in practice it
tends to reduce literature to a mere symptom of what are perceived to be
larger and more significant institutional or historical phenomena. These
readings tend to view textual analysis with suspicion; their indictments of
formalist criticism often seem to be a displacement of an anxiety about
literature itself, which, within the logic of such a system, must be seen as
a reflection or even celebration of bourgeois liberalism.

More significant for our purposes is the theological aspect of this
approach. Indeed, both Walter Benjamin and Fredric Jameson make explicit the sense in which hermeneutic Marxism takes its cue from scriptural
exegesis.[17] Understood allegorically, literary practice unfolds within a teleological system—figured as a symptom of struggle, it moves inexorably
toward the eventual *Aufhebung* of its dialectical terms. Needless to say,
this theological or allegorical historicism rests on a rigid binarism: mirroring the traditional Christian insistence on the opposition of matter and
spirit, these historicist critics read the past in terms of an ongoing tension
between public and private, outside and inside.[18] As in the Christian system, woman inevitably stands in for the discredited second term. In his
analysis of *Troilus and Criseyde*, for example, Stephen Knight asserts that
Criseyde

> is a figure of a new self-consciousness for both men and women; it is because
> women were in so many ways excluded from the authority of a patriarchal
> public order that Chaucer is able to exploit them as a terrain for the explora-
> tion of privacy—the Wife of Bath will be another striking case.[19]

Despite this seemingly sympathetic assessment, it is clear that the public
and collective realm is privileged in Knight's study. It is also clear that he
is at pains to maintain the distinction of public and private along the lines
of sexual difference, even to the point of distorting the text, as he does
when he tells us that the story of Thebes was "set aside by Criseyde to talk
of life and love with Pandarus"; it is in fact Pandarus who commands that
Criseyde "do wey" her historical book.[20] This insistence on the equivalence of feminine and private leads Knight to claim that Criseyde is the
"essence" of privacy and introspection, while Troilus is characterized as a
"private lover but inflexibly public man."[21] Similarly, Lee Patterson associates the Wife of Bath with a reactionary "internalization of value," a
privatized subjectivity that is the antithesis of class consciousness. In his

analysis of the sequence of the Canterbury Tales, he isolates what he takes to be Chaucer's individualist and transhistorical bias:

> . . . in substituting for the political threat posed by the Miller the Wife of Bath's insistence upon the priority of the individual self, Chaucer makes what we have come to recognize as the characteristic liberal move. What the Wife wants is not, despite her truculent tone, political or social change; on the contrary, the traditional order is capable both of generating her independent selfhood and of accommodating the marital happiness that would accomplish its fulfillment.[22]

What seems to be operative here is an implicit equivalence between the oppositions public/private and reality/fantasy, wherein the second terms are "scapegoated" to shore up their privileged opposites. Certainly the Wife of Bath's Tale problematizes these oppositions; the story of a rapist's metamorphosis into a courtly lover seems to me to be about the interiorization and neutralization of political challenge by a discursive system—romance—which is in fact parasitically dependent on sexual violence and voyeurism. For women, social and political protest has frequently found expression in fantasy; one could argue that the Wife's *Tale* illustrates the sense in which that challenge is always potentially undone by the representational systems it invokes.

The point, of course, is that private fantasies echo public or group fantasies; while literary conventions are certainly not unproblematic ideological "messages," neither are they a simple reflection of an individual (i.e., undivided) imagination. Private and public are always mutually implicated, and gestures toward the real inevitably carry with them the trace of a fantasmatic investment. The medieval association of textual "privetee" with the secrets of the feminine body is encrypted in this critical insistence on a correspondence between femininity and an apolitical private self; both are symptomatic of a male fantasy of feminine interiority, a fantasy that allows masculinist poets and critics to imagine for themselves an extra-textual and extra-semiotic speaking position.

Once again, the installation of sexual difference both reflects and enables a metaphysical distinction that grounds empiricist epistemology. The etymological relation of the term "private" to the Latin *privare*—to deprive—re-evokes the Freudian castration scene, the originary myth that links sexual difference to the perception of lack, and establishes the feminine position as *essentially* privative. The masculinist reading of the scene turns on the conversion of absence into loss, a conversion necessitated by the privilege accorded the penis. This conceptual leap from absence to loss turns the originary myth, the story of sexual difference, into a narrative of fetishism. As Dominick LaCapra puts it in his essay "History and Psychoanalysis,"

> What is missing is the very phallus that the woman (the phantasmatic phallic mother) had "in the beginning" but lost through some misdeed—an obvious lesson for the boy himself. The fetish, for Freud, is itself the narcissistically inverted surrogate for the phantasmatic lost totality—a totality that never existed and whose imaginary constitution requires a conversion of absence into loss on the basis of a nonperception.[23]

By representing privation and privacy, woman enables the fantasy of the "lost totality" or communal spirit that dialectical historicism celebrates. This fetishistic investment in the past masquerades as "purely objective" scholarship only to the extent that it succeeds in maintaining the boundary between private and public, fantasy and reality. As I discussed in the previous chapter, however, the fetishist's position is always an unstable one, implying as it does both a projection of lack and an identification with privation itself.

The current movement in medieval studies away from literature and into the archives may reflect, among other things, an unconscious awareness of this linguistic indeterminacy which continually effaces borders; literary texts are dangerous because they inevitably destabilize configurations based on sexual difference, and thereby threaten to reveal the homosocial and homoerotic desire that subtends collectivist nostalgia. Medieval historicism thus understands history as that which is neither literary nor contemporary; the past—like the phallic mother—is endowed with a fantasmatic plenitude, a potency beside which "presentist" hermeneutic concerns, like literary texts themselves, are shown to be dangerously indeterminate and privative. By defining history as "the real," dialectical historicism relegates literature to a transhistorical and apolitical realm of fantasy.[24]

Despite its undeniable ideological efficacy, however, this opposition is epistemologically very problematic, in that it seeks to veil the fantasmatic construction of historicity itself. Medieval historicism, like medieval and particularly Chaucerian literature, seems to move between the two mutually dependent poles of melancholia and disavowal. The lament for a lost past is inevitably accompanied by a denial of that loss, as Patterson's repeated polemical equivocations on the subject of the historical real illustrate.

While he admits that "textuality is inescapable" and that "we cannot repro-
duce the past *wie es eigentlich gewesen* [*ist*],"[25] these admissions are always
either preceded or followed by lengthy (and somewhat reductive) critiques
of "deconstructive formalism" by which we are to understand a critical
practice that "[sequesters] the world of events into a realm of presence
closed to the irreparably deficient activity of writing."[26] The undecidability that characterizes Patterson's treatment of this issue is, of course,
central to any historicist subjectivity, any practice that seeks to engage the
problematics of memory or memorialization. Caught between the event
itself and the imaginative reconstruction necessitated by memory, the analyst of history moves from a melancholic awareness of loss to a reparative
disavowal; in so doing, however, she or he gives up a commitment to the
real, and seeks refuge in the unstable realm of representation.

This is precisely the problem that Chaucer explores in his historical
romance, *Troilus and Criseyde*. Like the *Book of the Duchess*, to which it is
closely related conceptually, the *Troilus* begins as a drama of loss, and
then proceeds to show how this essentially historicist problem becomes,
through displacement, a problem of sexual difference. The privatization or
interiorization of Criseyde is the means whereby the poem disavows its
inaugural losses; as in the *Duchess*, however, sexual identifications and
identities are shown to be dangerously slippery. In the remainder of this
chapter, I will explore what I take to be the melancholic aspect of the
poem, and the sense in which the *Troilus*, like the *Duchess*, translates this
dilemma into a realm of sexuality centered on a feminine object; finally, I
will interrogate the problematic role of Troilus himself, both within the
poem and among its critics. I will suggest that the problem of historicity,
for Chaucer as for his readers, is bound up with the sexual politics of
representation. Moreover, in forcing us to confront the problem of difference per se, the reading and writing of history situates us—no less than
Chaucer—in an arena where our fantasies about the past have profound
ethical implications for the present.

## Meaning and Melancholia: A Poetics of History

Like the *Book of the Duchess*, Chaucer's *Troilus and Criseyde* begins in a
melancholic mood; the first two stanzas create an air of such pervasive
sadness and paralysis that the poem nearly dissolves before the story can
be told. The opening lines are littered with weeping bodies: Troilus,

Tisiphone and the narrator are all "sorwynge," and even the verses themselves weep as they are written. Thus corporealized, the text cannot sustain the dualist opposition between matter and meaning, cannot fulfill the ideological imperatives of its orthodox Christian context. All this weeping threatens to reduce the poem to inarticulate sound; the poet must surmount this "drive to dissolution" if the story is to be told at all.

It is the narrator's historical awareness of how it all turns out that nearly undoes the romance. His historical perspective on the events he must relate brings with it a sense of futility, a melancholic paralysis that calls the entire enterprise into question; paradoxically, it is only by forgetting the story's end that he can "memorialize" the romance as such. This traumatic opening isolates history as a threat to the romance, and thus initiates the generic instability that characterizes the poem throughout. In the opening lines of the work, the narrator explicitly promises his audience a romance:

> The double sorwe of Troilus to tellen,
> That was the kyng Priamus sone of Troye,
> In lovynge, how his aventures fellen
> Fro wo to wele, and after out of joie,
> My purpos is, er that I parte fro ye.
> Thesiphone, thow help me for t'endite
> Thise woful vers, that wepen as I write. (1. 1–7)

This attempt to fix or locate the poem generically—as a story about "lovynge"—is undermined by the syntactic intrusion of that other Troy, the Troy in which Troilus is but another of King Priam's many sons. Even before the narrative gets started, the specter of the classical Trojan saga threatens to trivialize this romance, just as the figure of Hector continually threatens to diminish the heroic stature of Troilus in the poem. Moreover, the intrusive second line of the poem links the classical past to the issue of paternity and, implicitly, to the question of inheritance. The invocation of Tisiphone which follows confirms the crucial importance of inheritance in the genesis of the poem, but also points to the indeterminacy of origins. In Statius's *Thebaid*, the blinded Oedipus calls upon the Fury to destroy his own sons, to "begin a work of vengeance that will blast their seed forever."[27] Behind the image of the Fury, the monstrous mother, lurks a figure equally dangerous to the poetic endeavor: the monstrous father. By invoking this unnatural maternal figure, Oedipus would wipe out the patrilineal continuum of this own house. It is a painfully delusive moment in the Statian text; although Oedipus posits himself as the originator of Theban destruction, the poem interiorizes his narrative of revenge within a larger historical cycle of violence, vengeance and loss that is presented as inexorable.[28] Thus the allusion to Statius, which ought to confer a measure of poetic legitimacy or hereditary rights upon the medieval text, succeeds only in destabilizing the father-son relationship, invoking sons who kill their fathers, fathers who kill their sons, and a historical world whose cycles of violence and loss preclude even the illusion of narrative autonomy. History emerges not as a paternal legacy, but rather as a testament to the impossibility of ever sustaining the relation of father to son; by identifying himself with Oedipus, the narrator establishes a connection to the literary past that can only be viewed as traumatic.

Given the fact that the *Troilus* is, at least peripherally, a poem about the fall of a nation, it is not surprising that here, as in the *Book of the Duchess*, the question of paternity is a troubling one. The story of Troy, as we all know, had considerable ideological significance for English poets and historiographers during the Middle Ages.[29] The fall of Troy was thought to have initiated the series of events leading to the founding of Britain; through the erstwhile Trojan Aeneas, Britain claimed the right to see itself as heir to the Roman Empire. Public and private fantasies are mingled in these opening lines: the poet's agonistic relation to his poetic fathers also reflects a nation's need to affirm, yet overcome, the powerful cultural precedent of the lost classical world. The allusion to a great Roman poet is an index for a great Roman state; in asserting a right to mourn for a lost past, the medieval poet also claims the right to inherit from it, a right that is essential to the founding of a specifically English literary tradition.[30]

It is typical of Chaucer, and fully in keeping with the metadiscursive issues raised by the *Book of the Duchess*, that this mourning—for Troilus, for Troy, and for the lost world of classical poetry—would slip into excess, becoming melancholic and potentially destructive. Through the narrator's identification with Oedipus, mourning for the lost past leads to an awareness of another, prior loss: the loss of the referential world or of the real necessitated by one's entry into language. In *Black Sun*, Julia Kristeva associates melancholic "asymbolia" with a denial of *dénégation* (Freud's *Verneinung*, or negation), or, more precisely, with a refusal to replace the lost archaic object—here, as in Freud's work, associated with the maternal realm of the real—with representation.[31] This inability to believe that the lost object can be replaced amounts to a denial of that loss; if the lost object is irreplaceable, its loss becomes intolerable. The melancholic subject, cut off from language and representation, is thus doubly alienated from the world of objects, which are inaccessible except through language. According to Kristeva, art mirrors psychoanalysis in attempting to restore language, and thus the phenomenal world, to the melancholic subject. In order to do this, however, it must somehow turn the lost real into an object that can be signified.[32]

It is easy to see how this emphasis on disavowal and displacement can turn into fetishism, particularly when the lost object is made synonymous with mother. In the *Book of the Duchess*, as we have seen, melancholia is reduced to mourning (made less traumatic) by substituting the absent Lady White for the lost referential world that haunts the narrator at the beginning of the poem.[33] In the *Troilus*, the opening allusion to Statius affirms the poem's right to mourn, and thus to inherit, but the narrator's identification with Oedipus encrypts a more archaic loss, and gestures toward the horrifying consequences of Oedipus's own denial of *dénégation*. In Book I of the *Thebaid*, Jupiter describes Oedipus's incestuous relations with Jocasta as an attempt to return to his own place of origin:

> scandere quin etiam thalamos hic impius heres
> patris et immeritae gremium incestare parentis appetiit,
> proprios—monstrum!—revolutus in ortus. (I. 233–35)

> (this unnatural heir has even ventured to climb his father's couch
> and defile the womb of the innocent mother, returning—oh!
> horror!—to his own life's origin.)

The narrator's identification with Oedipus leads him to the very conflict that, for Freud, marked the traumatic origins of normative sexuality. Identifying with the father's desire, the male child first seeks to kill the father that he may have the mother; eventually, the father's prohibition and the fear of castration persuade him to transfer that desire to an appropriate heterosexual object choice. What is horrifying about the oedipal *Urtext*, of course, is that the conflict is unresolved, leading to the defilement associated with incest. Thus, what Kristeva calls a denial or disavowal of *dénégation*—a refusal to negate the loss of the originary object through representation—also carries with it a trace of a forbidden desire, a desire to return to one's own origin in violation of the prohibition upon which patriarchal culture is founded.

Here, as so often in Chaucer's poetry, identification is shown to be the means whereby identity is at once established and destabilized. The narrator's ostensibly normative identification with a lost paternal figure returns him to the repressed origins of poetic speaking: the feminine body. What this difficult inaugural moment seems to suggest is that, although memory is essential to the ideological project of a cultural poetics, and thus to a nationalist-patriarchal continuum, it is also perilous to the poetic subject. Formed and informed by the uncanny traces of an archaic lost object—the real—memory is always nostalgic, always implies a painful longing for the place of origin (the etymology of "nostalgia" makes this explicit: from Greek *nostos*, "to return home" and *algia*, "a painful condition"). This longing, which is at the heart of melancholia, continually threatens to return poetic language to its lost maternal and material origins, thereby silencing any textual endeavor. To the extent that it depends on identification, memory—and thus history—always leads the subject into the unstable realm of desire, wherein meaning and materiality can no longer be constrained within a dualist metaphysical system. Identification with the lost fathers inevitably slips into desire for the lost mother, a desire that such a system can only understand as a drive to dissolution and death, a return to the origin, or to inanimacy.[34]

Of all the difficult beginnings in Chaucer's poetry, these opening lines of the *Troilus* are perhaps the most troubling. The generic and ontological problematics of history and memory are here linked to melancholia, to the body, and to death. It is therefore not surprising that the rest of the poem seems committed to forgetting the past. The narrator, Troilus, and Pandarus all contribute to the poem's disavowal of the historical real and its deferral of historical knowledge. We are repeatedly told that Troilus goes out to fight as a courtly lover, not as a Trojan warrior. Pandarus tells Criseyde that his news of Troilus's interest in her will banish all thought of the war from her mind. The narrator tells us to read Dares and Dictys if we want history—his "matere" is romance. It is significant that this disavowal is always associated with the male voice, since it goes hand in hand with a narrative effort to install sexual difference as the dominant opposition in the poem. In the next section of my analysis, I will explore this phenomenon in some detail, focusing on the sense in which sexual difference is made to compensate fetishistically for historical difference in the text. Expanding on my argument in the previous chapter, I will suggest some ways in which the very dynamic of fetishistic identification subverts this strategy, opening up a space for a feminist reading of the text, and just perhaps, for a feminist and psychoanalytic intervention in the larger historicist debate in the field.

## Criseyde Disfigured

Shortly after the narrative introduction to the poem, the problem of paternal textual authority re-emerges in the figure of Calkas. Calkas's historical foreknowledge, like that of the narrator, threatens the continuity of the romance. It is only by removing this "lord of gret auctorite" from the poem that the narrator can defer his knowledge of Troy's—and Troilus's—violent end. Significantly, Calkas is banished from the text at the same moment his daughter enters it; she is left to fill his place, and to absorb the gaps and losses that are the only legacy of the poem's absent fathers. The body of Criseyde, clad in mourning, replaces the weeping body of the text. Embodying loss, she enables the narrator and his poem to escape from the pathological and potentially paralyzing melancholy of the first two stanzas.

This displacement and projection of lack links narrative recuperation to a simultaneous refusal of history and affirmation of sexual difference. It is consistent with this strategy that the repressed communal/historical world should return, uncannily, through the women in the poem. The Trojan war becomes internalized as Criseyde's feminine paranoia; her concern for events outside the walls of Troy marks her as morally flawed, "slydyng of corage."[35] In addition, the names of Criseyde's mother and niece—Argyve and Antigone—bespeak a connection to the Theban Saga, which, from a medieval perspective, historically preceded the story of Troy.[36] In Book II, Helen's seeming flirtation with Diephebus looks forward to their marriage after Paris's death. Perhaps most striking is the fact that the poem's only historian is Cassandra, the classical exemplar of feminine discursive insufficiency. This feminization and marginalization of the past effects a fantasmatic division between meaning and materiality, between masculine poetic language and feminine bodies, a division that attempts to counteract the image of the corporealized text in the poem's opening lines, thus displacing lack from male subjects to female objects.

Paradoxically, then, the exteriorization of history comes to depend on the interiorization of woman. This fact is made explicit in the final glimpse of history we are afforded prior to the *Natureingang* that initiates the romance proper:

But though that Grekes hem of Troie shetten,
And hir cite biseged al aboute,
Hire olde usage nolde they nat letten,
As for to honoure hir goddes ful devoute;
But aldirmost in honour, out of doute,
Thei hadde a relik, heet Palladion,
That was hire trist aboven everichon. (1. 148–54)

The "relik" is of course the statue of Pallas Athene that protects the walls of Troy. The anachronistic term uncovers the statue's sacred value as a fetish; as long as this fetishized feminine image remains within the walls of Troy, the Greeks cannot transgress them. That Criseyde is a similarly fetishized sacred object is confirmed when she is exchanged for Antenor; Chaucer reminds us (as Boccaccio does not) that within Benoît's *Roman de Troie*, Antenor joins Aeneas in stealing the statue, thereby bringing about the "meschaunce" of Troy's fall. Criseyde's departure from the city prefigures the theft of the Palladium. Lacking the feminine fetish, the city walls cannot shut out the brutal reality of war, nor can Troy remain the *hortus conclusus* of Troilus's romantic fantasy. As the Palladium keeps the war outside Troy, so the fetishized body of Criseyde keeps the historical Troy outside the borders of the romance.

Because this exclusionary strategy requires an interiorized feminine object, it depends upon the establishment of stable sexual identities. Within the specular economy of the romance system, however, sexual identities can only be stabilized when man is associated with vision, and woman with spectacle.[37] The poem's disavowal of historical knowledge—and of historical difference—is thus dependent on the specular interiorization of Criseyde, who, according to the narrator, is the least "mannysh" character in the poem.

As in the *Book of the Duchess*, these specular moments reveal the points of resistance in the system; Criseyde proves to be a difficult object, Troilus a reluctant subject. Through her association with Calkas, Criseyde can be said to belong, initially, to the historical, extra-Trojan space beyond the city walls. Even after her father leaves, her status remains marginal—this marginality is figured in spatial terms when we see her standing in the temple,

. . . ful lowe and stille allone,
Byhynden other folk, in litel brede,
And neigh the dore, ay undre shames drede (1. 178–80)

Positioned near the door, she is almost out of narrative reach; it is up to Troilus to move her to the interior of narrative space, to make her the object of his gaze and his poetic desire. In the scopophilic exchange that follows, however, Troilus proves to be incapable of situating himself outside the specular economy he himself has initiated. When he first looks at her, his gaze seems to have a phallic potency, an ability to penetrate its object:

> And upon cas bifel that thorugh a route
> His eye percede, and so depe it wente,
> Til on Criseyde it smot, and ther it stente. (1. 271–73)

A careful reading reveals that, although his look pierces the crowd, it cannot penetrate Criseyde.[38] It is her look that penetrates him, literally "deflating" his attempt at specular mastery:

> And of hire look in him ther gan to quyken
> So gret desir and such affeccioun,
> That in his herte botme gan to stiken
> Of hir his fixe and depe impressioun.
> And though he erst hadde poured up and down,
> He was tho glad his hornes in to shrinke;
> Unnethes wiste he how to loke or wynke. (1. 295–301)

Sexual identities are inverted as Criseyde's look metaphorically pierces Troilus, leaving him "thorugh-shoten and thorugh-darted." Given that the poem's reparative agenda depends on the interiorization of an irreducibly feminine Criseyde, this moment of reversal and deviance can only be seen as dangerous.

Troilus's inability to sustain an active male role necessitates the intervention of his un-courtly double, Pandarus, who promises to restore Troilus to a state of potency and plenitude. Near the end of Book I, he begins to reconstruct Troilus's courtly subjectivity in phallic terms:

> "I thenke, sith that Love, of his goodnesse,
> Hath the converted out of wikkednesse,
> That thow shalt ben the beste post, I leve,
> Of al his lay, and moost his foos to greve." (1. 998–1001)

The double sense of "lay"—meaning either law or song—here confirms Troilus's dual role of lover and poet, while the word "post," as we will remember from the description of the Friar in the General Prologue to the *Canterbury Tales*, has decidedly sexual connotations.

In Book II, Pandarus begins to mediate in earnest, with the aim of moving Criseyde to the interior of his literal and figurative house. Once again, the intrusive presence of history threatens to destabilize the courtly fantasy. The narrator invokes Clio, the muse of history, as his guide, in an effort to distance himself from the "pandering" that is about to take place:

> . . . I nyl have neither thank nor blame
> of al this werk, but prey yow mekely,
> Disblameth me if any word be lame,
> For as myn auctour seyde, so sey I. (2. 15–18)

He attempts to give closure to the question of history by defining historiographic mediation as translation, an act "of no sentement." A few lines later, however, this linguistic and synchronic definition of *translatio* opens onto a diachronic perspective, spanning "a thousand yeer," and then further expands to include cultural difference as well: "in sondry londes," the narrator remarks, "sondry ben usages." Both historiography and translation exceed the boundaries which the narrator originally tries to establish for them, a fact which calls his own perspective on the past into question, and threatens to implicate him in the "traffic in women" Pandarus is about to initiate. By the end of the proem, he is no longer sure of his ability to mediate or "translate" at all. "Myn auctor shal I folwen," he asserts, and then adds uncertainly, "if I konne."

The expanding semantic boundaries of translation in the proem remind us that *translatio* also means "metaphor," and that this book concerns the translation or metaphorization of Criseyde herself. Given the narrator's still unresolved problems with history, and Troilus's inability to reduce Criseyde to the passivity of spectacle in Book I, much is at stake at this point in the narrative. It is up to Pandarus to install sexual difference as the dominant opposition in the poem, and thus to "shore up" the myth of male discursive plenitude, a myth which the narrator's uncertainty continually calls into question. Only when Criseyde's femininity is bound within a specular economy—and thus rendered irreducible and unproblematic—can she become the "ground" for Troilus's lyrical metaphors and the symptomatic reflection of the narrator's disavowal and repression of the communal and historical world.

It is through Pandarus, then, that historical difference as an effect of loss comes to be inscribed as sexual difference as an effect of lack. This strategic displacement is made most explicit early in Book II, when Pandarus finds Criseyde reading the story of the siege of Thebes. At this moment, Criseyde's exteriority as reader stands in the way of Pandarus's efforts to textualize her, to inscribe her in the romance he is writing for Troilus. What is more, the Theban matter has already been established as a threat to the continuity of the romance itself. It is thus significant that Pandarus simultaneously dismisses the book and demands that she remove her veil that he may look at her:

> "But lat be this, and telle me how ye fare.
> Do wey youre barbe, and shewe youre face bare;
> Do wey youre book, rys up, and lat us daunce,
> And lat us don to May som observaunce." (2. 109–12)

The parallel "do wey" commands link the foreclosure of history to the construction of the male gaze, and to courtly convention. The observances of May, the unveiling of female faces and the closing of historical texts are all bound together, as Pandarus attempts to close off all gaps and neutralize all threats to his erotic and poetic enterprise.

Throughout Book II, Pandarus's mediation manifests itself as an insistence on the visual. His fetishization of the look foregrounds the reader's complicity in the voyeuristic enterprise of romance. At one point his rhetoric suggests a relation between poetry and fetishism that is particularly significant. In attempting to get Criseyde to dance and make merry, Pandarus again suggests that she remove, or at least change, her clothes:

> ". . . cast youre widewes habit to mischaunce!
> What list you thus youreself to disfigure,
> Sith you is tid thus fair an aventure?" (2. 222–24)

Criseyde's widow's habit stands in the way of the visual pleasure romance generically promises. Refusing to submit to the male gaze "disfigures" or de-faces a woman, according to Pandarus. What interests me here is the implicit connection between material and rhetorical senses of the word "disfigure." By not allowing herself to be made into a spectacle, Criseyde also refuses to be figured rhetorically, to serve as the basis for the tropological substitutions that will enable Troilus to constitute himself as a poet in Books IV and V. This moment also has an uncanny resonance for the modern reader; in Henryson's fifteenth-century continuation of the story, Criseyde will suffer the literal disfigurement of leprosy. Henryson's reading of Chaucer's poem suggests that rhetorical figuration, and specifically metaphor-making, has at its origin the fantasy of a certain intractable feminine materiality which is either cherished fetishistically, as object of the gaze, or despised and jettisoned as what is most abject.[39] In Chaucer's text, as in Henryson's, the figuring or troping of the feminine body enables the ahistorical fantasy of courtly romance, but it exacts a price. For the feminine object, figuration always implies disfiguration—only by de-facing woman can man constitute himself as a subject who is immune to the predations of historical change.

So far, I have argued for a reading of the *Troilus* that emphasizes its normative and reparative function within a patriarchal courtly culture. Through Pandarus, the narrator disavows the irremediable difference of the historical or material world, by inscribing that difference onto the body of Criseyde; through Criseyde, material losses are made good as poetic or metaphoric gains. In situating itself over and against feminine interiority or lack, male subjectivity is shown to be coherent and whole. What is interesting about Chaucerian poetics in general, and the *Troilus* in particular, however, is the extent to which this masculinist strategy is shown to fail precisely at the points it seems to be most successful. By way of example, I would like to mention two more specular moments in Book II in which sexual difference is set up as a problem which Pandarus must solve if the romance is to continue. After Pandarus leaves Criseyde, she happens to look out her window, and sees Troilus riding home from battle. This moment becomes perilous not because Criseyde "un-mans" the hero, as in Book I, but because the narrator's identification with Troilus—an identification that is crucial to the poem's coherence—shifts from a homosocial affirmation of Troilus' masculinity to a homoerotic emphasis on his vulnerability and lack. The passage literally splits in two, as an index of the male subject's sexual undecidability:

> So lik a man of armes and a knyght
> He was to seen, fulfilled of heigh prowesse,
> For bothe he hadde a body and a myght
> To don that thyng, as wel as hardynesse;
> And ek to seen hym in his gere hym dresse,
> So fresshe, so yong, so weldy semed he,
> It was an heven upon hym for to see. (2. 631–37)

These last three lines emphasize Troilus's "fresh" and heavenly beauty, terms which are usually reserved for women in medieval lyrics. The next stanza contributes further to the slippage in sexual identifications by dwelling on Troilus's pierced and penetrated armor, thus emphasizing his vulnerability and lack of phallic wholeness:

> His helm tohewen was in twenty places,
> That by a tyssew heng his bak byhynde;
> His sheeld todasshed was with swerdes and maces,
> In which men myght many an arwe fynde
> That thirled hadde horn and nerf and rynde (2. 638–42)

Criseyde, by virtue of her superior position, is endowed with a specular exteriority that is usually reserved for the male subject. This slippage in identification leads to a reversal of gender positions that causes the narrator no small amount of anxiety. Although Troilus's love-at-first-sight was presented as "natural" and unproblematic, Criseyde's almost identical experience leads the narrator to problematize the matter unnecessarily by denying that her response denotes superficiality or fickleness.

Again, it is up to Pandarus to restore both Troilus and the narrator to a position of potency by re-staging the scene, this time with Troilus's complicity. Now the narrator can put Criseyde in her place; as Troilus passes beneath the window, the narrator expresses a hope that she "hath now kaught a thorn," which she "shal nat pulle out this next wyke" (2. 1272–73). Criseyde's metaphoric penetration here compensates for the narrator's own voyeurism in describing the vulnerability of his hero earlier. By rhetorically structuring Criseyde as lacking, the narrator covers over the sexual indeterminacy of his own desire, or, perhaps more to the point, the sense in which the desire that circulates within texts perpetually exceeds sexual difference.

Attempting to close off the oscillation and randomness of sexual identities and identifications, both Pandarus and the narrator expose the violence that subtends the romantic fantasy, the sense in which the language of romance slips easily into metaphors and images of rape and death. Sexual violence lurks just beneath the surface of the text. The *Natureingang* of Book II offers the seemingly innocent song of the swallow Procne, repressing its Ovidian subtext of rape and infanticide, Criseyde's dream of the eagle is one of violent but painless penetration, and just prior to the consummation scene in Book III, Troilus prays for sexual potency by invoking images of rape from classical mythology.[40] Interestingly, the images of power and violence tend to emerge at the most conventional, culturally over-determined moments in the text, threatening the innocence of both the romance and its hero. Troilus's resistance to the historical world that threatens his courtly fantasy is only heroic if the realm of romance retains its visionary idealism, that is, only if violence and death remain outside the privatized erotic space that is at the poem's center.

This latent violence blurs the boundary between public and private in the poem. In fact, the rhetorical and metaphoric violence that adheres to the problem of sexual difference mirrors the violence and loss that was associated with historical difference early in Book I. This mirroring of individual and communal fantasies will become more obvious in Book IV, when the romance is once again confronted with the historical Trojan saga, and Pandarus's metaphorical house falls to the exigencies of war. I want to look briefly at the moment when public and private are most clearly at odds in the poem, when the Trojan parliament is considering the exchange of Criseyde for Antenor. Troilus, true to the courtly convention of secrecy, remains silent as Criseyde's fate is decided. The private "traffic in women" which made Criseyde an object of exchange between Pandarus and Troilus is set against this public "chaungynge," which is dictated by national rather than individual desire. Even Troilus partakes of the public fantasy whereby "she is chaunged for the townes good." In fact, he seems to accept his loss of Criseyde as a foregone conclusion; he does not bother to tell her of the parliament's decision, but instead retreats into philosophical speculations about the perfidy of fortune and the impossibility of choice. Once Criseyde has been deemed exchangable, Troilus quickly—in fact too quickly—exchanges the role of lover for that of philosopher/poet. The romance becomes internalized as Troilus's male fantasy, just as the Trojan War had been privatized as Criseyde's feminine paranoia earlier in the poem.

Throughout Book V, we find Troilus in the grip of melancholic fantasies that seek expression in elegy. The connection between pathology and poetry is made explicit in the repetition of the word "fantasie" in connection with Troilus's poetic and narcissistic musings. It is within the logic of the Freudian *fort-da* paradigm that Troilus passes the time "refiguryng" the lost feminine object—these melancholic imaginings are a kind of artistic play that enables the lover to constitute himself as lyric poet. What is also clear is that for Troilus, these poetic fantasies are structured in opposition to the historical and communal "reality" of the extra-Trojan world. His belief in love, even in the face of Criseyde's faithlessness, is also a repudiation of a historical world that is seen to be violent and privative.

For Criseyde, as we have seen, the conventions of romance are also at least potentially privative, and certainly violent. If she is commodified by the community, she is also a fetishized object of exchange that enables the male fantasies of Pandarus, Troilus, and the narrator.[41] The distinction between fantasy and reality, romance and history, that subtends Troilus's poetic subjectivity is inaccessible to her; she is always already on the inside, never on the outside, of both social and poetic constructs. Her moral "disfiguration" is the price of Troilus's refusal of history: in a romantic fantasy where the violence of warfare and the victimization of women don't "count," Criseyde's inability to return to Troy and her acceptance of another male protector can only be seen as betrayal.

Clearly, then, there are two potential victims in the story. Within the Boethian logic of the poem's end, Troilus is the victim of feminine and material instability. This is, not surprisingly, the reading of the vast majority of the poem's critics. From a feminist point of view, Criseyde is victimized by male fantasies at both the private and the public level. Cast into the mutable realm of history by the Christian imperatives of closure, she is denied any kind of transcendence; at the same time, her "chaungyng"—as exchange and metamorphosis—allows Troilus to ascend to the eighth sphere, and thereby to assume the position of specular exteriority that he was denied in the romance proper. The difference of view that distinguishes these two readings lies precisely in their respective views of difference. The traditional reading affirms the poem's Boethian closure—despite the nagging doubts it leaves behind—because it closes off historical and sexual difference as a problem in the text. The feminist reading problematizes the gaps and absences in the poem as losses which the text recuperates by reducing all difference to sexual difference.

If I seem to displace the poem's obsession with sexual difference onto the criticism it has generated, it is because virtually all the critics interested in the ethical dimension of the poem identify strongly with either Troilus or Criseyde.[42] Identification is, of course, essential to the constitution of a critical subjectivity, and is in no way avoidable. It is also, as I have argued, epistemologically unstable, in that it simultaneously establishes and effaces the border between subject and object, resulting in the endocryptic tendency I discussed earlier. In the remainder of this study, I would like to continue the dialogue between the field of medieval studies and the *Troilus*, focusing specifically on the disavowal of historical knowledge that characterizes Chaucer's poem as well as historicist-medievalist arguments about the past. In so doing, I will suggest some ways in which we might begin to come to terms with a literary past which, like the Freudian hysteric, always knows more than it knows.

## Historical Innocence: What Chaucer Knew

In a recent article on the Prioress's Tale, Judith Ferster begins by discussing—through the distancing tactic of anecdote—some of her anxieties about "connecting Chaucer, feminism, and psychoanalysis." Her opening paragraph is in many ways typical of the traditional medievalist's view of history:

> Hearing that I was about to connect Chaucer, feminism, and psychoanalysis, some feminist historian friends of mine laughed. Their skepticism concerned two sides of the triangle. One side was the connection between Freud and feminism. They cited the fact—they called it a fact—that Freud was wrong about women. Their radically historical view of Freud and—I suspect—all theorists leads to skepticism about another side of the triangle. If I could not prove to them that habits of child-rearing in middle-class families in nineteenth-century Vienna replicated those of merchant families in fourteenth-century London, they would not grant that psychoanalysis might help us understand Chaucer's poems. They were sure I could not prove such an equation because the Middle Ages did not produce either selves or ideas of selfhood like ours. What could Chaucer know about the unconscious? [43]

What, indeed? The positivist assumptions of Ferster's friends—which, one may assume, echo doubts of her own about the validity of theory in general—are quite clear. There is a "right" and a "wrong" about women; there is a radical particularity about history that hopelessly alienates one "period" from another; and finally, methodology is only valid if it can be reduced to an "equation" that gives us a clear, visible answer. It is a testament to the power of this kind of thinking that Ferster—who purports to be sympathetic to the kind of approach her friends reject—continues her own argument in the terms defined by these empiricist assumptions, arguing from archival evidence that medieval families were, indeed, structured similarly to those of nineteenth-century Vienna. [44] All this, of course, ignores the very provocative question with which her paragraph closes: what could Chaucer know about the unconscious? What could the Middle Ages know about psychoanalysis? More to the point, what can history know about what we want to know from it? In answer to the first question, one may "straddle the line" by claiming, as many "modern medievalists" are doing these days, that Chaucer was an exceptionally precocious poet, who, like the hysteric, knew more than was probably good for him. The last question gets to the heart of the matter, the point where epistemology and ideology intersect: what does history know, or what should it know? More succinctly, where does historical knowledge come from? This last permutation of the question takes us back to the relation between origins, or originary fantasies, and epistemological structures—questions that occupied Freud throughout his career. In a manner typical of both Chaucer and Freud, I will defer my own response to Ferster's question, turning instead to the Freudian text that most problematizes the relation between temporality and knowledge: the celebrated case of the "Wolf Man."[45]

This young Russian aristocrat came to Freud with a variety of neurotic disturbances which Freud traced back to several childhood traumas. Chief among these were two events: an early seduction by a sister who was, as Freud puts it, "about two years his elder, lively, gifted, and precociously naughty,"[46] and the witnessing of a so-called primal scene between his parents at the age of one and a half. The case is perhaps the most vexing and intriguing in the Freudian corpus, with the possible exception of the aborted analysis of Dora. Where Dora's case constituted an explicit challenge to Freud's theory of sexuality, that of the Wolf Man raised finally unanswerable epistemological questions, questions about the relation between memory and knowledge, and about the role of identification or transference in transforming or translating the former into the latter. Freud's insistence on the reality of the primal scene turns on the idea of *Nachträglichkeit* or belatedness, whereby the scene is "reactivated" at some later point, when new events and new knowledge endow it with a meaning it could not have had for the infant observer. The key to the "exciting cause" of the illness proves to be a dream that the patient had in early childhood, in which he opened his window to find six or seven white wolves sitting in a tree, staring at him. Freud provides an elaborate reading of the dream that links the boy's subsequent animal phobia to a fear of castration by the father, a fear which in turn, Freud claimed, harked back to a traumatic spectacle of parental intercourse *more ferarum*. The primal scene is reconstructed from the narrative of the young man, now grown, through the mediation of a dream which he claims to have had at the age of four or five. Freud's own narrative of the case mirrors the non-linearity of the patient's memory; it is filled with equivocations and deferrals, looks backward and forward, seems always to be on the verge of collapse. As with any good mystery story, the emphasis shifts midway from the Wolf Man to the analyst/detective; the "answer" to the mystery is clearly the primal scene, but how to prove it? In attempting to refute all possible objections to the scenario he has proposed, Freud addresses two issues in particular: the possibility that the scene was "merely" a fantasy on the child's part, which led to the dream, and the problem of transference, which suggests that the analyst might have planted these ideas in the mind of the analysand "on account of some complexes of his own."[47] Throughout the narrative, Freud remains divided on the first point, which is, of course, closely related to the second. He suggests that the primal scene could have been a fantasy, and that its facticity is ultimately not all that important to the analysis. "Dreaming," he asserts, "is another kind of remembering."[48] Nevertheless he continues to insist stubbornly that in this particular case, the primal scene actually did take place. As proof he offers several more of the Wolf Man's recollections, which, through an impressive reading of screen memories and a dream involving a butterfly, finally enable the analyst to proclaim that the primal scene "which may in other cases be a phantasy, was a reality in the present one."[49] The complicated series of condensations and displacements that lead the analyst back to the "reality" of the primal scene reveal his fantasmatic investment in it. The linearity he seeks to restore is ultimately lost in the tropological twists and turns of the analysis; the putative origin is shown to be an effect of its recollection, rather than the other way around.[50]

The anxiety that adheres to the concept of the real in Freud's narrative seems to me very apropos of the objections raised by Ferster's feminist historians, which in turn echo those of the historicist readers I discussed earlier. The role of transference or identification in the constitution of a knowing subject always indicates a split subjectivity predicated on the alienation of reference, or the real. In light of Freud's epistemological dilemma, Ferster's provocative query gives way to another: how can we keep the Middle Ages from knowing what we know, when history itself is so informed by those "complexes of our own" that determine the questions we ask of it? To the extent that it is based on imaginary identifications, feminism is itself a trope that scrambles the positivist equation. Needless to say, more traditional interpretive tropes function similarly: a critical identification with the Christian faith, or with the poet as autonomous maker are equally constitutive of critical subjectivity, and have no greater access to the real than any other identification masquerading as method. This is not to say that an understanding of Christian theology, medieval literary conventions or historical events themselves are not valuable, even essential to the critical reading of medieval texts; it is rather to call into question the critical practice that would sequester history from literature, or ontogeny from phylogeny, imposing rigid barriers between categories and concepts which resist that binarism. Deconstruction has taught us that all binary oppositions have a built-in scapegoat mechanism—they can only yield a unified, transcendent vision by sacrificing some other who inevitably stands in for the discredited half of the dyad. The issue for a political criticism should not be the preservation of a contextual reality that is innocent of modern prejudice, but rather the preservation of the differences that are threatened by the reduction of history to an equation, or of woman to a simple matter of "right or wrong" reading. The more significant feminist issue is not, I think, "what could Chaucer know," but rather, what are the consequences—for women and other marginalized groups—of this binarist insistence on the fully present reality, and thus the ethical neutrality of history? Certainly this binarism facilitates the kind of slippage between historical and sexual anxieties that we have noted in the *Troilus* as well as in historicist readings of the Middle Ages. Because sexual difference is assumed to be empirically verifiable and thus irreducible, it can be made to stand in for other distinctions that are perceived to be less stable. In this final section of my study, I would like to look at one last way in which historical problems and anxieties are sexualized in the poem, and thereby to address the epistemological dilemma of historicist reading from a position that is both feminist and Chaucerian.

## Sexual Innocence: What Troilus Knew

I have already mentioned several moments in the *Troilus* when historical knowledge is actively disavowed or repressed in the service of poetic continuity. The problem of historical foreknowledge is a *leitmotif* in the poem. Calkas knows the story's end, but quickly moves beyond the boundaries of the romance. The "romaunce" of Thebes contains the seeds of Troy's destruction, but Pandarus interrupts Criseyde's reading of the story before anything can be learned from it; significantly, his interruption coincides with the rubric announcing the exit of yet another knowing historical subject, the seer Amphiarus. In the proem to Book II, the narrator's invocation of Clio paradoxically leads him away from history and into romance: the problem of historical difference is subsumed under cultural and finally sexual difference, as the narrator begins to relate "how Troilus com to his lady grace."

The need to keep the poem innocent of history parallels the need to keep Troilus innocent of sexuality. Troilus' consistently lyrical and "bookish" approach to love, his seeming inability to cope with the materiality of sexual desire and consequent swoon just prior to the consummation scene all encourage the reader to agree with Troilus's assessment of himself in Book III. "When al is wist," he asserts, "than am I nought to blame." Certainly this is true within the epistemological boundaries established by the poem's Boethian ending. The radical dualism of the Boethian system exculpates Troilus by associating Criseyde with materiality and instability; "whan al is wist," Troilus is guilty only of misplaced love.

Both within the poem and among its critics, Troilus's sexual innocence is consistently set against the sexual knowledge possessed by Criseyde and Pandarus. Chaucer encourages this reading by making both characters seem older than in Boccaccio's version; Pandarus is now Criseyde's uncle rather than her cousin, and Criseyde's age and possible maternal status are rendered gratuitously mysterious by the narrator. The triangle thus takes on the characteristics of the family romance, with Troilus rather than Criseyde in the role of seduced innocent.[51]

Nevertheless, there are several moments in the poem when Troilus's innocence is called into question. One of the most disturbing for the poem's "pro-Troilus" readers is the explicitly homosocial and implicitly homoerotic exchange between Pandarus and Troilus at the beginning of Book III. Pandarus voices doubts about the ethics of his role in the seduction of Criseyde, although he seems to worry more about his own reputation than hers:

> "And were it wist that I, thorugh myn engyn,
> Hadde in my nece yput this fantasie,
> To doon thi lust and holly to ben thyn,
> Whi, al the world upon it wolde crie,
> And seyn that I the werst trecherie
> Dide in this cas, that evere was bigonne,
> And she forlost, and thow right nought ywonne." (3. 274–80)

Troilus assures Pandarus that he considers his actions to be completely admirable, in that they are motivated by "gentilesse, / compassion and felawship, and trist." Then, as a gesture of gratitude, he makes this shocking suggestion:

> "And, that thow know I thynke nought ne wene,
> That this servise a shame be or jape,
> I have my faire suster Polixene,
> Cassandre, Eleyne, or any of the frape—
> Be she never so fair or wel yshape,
> Tel me which thow wilt of everychone,
> To han for thyn, and lat me thanne allone." (3. 407–13)

This moment is particularly ugly in light of the fact that these women are all victims of male violence and sexual desire in classical as well as medieval versions of the Troy story. Helen is the most famous victim of male "ravysshyng," but we are also compelled to remember the grisly fate of Polyxena, slaughtered on the grave of Achilles, and Cassandra, blessed and cursed by Apollo, whose advances she refused.

This passage always provokes strong responses in the poem's critics. D. W. Robertson sees it as Troilus's moral nadir, a descent to the level of Pandarus brought about by misplaced values.[52] Donald Howard affirms the homosocial aspect of the scene, reading Troilus's offer as a gesture of fraternal loyalty.[53] Winthrop Wetherbee assumes that Troilus is as innocent of the sexual implications of his offer as he is of sexuality in general; although this seems improbable given what follows, it is in keeping with what would seem to be Troilus's purely metaphoric understanding of love up to this point.[54] Carolyn Dinshaw, on the other hand, suggests that at this moment Troilus enacts a split between an "individual courtly response" and a societal attitude committed to the traffic in women that sustains patriarchy.[55]

However one reads the passage, one thing is clear: at this moment Troilus certainly *seems* to "know more than he knows" about what really underlies the idealizing tropes of courtly love. Once again, I see this transgressive knowledge as an effect of transference—Troilus's imaginary identification with Pandarus as ego ideal here pushes him to the vanishing point of courtly ideology, the point when it exceeds its own ethical limits. The passage is disturbing because it marks the return of the repressed, the re-emergence of the material conditions of courtly discourse. It uncannily blurs the boundary between complicity and innocence, between knowing and unknowing.

There are several other instances in the poem when Troilus appears to know more than his courtly idealism can contain. I will limit my discussion here to one more, which bears specifically on the relationship between language, knowledge, and sexuality. After Criseyde has been traded to the Greeks, Troilus retreats into the realm of "fantasie." This word appears again and again in Book V as an index of Troilus' state of mind; as a symptom of melancholia, these narcissistic imaginings constitute a point of intersection between courtly/metaphoric discourse and its erotic/material basis, that is, between textual and sexual desire. Again, the border between knowing and unknowing is effaced, this time with decidedly comic effect. When Troilus visits Criseyde's empty house, neither he nor the narrator can avoid descending into the realm of the *double entendre*: the house becomes the body of Criseyde, with its "dores spered alle," and Troilus's lament is somewhat undone when he compares the house to a "lanterne of which queynt is the light." For the melancholic subject, language always returns to the body, the ma(t)ter whence it derives.

Courtly language, like Troilus himself, knows and yet doesn't know. Disavowing both its origin and the "fyn of his entente," the lover's metaphoric discourse becomes stagnant and absolute, except at those uncanny moments when the encrypted lost object returns to efface boundaries and restore forgotten knowledge. Troilus's desperate effort to keep history beyond the borders of the romance makes Troy itself into a "prisoun," as Diomede calls it, of empty rhetoric and knowledge denied.

The pathologized Troilus of Books IV and V is a type of the historically traumatized medievalist, for whom history is an all-or-nothing proposition. By insisting on the boundaries between text and context, source and supplement, the traditional historicist reader becomes trapped, like Troilus himself, in a war between inside and outside, formalism and historicism, fantasy and reality. Historicist readers like those cited by Ferster must protect the past from knowledge of the present in much the same way that Pandarus protects Troilus from the unethical preliminaries to the romance, as the poem's narrator attempts to protect his story from the intrusion of "sentement" or narrative desire, and from the destabilizing effects of "oure tonges difference."

The *Troilus* uncovers the price, for the marginalized other, of this melancholic disavowal. By knowing more than the courtly system can or will allow, Criseyde earns only obloquy; by the end of the poem, she is well on the way to becoming the "abject odious" of Robert Henryson's poem and the heartless wanton of Shakespeare's drama. The possibility of a feminist historicism, and, for that matter, of a politically aware medieval critical discourse, turns on this issue of historical knowledge. Only by acknowledging the instability of the border between past and present or public and private can we begin to move beyond our melancholic and static investment in the idea of history, and thus finally begin a productive dialogue with the literary and social past. In yet another uncanny and transgressive moment, Criseyde herself speaks movingly of her own historical fate; it seems to me that her words also speak to the dilemma of the feminist medievalist who knows, yet must not know, the past in terms of the present:

> To late is now to speke of that matere.
> Prudence, allas, oon of thyne eyen thre
> Me lakked alwey, er that I come here!
> On tyme ypassed wel remembred me,
> And present tyme ek koud ich wel ise,
> But future tyme, er I was in the snare
> Koude I nat sen; that causeth now my care. (5. 743–49)

# 6. Father Aeneas or Morgan the Goddess

The relationship between epic as a genre and ideologies of nationalism is not news; texts such as the *Chanson de Roland*, the *Nibelungenlied* and the *Aeneid* have all played, at various points in history, a significant role in the consolidation or reaffirmation of nations or empires.[1] Literary epics constitute a kind of communal fantasy of paternal origins, a fantasy of which the erasure or abjection of the maternal or feminine origin is an essential component. In a sense, the national epic functions as an extended elegy, insofar as it constitutes itself negatively; "father Aeneas" can be established as the paternal progenitor of the Roman State only against the claims of Juno and the various other *matres* who continually threaten the patriarchal agenda.

This metaphysical tension between maternal (corporeal) and paternal (discursive) origins takes us back to originary and originating concerns of this book, back to the *Book of Margery Kempe*. Margery's efforts to establish a maternal metalanguage that might challenge the assumptions of the "ghostly fathers" and affirm the libidinal component of mystical *jouissance* can be seen as an inversion of the epic poet's anxieties about femininity and desire, anxieties that often seem to circulate around maternal figures.

In this final chapter, I would like to pursue the question of origins and difference a few steps further, in the context of a reading of *Sir Gawain and the Green Knight*. *Sir Gawain* echoes Chaucer's *Troilus* in situating the epistemological problematic of textual origins within a dialogue between epic and romance, a dialogue predicated upon the male subject's mastery of a feminine Other. In *Sir Gawain*, however, this conversation is much more explicit; the filial relation between Aeneas and Arthur is the opening assertion in a text obsessed with the problematics of origins and endings. The issue of genre is also, it seems to me, crucial to an understanding of those previously intractable aspects of the poem: the poet's references to "Morgne the goddes," to Gawain's "surfet," and his or her opening invocation of the concept of *translatio studii et imperii* can, I think, be understood in relation to Virgil's *Aeneid*. Before looking at the medieval poem itself, then, we'll be taking a detour into the classical past, in an effort to elucidate the fascinating but hitherto unacknowledged relation between a great Latin epic and the medieval romance that seems so self-consciously to supplement it.

## Junoan Versus Virgilian Narrative

Very little has been written about the enigmatic opening of *Sir Gawain and the Green Knight*; several critics have even suggested that the Trojan frame has no significance whatsoever for any reading of the poem itself.[2] As for those who have acknowledged the importance of the introduction, nearly all have concluded that the Trojan Saga—another tale of "blysse and blunder," of tradition and treason—provides an allegorical frame for the Arthurian epic, which in turn "frames" the romance generically.[3] This is an insightful and provocative suggestion, one which constitutes the basis of the reading I will propose here. It is my belief, however, that more can be learned about the historical assumptions and literary aspirations of the medieval poem if we look closely at the classical text which most effectively translated the Trojan story to the medieval audience.[4]

The *Aeneid* is clearly a poem that reflects epic's generic concern with patrilineal foundations, with national origins and the legendary reputations that sustain them. Within the Virgilian text, the founding of an empire is specifically linked to the quest for the dead father and to anxieties about textual deferral and dilation, anxieties which attach themselves, quite readily, to the problem of sexual difference. Dido and Juno represent obstructions—both pleasurable and unpleasurable—that delay and ultimately threaten the linearity of Aeneas's epic voyage. The paternal legacy that Aeneas literally bears out of Troy can only be "translated" to Rome if he can successfully resist these feminine distractions.

Textual and national origins are linked in the poem's opening lines: Virgil begins his poem with the assertion that he will sing of arms and the man "who first from the coasts of Troy (*Troiae qui primus ab oris*), exiled by fate, came to Italy and Lavinian shores" that he might "build a city and bring his gods to Latium; whence came the Latin race (*genus Latinum*), the paternal lords of Alba (*Albanique patres*), and the walls of lofty Rome." The establishment of a patriarchal legacy and Aeneas's claim to national fatherhood is syntactically disrupted by the intrusion of "cruel Juno," whose "unforgiving wrath" threatens Aeneas's paternal quest and the poet's assertion of the primacy of fathers. It is significant that Juno's lack of forgiveness is articulated as a refusal to *forget*; Aeneas' founding of Rome and memorialization of its Trojan fathers is syntactically and thematically deferred "through cruel Juno's unforgiving/unforgetting anger" (*saevae memorem Iunonis ob iram*).

The next stanza reveals the sense in which the assertion of origins depends upon the triumph of one version of history—one sort of memory—over another:

> Musa, mihi causas memora, quo numine laeso
> quidve dolens regina deum tot volvere casus
> insignem pietate virum, tot adire labores
> impulerit. (1. 8–11)

> (O Muse, help me to recall the causes; wherein thwarted in will or wherefore angered, did the Queen of Heaven drive a man, known for devotion, to traverse so many perils, to face so many toils.)
> (trans. modified)

In these opening lines, the maternal and vindictive memory of Juno is set against the paternal memory of the poet: the war between Juno and the Trojans is explicitly seen as a war of memory whereby the feminine refusal to forget endangers a masculine ability to remember the fathers of legend. One might also read this contest as a struggle between two competing origins; a paternal and textual notion of origin, which would locate the beginnings of the Roman State in the heroic legend of Troy, is obstructed by a maternal and implicitly corporeal origin that calls the very idea of fatherhood and "legitimacy" into question.

The notion of competition is further developed in the next lines (1. 12–33), where we learn that Carthage, chosen by Juno to be the "capital of nations," constitutes a kind of feminine alternative to Rome as the origin of empire. Carthage and its queen are hereby established as the Junoan and maternal Other of the paternalist narrative, a threat that must be either evaded or neutralized if the poem's ideological agenda is to be realized.

Just as Aeneas himself goes astray and exceeds his linear trajectory in landing at Carthage, so poetic inspiration itself seems to become errant, metamorphosing into a narrative inflation that is linked to feminine excess. The metaphoric "breath of inspiration" is subjected to a dangerous feminine literalization when Junoan winds "rush forth where passage is given, and blow storm-blasts across the world" (1. 82–83). The maternal winds cause a perilous delay, a narrative digression which leads to Aeneas's nearly fatal dalliance with Dido. Not surprisingly, the storm is said to derive from a usurpation of paternal prerogative: the seas become "swollen" (*tumida*) when Aeolus, following Juno's command, subverts the ordered hierarchy of divine rule, assuming the role that properly belongs to Neptune (1. 132–41). Behind this usurpation we may see the traces of yet another: Juno's violation of Jupiter's plan for Aeneas and his sons. By implication, then, the digression to Carthage may be seen in light of Juno's subversion of paternal authority; the narrative itself becomes "swollen" when women fail to acknowledge their secondary status.[5]

Throughout the first part of Virgil's text, delay is figured as feminine and dangerous. In Book 3, the harpies, with their "maiden faces" and foul droppings, threaten Aeneas and his men, promising further delays to come:

> Italiam cursu petitis, ventisque vocatis ibitis
> Italiam portusque intrare licebit; sed non ante
> datam cingetis moenibus urbem, quam vos dira
> fames nostraeque iniuria caedis ambesas subigat
> malis absumere mensas. (3. 253–57)

> (Italy is the goal you seek; wooing the winds, you shall go to Italy and freely enter her harbors; but you shall not gird with walls your promised city until dread hunger and the wrong of violence towards us force you to gnaw with your teeth and devour your own tables!)

Later in Book 3, this feminine threat recurs in the form of Scylla and Charybdis; the latter is described as "insatiable" (*implacata*), sucking the waves into her "abyss" (*barathrum*),[6] while the former is said to be a woman with monstrous nether parts. The fear of delay is here figured as a fear of feminine sexuality—implacable, monstrous, and devouring. In Book 5, the poet returns to the struggle between fathers and mothers. During the funeral games for Anchises, the Trojan men rejoice in the parade of youths who recall to them their own paternal ancestors:

> excipiunt plausu pavidos gaudentque tuentes
> Dardanidae veterumque adgnoscunt ora parentum.
> (5. 575–76)

> (The Dardanians greet the bashful boys with cheers and rejoice as they gaze, seeing in them the features of their sires of old.)

Immediately following this celebration of the father-son bond, the figure of the mother returns to subvert the continuation of the journey, and, by implication, the continuity of the patrilineal legacy. Juno causes the Trojan matrons to burn the ships that will bear them to Italy. The matrons, like Creusa before them, must be left behind if this cultural translation is to be successful; on the advice of the aged Nantes and the ghost of his own father Anchises, Aeneas leaves the fearful mothers in Sicily:

> transcribunt urbi matres populumque volentem
> deponunt, animos nil magnae laudis egentis.
> (5. 750–51)

> (they enroll the matrons for the town, and set on shore the folk who wish it so—souls with no craving for high renown.)

This is the last point at which the maternal Other of the paternalist narrative holds any genuine power over Aeneas's fate. The re-emergence of Anchises at this point is significant; in the following Book Aeneas will descend to the underworld, reaffirming the connection between dead fathers and living sons. This sixth book is the literal and thematic center of the poem, a turning point at which Aeneas reaches the true goal of his journey by returning to his own *paternal* origin. Juno's power over the narrative is hereafter diminished. No longer able to offer an alternative to the poem's patriarchal agenda, she can only delay the inevitable founding of Rome:

> non dabitur regnis, esto, prohibere Latinis,
> atque immota manet fatis Lavinia coniunx:
> at trahere atque moras tantis licet addere
> rebus. . . . (7. 313–15)

> (not mine will it be—I grant it—to keep him from the crown of Latium, and by Fate Lavinia abides immovably his bride; yet to put off the hour and to bring delay to such great issues—that may I do. . . .)

In this cause she enlists the help of the Fury Allecto, and becomes the maternal progenitor not of an alternative empire, but rather of the senseless bloodshed and violence that dominate the remaining five books. The Fury first infects the mother of Lavinia with her venom, who in turn spreads the frenzy of Bacchic violence among the matrons of Latium.

Once again, Junoan delay is figured as a maternal corruption of poetic inspiration—Queen Amata takes on not only the will, but also the "viperous breath" of the mother-as-origin:

> huic dea caeruleis unum de crinibus anguem
> conicit, inque sinum praecordia ad intima
> subdit, quo furibunda domum monstro permisceat
> omnem. ille inter vestis et levia pectora
> lapsus volvitur attactu nullo fallitque
> furentem, viperam inspirans animam. . . . (7. 346–51)

> (On her the goddess flings a snake from her dusky tresses, and thrusts it into her bosom, into her innermost heart, that maddened by the pest she may embroil all the house. Gliding between her raiment and smooth breasts, it winds its way unfelt, and, unseen by the frenzied woman, breathes into her its viperous breath.)

Having been "impregnated" by the phallic serpent, the symbol of a horrifying sexual inversion and yet another "usurpation" of male prerogative, Amata may be said to "give birth" to the morbid excesses of Books 7 to 12. The bloody conflicts of the second half of the poem are thus structured as a heroic Trojan resistance to the deadly Junoan tactics of delay; Virgil prefigures more recent military narrators in attempting to frame violence as a heroic opposition to irrationality. Only through death can the male subject negate/transcend the chaos of maternal desire, and thereby affirm the father as origin. "From Jove," claims the Trojan Ilioneus, "is the origin of our race; in Jove, as ancestor, the sons of Dardanus glory" (7. 219–20).

The myth of male generativity lies at the heart of nationalist epic; the genre's investment in history, in the reparative recollection of lost fathers, marks it as fundamentally elegiac. The notion of regression is itself unstable, however—as we saw in the previous chapter, the return to origins that history implies threatens the male subject with corporealization and silence, with a return to the *hystera* as the irreducible source of life itself. This threat underwrites the *Aeneid*'s investment in the illusory distinction between feminine and masculine regression: the former is shown to be paralyzing and static, while the latter carries with it the potential for transcendence and redemption.

Nowhere is this difference more apparent than in Books 1 and 2, wherein the paralyzing effects of Junoan history are set against the liberating and ideologically potent impact of history-as-discourse. As Aeneas gazes at the pictorial narrative of the Trojan War in Juno's temple, he becomes immobilized by the *picturae inanes* that commemorate Juno's triumphs over her Trojan enemies. Within Junoan history, Aeneas himself is a minor player; he is mentioned in only one line, between the description of Priam's "weaponless hands" and the final reference to Penthesilea *bellatrix*, the maid who "dares battle with men." The Junoan narrative would leave us with this final image of castrated men and phallic women; Aeneas must counter it with a narrative of his own, a history that restores the weapons to the hands of the fathers and simultaneously neutralizes the symbolic threat of the *bellatrix*, the woman who would usurp rather than sustain patriarchal authority.

That Junoan history constitutes a threat to the paternalist epic is clearly revealed in the effect it has on Aeneas himself: he is entranced—"in amazement he hangs rapt in one fixed gaze" (*stupet obtutuque haeret defixus in uno*)—he is, as Lee Patterson puts it, "rapt with pleasaunce."[7] In a provocative article on specular moments in epic narrative, Patterson uncovers the dialectical relation between visual and discursive diegesis in the poem:

> The point is not simply that full knowledge cannot be mediated by images, but that the gaze is one pole of a dialectic of which the other is some form of discursive exposition. The gaze implies a nostalgic evasion of understanding, a lowered state of consciousness that is figured by a trance-like stupor that must be broken, both to disarm its dangerous seductions and to unlock the riches its object contains. Indeed, even in intellectual contexts in which visionary experience is regarded less dubiously, such as Neoplatonic philosophy and the traditions of medieval mysticism cognate to it, the gaze is still seen as needing a discursive complement for its potential to be realized.[8]

Junoan history, with its "disarming" potential and "dangerous seductions," prefigures the dalliance with Dido which follows: both are distractions, "evasions" that threaten the paternalist re-writing of Trojan and Roman history. Both must be annulled in the dialectical synthesis that will reconstitute history as redemptive rather than retarding, masculine rather than feminine. Significantly, it is yet another spectacle, the beauty of Dido (*forma pulcherrima Dido*) that breaks the spell; moreover it is Dido who prompts Aeneas's discursive reconstruction of Trojan history in Book 2. The interiorization of woman-as-spectacle releases Aeneas from the seductions of Juno's specular history, enabling him to construct the discursive or paternalist "complement" that will nullify the disarming maternal narrative.

## *Fama* and *Femina*: From Epic to Romance

The ideological efficacy of epic thus depends upon the distinction between digression and regression, upon the metaphysical opposition of history as distraction (the Junoan mural) and as recuperation (Aeneas's reconstructive narrative). A similar metaphysical imperative adheres to the concept of fame: even before Aeneas fulfills his destiny by landing safely in Italy, his considerable reputation precedes him to Carthage. When Dido meets him in the temple in Book 1, her words seem to look both backward, to the glory that was Troy, and forward, to the glory that will be Rome:

> quis genus Aeneadum, quis Troiae nesciat urbem
> virtutesque virosque aut tanti incendia belli?
> (1. 565–66)

> (who could be ignorant of the race of Aeneas's people, who of Troy's town and its manly deeds and brave men, or of the fires of such a war?) (trans. modified)

Here, as elsewhere, Aeneas's reputation threatens to exceed his ability to act and thereby to create it: throughout the poem, *fama*—as both reputation and rumor—represents a kind of discursive excess that is at once both necessary to the ideological agenda of the imperial epic, and potentially subversive of the hero's linear journey from one great patriarchal culture to another.

Not surprisingly, it is in Book 4, Dido's book, that the concept of reputation is forcibly separated from that of rumor. The former sense of *fama* becomes linked to the continuity of the journey, of the poem itself, while *impia fama*—in the explicitly feminine sense of rumor—becomes associated with dangerous, uncontrollable rhetorical excess, a threat to the legacy of *pius Aeneas*.[9] The excesses of *fama* are projected onto this feminized notion of rumor so that the paternalist ideal of reputation-as-legacy, of a specifically *rhetorical* inheritance, may be identified with presence and plenitude. Within Book 4, the description of Rumor running amok in Libya metaphorically reflects Aeneas's digressive and excessive sexual pleasures with Dido; as such, it must be set against that "nobler fame" (*fama melior*) that Aeneas neglects in his "wanton ease" and "shameless passion" with Carthage's Queen.

extemplo Libyae magnas it Fama per urbes,
Fama, malum qua non aliud velocius ullum.
mobilitate viget virisque adquirit eundo;
parva metu primo, mox sese attollit in auras
ingrediturque solo et caput inter nubila
condit. (4. 173–77)

(Forthwith Rumor runs through Libya's great cities—Rumor, of
all evils most swift. Speed lends her strength, and she wins vigor as
she goes; small at first through fear, soon she mounts up to heaven,
and walks the ground with head hidden in the clouds.)

This artificial separation of one sense of *fama* from another is consistent
with the poem's continual efforts to distinguish one sort of digression
from another: Aeneas's errant journey to Carthage threatens the poem's
patrilineal and nationalist aspirations with Junoan delay, while his equally
digressive quest for Anchises in Book 7 is completely in keeping with the
ideological concerns of the poem. In both cases, a dialectical relation is
established along the lines of sexual difference. In short, the association of
femininity with excess enables the oxymoronic concept of rhetorical plenitude. Once again, the paternalist poet's anxieties about language and
origins are mitigated through the projection of discursive lack/excess onto
woman-as-other.

   All this seems to set the stage for a much later text with similar
concerns, and a similarly problematic relation to the question of origins
and endings, reputation and rumor. The hero of *Sir Gawain and the
Green Knight*, like Virgil's Aeneas, is forced to undertake a perilous journey in which the related issues of national reputation and origins are
paramount. Gawain's linear journey is also "dilated" or interrupted by
feminine dalliance, and here, too, the pleasurable interlude threatens both
the continuity of the journey and the ideological assumptions it represents.[10] In the remainder of this chapter, I would like to explore the sense
in which the nationalist/paternalist concerns of both classical and Christian epic are set against an explicitly feminine and dilatory romance discourse in the medieval poem. Ultimately, I will argue that the poem's
failure to resolve the problem of signification and reputation must be
understood in the context of Gawain's final repudiation of women, and
particularly of the quasi-maternal sorceress, Morgan le Fay. Here, as so
often, misogynist rhetoric constitutes a defense against the gap between

signifier and signified, the primal "wound," according to Lacan, of the subject-in-language. This projection of lack onto woman thus creates the illusion of masculine discursive presence, an illusion which grounds paternalist originary narratives, and which romance as a genre continually calls into question.

Invoking the concept of *translatio studii et imperii*, the opening lines of *Sir Gawain and the Green Knight* establish a connection between cultural heritage, political power, and the poetic endeavor itself. "Ennias the athel" and his noble kindred subjugated realms and became the "patrounes" or paternal rulers "welneȝe of al þe wele in þe west iles," we are told. Given Britain's claim on this legacy, much is at stake in the text that is about to unfold—both national legitimacy and the establishment, through literature, of a cultural elite hinge on the outcome of the challenge to "Arthures hous" that will follow.

Nevertheless, the "childgered" Arthur and his beardless knights hardly seem to be the stuff upon which national mythologies are founded. Despite the fact that "þe best burne [sat] ay abof, as hit best semed," the Green Knight has trouble discerning any obvious paternal authority in the Court:

> Þe fyrst word þat he warp, "Wher is," he sayd,
> "Þe gouernour of þis ging? Gladly I wolde
> Se þat segg in syȝt, and with hymself speke
>     raysoun."
>     To knyȝtez he kest his yȝe,
>     And reled hym vp and doun;
>     He stemmed, and con studie
>     Quo walt þer most renoun. (224–31)

(The first words that he uttered, "Where is," he said, / The governor of this company? Gladly would I / See that man in sight, and have some words with him." / Toward the knights he cast his eyes, / And swaggered up and down; / He halted, and watched to see / Who there possessed the most renown.)

The challenge to feudal ideology implicit in this failure/refusal to recognize hierarchical relations is intensified when Gawain himself suggests, with a certain false modesty, that his own worth might more readily be called privilege: his only "bounté," he tells Arthur, is more an accident of birth than the result of merit:

"Bot for as much as ȝe ar myn em I am only to prayse,
No bounté bot your blod I in my bodé knowe . . ." (356–57)

("Only because you are my uncle am I praiseworthy, / No virtue but
your blood in my body do I acknowledge . . .")

At issue, then, is not only the right of English romance to inherit from its
epic fathers, but also the right of the aristocracy to rule at all. In establishing a referential basis for the court's "renoun," Gawain will also establish
an ethical basis for class privilege.

Here, as in the *Aeneid*, the concept of "renoun" has two sides—it is
essential to the literary and cultural legacy of the Arthurian myth, and, to
the extent that it is shown to be undeserved, mere "inflated rhetoric," it is
the site of the greatest instability and anxiety in the text. The Green
Knight's characterization of the Court's reputation echoes Virgil's description of Rumor's wanton excesses:

"What, is þis Arthures hous," quoþ þe haþel þenne,
"Þat al þe rous rennes of þurȝ ryalmes so mony?" (309–10)

("What, is this Arthur's house," said the knight then, / Of which so
much fame has spread through so many realms?")

It is up to Gawain to sustain the illusory opposition between the collective
and public reputation of the Court, and the private rumors—presumably
rumors of Guenevere's infidelity, and of Gawain's own sexual excesses—
that seek to undermine it.[11]

Indeed, many readers have noted the sense in which this romance,
like its continental predecessors, seems uncannily aware of the epic Arthurian "frame" it excludes: the "rechles merþes" of the Court, Morgan's an-
tipathy to Guenevere, and Gawain's alleged erotic talents all point beyond
the borders of the romance itself to the linear story of the rise and fall of
the Arthurian Court.[12] These moments may be seen as metonymic displacements that link this tale to the larger inevitabilities of its literary context; like its predecessors, this romantic *entrelude* can only defer the
moment of judgment, the final instance when words and deeds, rumor
and its referent, will come together such that disavowal is no longer possible. Arthurian romance unfolds during this period of delay, a period
metaphorically linked to the Christian notion of an Age of Grace;[13] the
crucial difference, of course, is that the continuity of the soul depends

upon the subject's awareness and acceptance of the story's end, while the continuity of the romance world demands, on some level, that we disavow our knowledge of the "final judgment" to come. Like Chaucer's *Troilus*, *Sir Gawain* exploits this epistemological uncertainty: the tension between literary and theological assumptions about history and knowledge forecloses the possibility of ideological resolution, even as it informs and enables the poem thematically. This tension/ambivalence explains the radical disjunction between Gawain's self-reproaches and the Court's celebratory disavowal in the final scene of the poem; the Court's inability to understand marks the failure of romance to fulfill its ethical function, to dialectically synthesize the public and private realms, thereby sublimating the latter to the ideological imperatives of the aristocratic collectivity.

Here, as in the Virgilian text, the digressive interlude is coded as feminine and private, and set in opposition to the masculine and public world that ideologically and ethically sustains the narrative. Here, too, private rhetorical excesses threaten to unveil the excessiveness of public reputations: Gawain must silence the rumors of his sexual exploits if he is to reaffirm the now-tenuous public renown of the Court. He must, like Aeneas, escape from this pleasurable period of delay unscathed; the continuation of Arthur's world, like that of his classical fathers, depends upon the triumph of public reputation over private rumor—although, as I suggested earlier, this binarism is as artificial as it is necessary.

The romance text is in fact committed to the systematic installation of binary oppositions, most notably nature/culture, private/public and feminine/masculine. Invariably, it is sexual difference—the most ostensibly "natural" of these oppositions—that works to sustain the others. Within the romance system, the supplementary realm of the private and erotic exists to legitimize or shore up a communal and public aristocratic hegemony. The often violent imposition of sexual difference conceals the sense in which the erotic and indeterminate "inner world" of medieval romance narrative continually exceeds the masculinist and hierarchical ideological agenda of the genre itself. The specter of rape, which haunts the periphery of all romance, represents an attempt to install sexual difference by forcibly projecting lack onto women, and thereby to protect the male subject against the ever-present threat of feminization and privatization. Thus, when Bertilak's wife tells Gawain that he is "stif innoghe to constrayne wyth strenkþe" if he so desires, she acknowledges both his prior literary/erotic exploits and the sexual politics of the genre itself.[14] Within the romance world, ideological and epistemological assumptions about history, culture, and class are always propped upon the male/female opposition, since only stable sexual identities can guarantee the male subject's access to the point of textual origin. In Chapter Three we saw how this metaphysical imperative is played out in the quasi-romance world of the pastourelle. Chrétien's *Erec et Enide* offers an equally revealing example: Erec neutralizes the dangers of private and erotic excess by re-writing the romance itself, forcing Enide into the role of specular object and victim again and again. By silencing and interiorizing her, he attempts to claim for himself a position of discursive exteriority, and to master the inside/outside antithesis that is both the structural and metaphysical basis of the genre.

This formula operates self-consciously in *Sir Gawain*, a romance in which the twin dangers of privatization and rhetorical excess are explicitly seen in terms of the metaphoric castration of the hero. R. A. Shoaf has pointed out the significance of the fact that the beheading game takes place on New Year's Day: the Church calendar claims New Year's as the Feast of the Circumcision.[15] This cutting away of corporeal excess was associated in Jewish law with religious purification, taking place eight days after the child's birth, and the day after the mother of the male child ceased to be considered unclean. In *Powers of Horror*, Julia Kristeva identifies circumcision with a symbolic separation from the defilement of the maternal body, and with the establishment of a "clean and proper" boundary both *for* the male body and *between* the sexes.[16] In *Sir Gawain*, however, the cutting that takes place works instead to establish a *connection* between Gawain, the son of the Round Table, and Morgan le Fay, the sinister maternal figure. What is more, this beheading or cutting game points not to the filial relation between man and God as paternal origin, but rather to the maternal origin which patriarchal narratives, and particularly epics, consistently reject. At the end of the story we aren't sure whether to see the paternal epic as the progenitor of the poem, as the opening lines suggest, or whether in fact the poem-as-game owes its existence to "Morgne the goddes."

The unexpected emergence of Morgan as the origin of the game has perplexed the poem's readers more than any other issue. Because the problem of Morgan seems both central and marginal to the critical history of the poem, it seems necessary and potentially useful to explore her role further.[17] Ultimately, I will suggest that the "Morganian" ending of the romance takes us back to the problem of loss with which I began this second half of the book, and finally back to the question of the body and the word that so troubled Margery Kempe and her readers.

## *Fata Morgana*, or, A Woman with an Axe to Grind

> The reader cannot avoid the feeling that the last-minute revelation of
> Morgan's scheme is too weak a foundation for this poem.[18]
> —Larry D. Benson

> For though the poet . . . would clearly like us to think of Morgan as
> the "only begetter" of Gawain's adventure, effectually she is not.[19]
> —Albert B. Friedman

The problem of Morgan le Fay is a problem of origins—to "blame" Morgan for the adventure is, paradoxically, to give her credit for the romance itself, for Gawain's fall as well as his ethical development during the course of the story. With the revelation of Morgan's generative role in the poem, what appeared to be a game between two men with a woman in the middle is revealed to be a matter between women; Gawain becomes a mere pawn in this feminine game of revenge.[20] According to Bertilak, moreover, Morgan's power derives from a usurpation of male power and authority; Morgan's sexuality, like Eve's, is linked to forbidden knowledge:

> "Þat schal I telle þe trwly," quoþ þat oþer þenne,
> "Bertilak de Hautdesert I hat in þis londe.
> Þurȝ myȝt of Morgne la Faye, þat in my hous lenges,
> And koyntyse of clergye, bi craftes wel lerned,
> Þe maystres of Merlyn mony hatz taken—
> For ho hatz dalt drwry ful dere sumtyme
> With þat conable klerk . . ." (2444–50)

("That shall I tell you truly," said the other then, / I am called Bertilak de Hautdesert in this land. / Through the power of Morgan le Fay, who is staying at my house, / and [who, through] cunning in magic, by crafts well learned, / Many of the magical arts of Merlin has acquired—/ For she once had intimate dealings with that notable wizard . . .")

Like Virgil's Juno, this "goddes" usurps masculine authority and appropriates masculine power because she has, if you will, an axe to grind: Juno's hatred of Troy is echoed in Morgan's grudge against Camelot. In both the *Aeneid* and *Sir Gawain*, this quasi-maternal usurpation results in pleasure and unpleasure, in narrative dilation and delay. In both cases, the ultimate challenge is to the patrilineal nation itself: as Carthage is established as a feminine alternative to Rome, so Bertilak's court has been seen as a threat to the primacy of Camelot. Like Juno, Morgan is a woman who can't let bygones be bygones, a woman with a long memory. Like Chaucer's Criseyde, she represents the point at which the romance fails to exclude the larger epic frame of which it is a part; as Criseyde challenges the narrator's disavowal of Trojan history, so Morgan "opens" the romance to its own linear context—to the figure of Merlin, to the threat represented by sexual excess in general and Guenevere in particular. In short, she challenges the disavowal on which the romance world depends.

One of the most common sources of discomfort for the poem's critics is the fact that Morgan is inserted into the narrative "too late," that is, that she seems to be an afterthought, an inadequate attempt to rationalize or motivate Gawain's adventure. It seems clear, however, that the sudden intrusion of Morgan must be considered in light of another "difficult moment" that precedes it: Gawain's rather excessive and ethically troubling antifeminist outburst near the end of the fourth fitt. After he confesses to the Green Knight, he seems, rather oddly, to deny responsibility for his actions:

> "Bot hit is no ferly þa3 a fole madde,
> And þur3 wyles of wymmen be wonen to sor3e,
> For so watz Adam in erde with one bygyled,
> And Salamon with fele sere, and Samson eftsonez—
> Dalyda dalt hym hys wyrde—and Dauyth þerafter
> Watz blended with Barsabe, þat much bale þoled." (2414–19)

> ("But it is no wonder if a fool act madly, / And through the wiles of women be brought to grief, / For just so was Adam beguiled by one, / And Solomon by many, and Samson besides—Delilah dealt him his fate—and David thereafter / Was deluded by Bathsheba, and he suffered much woe.")

The belated reference to Morgan is thus linked, retrospectively, to another woman who came too late. Established within Christian mythology as the origin of the Fall, Eve is nonetheless said to be something of an afterthought; she is a supplement to the originary creation of man, human only insofar as she has a soul—a soul that is coded as masculine.[21] Gawain's attempt to shift the blame to Eve and her female descendants is mirrored in the poet's attempt to "blame" the game itself on Morgan; the origins of the romance are thereby associated with the origins of sin, and both are allied with feminine sexuality as the material trace of an originary fall into difference and lack.

Throughout this book, I have drawn on R. Howard Bloch's assertion that medieval theologians and rhetoricians linked tropological "usurpation" to the originary subversion of divine and masculine authority in the Garden. This reading of the Fall helps explain why, as Bloch has pointed out, "the reproach against women is a form of reproach against language itself."[22] Eve's perfidy stands in for the perfidy or arbitrariness of signification, for the foreclosure of the real that tropological substitution necessitates. If, as Augustine asserted, humankind has existed since the Fall "in the land of unlikeness," it is an unlikeness or difference of which sexual difference is only a symptom—the first alienation is that of the subject in language. Gawain's misogynist rhetoric can thus be traced to the difference or gap between his name and his reputation, between the perfect pentangle and his ethical imperfection, and finally, to the slippage that obtains between an aristocratic/paternalist ideal and the poem that ultimately fails to re-present it.

The problem of origins, then, is inextricable from the problem of signification. Gawain's failure to live up to the seamless pentangle, to rhetorically master the erotic encounter with Bertilak's lady, and finally, to affirm the significance of his adventure within a communal and public context at the tale's end all point to the "nick on the neck" as a sign of lack which the girdle as fetish can only inadequately veil. By focusing so emphatically on the issue of reputation, the poem asks us to interrogate the referential value of signs and names; Arthur's court, Gawain, the pentangle and even the poem itself all fail on some level to *refer*, or to point to any extrasemiotic reality. It is even hinted that the Court sustains itself through stories rather than deeds. Early in the poem we learn that, for Arthur, tales are an acceptable substitute for actual "marvels":

> he wolde neuer ete
> Vpon such a dere day er hym deuised were
> Of sum auenturus þyng an vncouþe tale,
> Of sum mayn meruayle, þat he myʒt trawe,
> Of alderes, of armes, of oþer auenturus . . . (91–95)

(he would never eat / On such a festive day until someone related to him / A strange tale of some adventurous matter, / Of some great marvel, that he might believe in, / Of nobles, of arms, or of other adventures . . .)

The moral stasis of the Court expresses itself as a retreat into "literariness" and away from actual adventure. The literary reputation of Arthurian society seems to be based *only* in literature: the Court's renown slips into a literary *mise en abyme*, ungrounded in any extratextual reality. As the Court cannot bear the burden of the literary reputation that precedes and exceeds it, so Gawain fails both to master the erotic moment, and to live up to the phallic promise of the pentangle; one might also argue that the poem fails to provide us with the unequivocal affirmation of aristocratic chivalry that its opening leads us to expect.

In the poem, as in the creation myth, the failure of signs to proclaim their referential origins is blamed on woman; the putative supplementarity of language, here as so often, is linked to the supplementarity of the feminine. As Eve is to blame for the alienation of man from meaning, so Morgan le Fay is to blame for this disturbing play of signifiers. This projection of lack onto woman brings with it a certain epistemological uncertainty, however—an anxiety that can only be relieved by a fetishistic displacement. In short, Gawain's own discursive inadequacies lead him first to blame womankind, and then, as if this were not sufficient to relieve the unpleasure of his situation, to recognize finally the significance of the green girdle. It is not coincidental that his misogynist outburst is followed immediately by his realization that the girdle has value:

> "Bot your gordel," quoþ Gawayn, "God yow for3elde!
> þat wyl I welde wyth guod wylle . . .
> in syngne of my surfet I schal se it ofte,
> when I ride in renoun . . ." (2429–34)

("But for your girdle," said Gawain, "May God repay you! / That will I use with good will / . . . / As a sign of my sin of excess I will look at it often, / When I ride in renown. . . .")

The green girdle is acknowledged explicitly as a specular displacement, a supplement that veils the excessiveness of Gawain's—and the Court's—aristocratic "renoun." The romance itself fetishistically compensates for a similar lack vis à vis the epic tradition evoked in the first stanza. While Gawain's quest is ideologically similar to Aeneas's, he does not manage to escape from the feminine dalliance unscathed; the dilatory interlude proves to be the source of the romance itself, not a mere supplement to the linear narrative.

Freud reminds us that fetishistic displacement is a kind of deferral of knowledge: the term *Verschiebung* means both displacement and deferral. In terms of the Christian/allegorical aspect of the romance, Gawain's dalliance with Bertilak's wife can be seen as a deferral of the final judgment that awaits him—and all humankind—at the end of his linear life-journey. In this crucial period of delay, whether it be read as the lifetime of a man or the so-called Age of Grace that is the interlude between Christ's Ascension and the Last Judgment, the Church itself will expand or dilate to take in the Faithful. In her book *Literary Fat Ladies*, Patricia Parker points out that the trope of dilation is associated in both religious and secular literature with the feminine body—the dilated text in its potential vagrancy or refusal to come to a point, so to speak, is often figured as a kind of excessive feminine corporeality. This brings us to the Gawain-poet's own literary fat lady, who appears just prior to the dilatory bedroom/hunt sequence in the text. I refer to the ugly old woman—presumably Morgan—with her "short and thick body, her buttocks round and broad" who represents what Kristeva has identified as the other, abject side of courtly idealization. The connection between courtliness and abjection emerges clearly in the specular description of the two women at Bertilak's castle:

> Bot vnlyke on to loke þo ladyes were,
> For if þe ӡonge watz ӡep, ӡolӡe watz þat oþer;
> Riche red on þat on rayled ayquere,
> Rugh ronkled chekez þat oþer on rolled;
> Kerchofes of þat on, wyth mony cler perlez,
> Hir brest and hir bryӡt þrote bare displayed,
> Schon schyrer þen snawe þat schedez on hillez;
> Þat oþer wyth a gorger watz gered ouer þe swyre,
> Chymbled ouer hir blake chyn with chalkquyte vayles,
> Hir frount folden in sylk, enfoubled ayquere,
> Toreted and treleted with tryflez aboute,
> Þat noӡt watz bare of þat burde bot þe blake broӡes,
> Þe tweyne yӡen and þe nase, þe naked lyppez,
> And þose were soure to se and sellyly blered;

A mensk lady on molde mon may hir calle,
> for Gode!
>> Hir body watz short and þik,
>> Hir buttokez bal3 and brode,
>> More lykkerwys on to lyk
>> Watz þat scho hade on lode. (950–69)

(But unlike to look on those ladies were, / For if the young one was fresh, the other was withered / Everywhere was rose-hue richly arrayed on the one, / Rough wrinkled cheeks hung on the other; / The kerchiefs of the one, with many clear pearls, / Her breast and bright throat bare displayed, / It shone brighter than the snow that falls on the hills; / The other with a scarf was bundled around the neck, / Bound over her black chin with chalk-white veils, / Her forehead muffled in silk, wrapped up everywhere, / Embroidered and adorned about with detailed work, / So that nothing was bare on that lady but the black brows, / The two eyes and the nose, the naked lips, / and those were unpleasant to look at and exceedingly bleared; / An honored lady on earth one may call her, / By God! / Her body was short and thick, / Her buttocks broad and rounded, / More delicious to look at / Was the one she had in tow.)

Part of what is frightening about the old woman here is that she is covered almost completely—"no3t watz bare of þat burde bot þe blake bro3es"—while the younger is exposed to the male gaze in a manner consistent with romance scopophilia. The old woman's swollen body, her refusal to be interiorized within the scopic regime of the genre mark her as irreducibly *other*; what is more, the "doubling" or interweaving effect of the passage itself gives the lie to the poet's assertion that these two women are fundamentally "vnlyke." The two women seem, as many critics have noted, to be two sides of the same coin. More succinctly, they seem to represent the duplicity that is so often associated with women in medieval literature and theology: the young and beautiful woman can be seen as the seductive exterior, the object of the gaze and of masculine desire, while the old hag signifies the veiled and horrifying interior, the maternal abject.[23] The dangers of rhetorical and erotic dalliance are made tangible in this portrait of the excessive and frightening feminine body—a feminine corporeality that cannot be mastered, like the unruly body of the dilated romance, becomes "something to be scared of," as Kristeva puts it.[24] The problem of difference and deferral—deferral of judgment, deferral of the end of the Round Table itself—circulates around the feminine body as a symptom of both symbolic lack and imaginary excess.

We will remember that the drama of fetishism also circulates around the feminine body—specifically the "castrated" maternal body. According to Freud, the fetishist protects himself from the threat of castration by fantasizing the existence of a maternal penis. Although he knows this is a fantasy, he nonetheless sustains himself in this situation of epistemological ambivalence—he sees, knows, and yet disavows his knowledge of the mother's lack:

> It is not true that, after the child has made his observation of the woman, he has preserved unaltered his belief that women have a phallus. He has retained that belief, but he has also given it up. . . . Yes, in his mind the woman *has* got a penis, in spite of everything; but this penis is no longer the same as it was before. Something else has taken its place, has been appointed as its substitute, as it were, and now inherits the interest which was formerly directed to its predecessor. But this interest suffers an extraordinary increase as well, because the horror of castration has set up a memorial to itself in the creation of this substitute.[25]

We saw in chapter four how the fetishism creates an epistemological and sexual dilemma for the male subject in that it is based on identification which transgresses the "rule" of sexual difference. The mother's lack of discursive potency unveils the symbolic castration of the male subject, and threatens to silence him altogether. Because this symbolic lack is the condition of the subject in language, regardless of gender, it can only be disavowed by asserting a "natural" difference between the sexes: within the scopic regime that underwrites the fetishistic drama, women can be said to lack something, that is, something visible, that men have. The assertion of this lack necessitates the continual re-staging of the specular castration scene—women must be exposed to the male gaze in order to reaffirm what *isn't* there, that is, to affirm that men possess something that women don't. The fact remains, however, that desire—and thus pleasure—are grounded in lack or absence. The fetish allows the subject to lack and yet not really lack, to have and have not.

Within representation, sexual difference is the afterthought that enables this play of pleasure and unpleasure, this lacking that seems like having. To the extent that it is a function of desire and absence, discourse is itself coded as feminine. To the extent that it is the very foundation of

patriarchy—a legacy that passes from fathers to sons—it must be dissoci-
ated from the feminine and maternal. The poet who would inscribe himself within this patrilineal system must, like the fetishist, know and yet not
know that something is missing.

In the Arthurian world of *Sir Gawain*, a good deal seems to be missing. As we have seen, the poem seems self-conscious of the fact that the
real is forever receding, that the extrasemiotic realm is conspicuously *not
there*. It is thus not surprising that Eve and Morgan are inserted within
the story as an afterthought; once again, sexual difference is installed retroactively as a defense against the specter of male (discursive) lack. The
poem goes further, however. The shift from the pentangle to the green
girdle foregrounds the romance hero's failure to identify himself with the
sign of pure exteriority, the shield with no "sunderings," no gaps. Significantly, the pentangle shield also bears the image of the Virgin. The body
of the Virgin mother is linked to the pentangle metaphorically: both are
fully coherent, unpenetrated, both "samned neuer in no syde, ne sundred
nouþer." Allied with the pentangle, the Virgin can be seen as the phallic
mother of the fetishist's fantasy: she represents the male subject's attempt
to *shield* himself from the realization of (symbolic) castration. Forced to
acknowledge that he "lakked a lyttel," Gawain abandons the pentangle
shield for the feminine girdle that merely veils the wound, thereby "setting
up a memorial" to "the horror of castration." The Court's focus on the
girdle rather than the event itself, and their obvious pleasure in doing so,
are perfectly in keeping with the dynamic of fetishistic displacement; in
celebrating the substitute, the Court distances itself from Gawain's trauma
of loss, choosing instead to affirm the pleasure of tropological substitution
and the impossibility of closure.

The poem leaves us in a state of epistemological ambivalence: should
we celebrate the self-referential text, that is, take our pleasure in the fetish
that veils an absence, or should we identify rather with Gawain's melancholic lament over "þe laþe and þe losse" that the poem has revealed?
These are, it seems to me, very pertinent questions for medievalists today,
questions which take us back to the tension between the linear agenda of
epic and the digressive pleasures of romance. In hermeneutic terms, we
might see the Arthurian court as a gang of "transhistorical deconstruction-
ists" who are not bothered at all by the fact that signs can only refer to the
*absence* of an extradiegetic realm. Gawain thus becomes a type of the medievalist traumatized by historical difference and lack, who is not altogether certain that the romance text, the green girdle, is sufficient to cover

over this originary absence. For that matter, "theory" itself is often spoken of in our field as a kind of rhetorical dalliance, a fetishistic deferral of the medievalist's linear and epic journey back into the past. A good deal of the anxiety in the field surrounding the issue of theory is, I think, precisely the kind of anxiety that adheres to the erotic interlude that momentarily obstructs epic narrative. If we stay in Carthage with Dido, we'll never get to Italy and build a legacy for our sons. Worse, yet, we may realize that what seemed to be a momentary dalliance was in fact the *raison d'être* for the whole narrative, and find ourselves, like Gawain, hopelessly alienated from the community as a whole, a community that is, unlike the Arthurian court, very invested in the recuperation of the Event.

These are difficult questions, none of which I can pretend to answer here. Somehow I'm drawn back to the figure of Morgan le Fay as the cause of Gawain's dangerous dalliance as well as his ethical development in the poem. The Christian reading of the poem would stress that Gawain's test at Bertilak's castle, his digression on the way to Judgment, is and should be the ethical center of the romance, insofar as it frees both the reader and the hero from the moral and spiritual stasis of the poem's aristocratic opening. While I believe that this emphasis on Gawain's spiritual growth—an emphasis that would discern an unproblematic binarist movement from secular to spiritual values in the text—is far too reductive in its axiological and ideological insistence on closure, it is far from invalid. Certainly the digressive interlude opens the text to epistemological possibilities that challenge the limits of romance convention. Gawain's self-realization is neither unproblematic nor absolute; as a reader of his own adventure, he is bound by assumptions about class and gender, assumptions that fore-close the possibility of deeper understanding. Nevertheless, the adventure works to radically destabilize the relation between public and private, out-side and inside. The reader shares Gawain's sense of disjunction, as well as the Court's collective desire to disavow it—caught between two mutually problematic responses, we find ourselves somewhere else, perhaps at the beginning of something new.

This is, admittedly, an idealistic and transferential reading, one that privileges Morgan's challenge—the challenge from outside—as the basis for new ways of knowing, new conditions of representation. My intent, like Morgan's, has been to subvert. Within the signifying system of ro-mance, however, Morgan's adventure also works to affirm the ability of Arthurian culture to respond, however tentatively, to the challenge from outside. In a sense, Morgan's game offers us a model for extracanonical reading; effacing the boundary between the margin and the center, it opens up a space for rethinking the relation between the "epic" ideal of the past and the supplementary or "romantic" lure of the present. The analogy can, I think, be taken even further. If, as many critics have suggested, the challenge posed by feminist and poststructuralist theory is digressive in terms of the epic assumptions of medievalism, it is also dilatory, providing a space for debate and a reconceptualization of the journey itself. In short, while she may have shown up rather late in the game, Morgan le Fay remains for me a figure of beginnings rather than endings, of possibility rather than perfidy. This is by no means a disinterested reading, of course; I'll be the first to admit that, as a feminist reader, I too have an axe to grind.

# Afterword: The Medieval Thing

In his essay, "The Freudian Thing," Lacan explored the historical and intellectual conditions for a "return to Freud."[1] In a sense, this book has attempted to interrogate some of the ethical and epistemological conditions for a "return to" the medieval past—not a direct return, in the manner of a time traveler, but rather a circuitous and difficult move that looks both backward and forward at the same time. What does it mean "to return?" Traditionally, the notion of a return to the past has implied a faithful reconstruction of the material and moral reality of history. This was the return mandated, for example, by D. W. Robertson in the early 1960s. More recently, historicist readers of the Middle Ages have attempted to turn away from the politically conservative "compulsion to repeat" upon which Robertsonianism seemed to insist, seeking instead to foreground different histories. In Caroline Walker Bynum's work, this new emphasis resulted in fascinating new evidence for a feminine religious sub-culture; in the work of literary historicists, the Peasants' Revolt of 1381 has taken on unprecedented importance. What remains unchanged, however, are the terms within which this new "return" is couched: both new and old historicisms position themselves emphatically against the lure of the present, and, in many cases, the seductions of theory. Despite their debt to the social and cultural changes of the last two decades, new histories mirror old in their insistence upon the recoverability of the past-as-event: historicists, like historians, see themselves as archaeologists or "translators" rather than Pandarus-like mediators. This return differs from its predecessors only insofar as the artifact, the medieval "thing" itself, is perceived to be a new thing.

But what is this medieval thing, to which we must return? Within psychoanalytic discourse, the "thing" is the originary lost object, jettisoned into the irrecoverable real with the entry into language. It is explicitly a maternal and corporeal thing, and thus, belatedly (*nachträglich*), a gendered thing. In his seminar on the ethics of psychoanalysis,[2] Lacan explores the concept of the Thing (*das Ding*) in philosophical as well as psychoanalytic terms, that is, as both the guarantor of moral law and the "blank place" within which we have inscribed our culturally-specific notion of femininity. For the Middle Ages, this nexus of woman, origin, and law finds its clearest and most significant expression in the myth of the Fall, whereby Eve as feminine supplement becomes the symptomatic reminder of our debt to the "Big Other," of our obligation to the Law of the Father. Only our rejection of the "bad" maternal object can guarantee our access to the "good" paternal origin. Lacan also points out, however, that this dual notion of the thing conceals a paradox: if the archaic thing is the basis of moral obligation, it is also the locus of drives that operate in excess of any law. Although structured as supplementary, feminine *jouissance* in fact underwrites the myth of a paternal origin and the moral urgency of paternal law.

Because of the mediating function of the unconscious, the thing—or more precisely the object that stands in for it—is constantly changing. At every historical moment, new objects—often explicitly gendered objects—are "raised to the dignity of the thing" such that their place in the moral order seems not only natural but essential to our ethical understanding of ourselves as subjects. This is one reason why the relationship of women to the concept of sexism is neither simple nor unparadoxical: in ceasing to be objects, we lose as well "the dignity of the thing" that links our mythic "excessiveness" to the ideals of universal Truth and Beauty. In other words, the distance between the Wife of Bath and Boethius's Lady Philosophy is not so very great.[3]

Lacan's theorization of the thing thus foregrounds the epistemological connection between memory and sexuality that I have been attempting to outline here. Each of the texts I have discussed problematizes the medieval subject's relation to the past: Margery Kempe attempts to remember her life in terms of the teleological narrative of sacred history, the hagiographer seeks to integrate ethnic nostaglia with the origins of the Christian church, and the Harley lyricist links the slipperiness of language to the originary transgressiveness of the feminine body. Within the work of Chaucer and the Gawain-poet, the problem of memory is more explicitly a literary and historical dilemma, whereby the "legitimacy" of the poetic artifact hinges on the abjection of a feminine and implicitly maternal object. Because memory does not unfold in a way that is linear and therefore unproblematic—that is, because repression is bound to fail—the relation between the putative source and its supplement remains unstable.

The archaic maternal thing re-emerges in the form of libidinal traces that continually disrupt the hierarchy of past and present, source and supplement, masculine and feminine. In short, memory doesn't move in only one direction—in our nostalgic longing for the past, we effectively remember the future as well.

Medieval writers, with their curious relation to the concept of anachronism, were more sensitive to and tolerant of the slipperiness of chronology than we have become.[4] As a particularly striking example of this peculiar understanding of history, I would like to turn momentarily to a Middle English text that has been both marginal and central to the field: central because it constitutes the most thorough elaboration of a mythic framework that is ideologically foundational to our understanding of ourselves as medievalists, and marginal because it continually disrupts the teleological assumptions that subtend that very mythology. I'm referring to Malory's *Morte D'Arthur*. As a work of literature Malory's text has always been troubling to its readers; like Freud's case histories, it seems to move backward and forward at once, and always seems on the verge of collapsing under the weight of its own temporal paradoxes. Following the psychoanalytic assumption that memory is both non-referential and non-linear in expression, however, we might begin to look at Malory's difficult text in another way: as a work that both explores and represents the internal contradictions and ethical dilemmas of historicist subjectivity.

The *Morte* is a story about origins and endings which cannot be prised apart. Even as Merlin "creates" the Arthurian Court, he is busy memorializing it, establishing monuments and tombs—historical records, if you will. To paraphrase Freud, the future of these characters is already behind them.[5] Merlin himself is the objective historian par excellence—he knows what has happened and what will happen, and despite his role in Arthur's origin, his own desires are not represented as such. Because of his knowledge of past and future, he quickly becomes a tiresome, even annoying figure, always turning up in some disguise or another to remind the characters of their fate, or of their moral obligation to the future. We are almost relieved when the sorceress Nyneve succeeds in silencing his voice, thereby enabling us to believe in the free will of the narrative and its characters. Significantly, it is precisely Merlin's desire that traps him; once the most exterior of characters, he becomes the most interiorized, imprisoned by a lust that has no place in the teleological narrative he has set in motion.

Once Merlin has become "entombed," the ethical focus of the narrative shifts to Lancelot; indeed, there is a logic to this shift that has, to my

knowledge, never been noted. Both Merlin and Lancelot become impris-
oned by a "painful longing": Merlin desires Nyneve as Lancelot desires
Guenevere. Lancelot's adulterous and heterosexual relationship with Ar-
thur's queen is circumscribed by a desire that is in many ways more problematic, however. At the literal and figurative center of the narrative is
Lancelot's desire for his chivalric "mirror image"—Sir Tristram de Lyones.
To be more precise, Lancelot desires what Tristram represents in the
*Morte*, and it is this moment of transference or identification that proves
to be his undoing. Lancelot nostalgically longs for the ethical simplicity of
Tristram's Cornwall, where adultery is morally justified by Mark's villainy,
where Isode is the passive and submissive love-object that Guenevere so
obviously is not. His transferential relationship to Tristram is explicitly
linked to his self-delusion near the end of the narrative, when Sir Bors
advises him to take Guenevere to Joyous Gard. Lancelot replies that

> That is hard to do . . . for by sir Trystram I may have a warnynge: for whan
> by meanys of tretyse sir Trystram brought agayne La Beall Isode unto kynge
> Marke from Joyous Garde, loke ye now what felle on the ende, how shame-
> fully that false traytour king Marke slew hym as he sate harpynge afore hys
> lady, La Beall Isode. Wyth a grounden glayve he threste hym in behynde to
> the harte, whyche grevyth sore me . . . to speke of his dethe, for all the worlde
> may nat fynde such another knyght.[6]

Bors must remind him that "kynge Arthur and kynge Marke were never
lyke of condycions, for there was never yet man that ever coude preve
kynge Arthur untrew of his promyse."[7] Seduced by the ethical absolutes
that characterize Tristram's situation, Lancelot misreads his own; like Malory himself, Lancelot sees the present in terms of an idealized, and always
already lost, past. Within Malory's fictional universe, the dissolution of the
Arthurian ideal bears an immediate relation to this moment of misrecognition, this longing or nostalgia for a lost golden age of ethically unam-
biguous chivalry.

If Merlin is a figure for the historian interiorized and imprisoned by
his own unacknowledged desire, Lancelot represents an historical subject
whose imaginary relation to an idealized past has serious ethical implications for the present and future. Nevertheless, there is a sense in which
Malory's celebration of and mourning for the Arthurian world returns the
ideal to history in a way that Lancelot's parallel relation to Tristram and
Cornwall cannot. Lancelot remains trapped in the narcissistic moment of

transference, but Malory's look back into the chivalric past quite literally explodes at the sound of Mordred's "grete gunnes." The sound of gunfire at the end of the *Morte* ruptures the imaginary mirroring of fifteenth-century present and idyllic chivalric past; this traumatic intrusion of technology both "causes" Malory's nostalgic narrative (in that it initiates the look backward to a "simpler time") and, within the diegesis proper, is caused by it.[8] In Lacanian terms, this moment of technological trauma is the "kernel of the real" that resists integration into the system of the narrative: it violates the boundary between history and fictionality, marking the end of the story as the end of an era, and sending us, quite against our will, back to the future.[9]

The historical problematic of Malory's "epic romance" provides a useful—albeit merely suggestive—addendum to the ethical and epistemological ambivalence I discussed in Chapter Six. If *Sir Gawain* can be read as a failure to decide between an epic and paternalist obligation to the past and the feminine and romantic lure of the present, the *Morte D'Arthur* might be said to explore the ethical costs of a pleasurable but static identification with an idealized golden age—with the lost chivalric thing, if you will. In our pursuit of or mourning for the lost medieval thing, we would do well to remember that our relation to the past is always bound up with the dynamic of desire and identification; our historical memory grounds our fantasies of who we are, fantasies which in turn effect the political/material reality of what we will become.

It seems to me that there are other ways in which we might begin to rethink—or return to—the thing without turning away from the issue of gender or the ethical problematic of the origin. Medieval history and philology remind us that the Germanic word "thing" has a specific cultural resonance: the Icelandic Þing-völlr (literally, the "thing-field") was a place wherein legal disputes were argued and decided, alliances made and broken. If we follow the logic of this particular "return," we might begin to explore the thing, the event, less as an object to be mourned or reconstructed in its supposedly "original" form, and more as a space for disputation and inquiry that holds out the possibility for alliances as yet unthought within the axiology that structures the ideal of medieval studies today. The institutional and cultural survival of our field may in fact depend upon our ability to renegotiate and thereby reconceptualize our relation to both the past and the present in their specificity. Our return to the past need not be an intellectual apostrophe, a "turning away" from the urgency of the our own political context; the ethical demands of our own pedagogy insist that the thing-field remain a contested space, wherein past and present might speak to one another without priority or privilege.

Implicit in the concept of the historical return is, as I have argued, the return of the repressed. Throughout this book, I have insisted that the fantasy of the origin—because it is a fantasy—exceeds the sexual and ethical neutrality presumed by what we might call a normative aesthetics. The aesthetic judgments that have hitherto structured the literary canon and its relation to its historical context are themselves informed by the fantasmatic nexus of femininity, the body, and the past. In an effort to foreground what has been unspoken in our traditional understanding of medieval literary history, I have focused throughout on moments of excess, moments when language fails to cover over its own inability to fully re-present theological, aesthetic, or historical truths. It has been my contention that these moments of failure or impossibility can in fact provide the basis for a new kind of dialogue between past and present, masculine and feminine—a new field wherein we might continue to interrogate our relation to the elusive but compelling medieval thing. In keeping with this admittedly idealistic but as yet unarticulated critical scenario, I would like to end not with a bang, or a whimper, but with a laugh.

Both *Troilus and Criseyde* and *Sir Gawain and the Green Knight* end in laughter. Troilus laughs at the false felicity of his previous life from the perspective of the eighth sphere, and the feudal aristocrats of Arthur's Court laugh when Gawain presents them with the girdle and the narrative it generates. It seems appropriate that this book, which began with the solitary yet spectacular weeping of Margery Kempe should end with the collective laughter of that most revered of literary institutions, the Arthurian Court. Had I ended this study with Chaucer's *Troilus*, the book would have resolved itself into a rather neat binarist configuration: the tortured beginning of Margery Kempe's *Book* would finally have led us to the equally problematic ending of Chaucer's *Troilus*. Margery's weeping and Troilus's laughter both represent points of impossibility within the teleological system of medieval narrative; both of these inarticulate sounds gesture toward an extrasemiotic truth which the linear text can neither supply nor sustain. Here the similarity ends, however. While Troilus's laughter signifies his triumph over Criseydan materialism, his dialectical negation of body and desire, Margery's tears have been read as a refusal or failure of the "metaphoric imperative" that structures our understanding and appreciation of mystical piety.

This juxtaposition of the weeping feminine body and the disembodied masculine laugh would thus seem to resolve or answer the question of canonicity that I raised at the beginning of the book. Within this conceptual frame, the history of canonical reading would be understood as a history of effacements and erasures leading toward the final transcendence of the disembodied male voice: a history of the sublimation of particulars in universals, of the maternal *lich* in the paternal *lichnesse*.

In Chapters Four and Five, I attempted to show how Chaucer's poetry calls this imperative into question by uncovering its "hidden history," even as his texts move toward their own dialectical resolution. Throughout Chaucer's work, the literary "problem" of sexual difference encrypts a more profound tension between ethics and aesthetics, between genetic and teleological causality. Chaucer's texts continually problematize the logic of dialectical configurations, even to the point of inverting the movement of *Aufhebung* completely in the opening "fragment" of the Canterbury Tales. The dialectical game of "quiting" ultimately leads not to a transcendence of ma(t)ter and affirmation of a paternalist poetics, but rather to the feminine body that sustains the libidinal economy of the system itself. At the end of this first sequence, we are left not with a disembodied male voice, but with the image of the commodified woman who "swyved for hir sustenance." That the Cook's Tale is unfinished attests to the epistemological impossibility of sustaining a poetics that moves in the wrong direction, that is, from Theseus's patriarchal triumph over "Femenye" back to the freely circulating feminine body with which the Cook's narrative ends—or doesn't end. Like Margery Kempe's tropological inversions, this reversal can only be understood as pathological, a violation of the law of discourse that always moves from feminine bodies to masculine voices.

It seems to me that *Sir Gawain and the Green Knight* offers yet another possibility. The Court's laughter may be read as a moment of undecidability, a refusal to join Gawain in his condemnation of the implicitly feminine adventure, and thereby to negate the specifically textual pleasures the narrative has produced. The poem itself inscribes that ambivalence in refusing to subsume the feminine corporeal origin within a linear and patriarchal textual system—Aeneas and Morgan remain equally marginal, and equally central, to the romance narrative. Finally, the poem fails to fulfill the structural imperative of medieval romance, which mandates that private pleasures be finally annulled in a dialectical affirmation of public, collective, and androcentric ideology. Gawain and the Court remain at odds, the final meaning of the adventure is never fixed in either secular or religious terms. This "failure to sublimate" links the canonical medieval poem to the "excessive" texts I discussed in the first part of the book. Both the Court's celebratory laughter and Gawain's melancholic self-reproaches are somehow too much; neither response seems capable of sustaining the epic/allegorical reading many of the poem's critics have proposed.

In seeking to restore the hidden history of canonical reading, this study lends support—albeit indirectly—to the recent historicist call for a new emphasis on the local and contingent. If canonical interpretive strategies work to annul the body behind the trope, they also efface the particularity of context, the historical conditions of meaning. My project differs from that of most historicists, however, in arguing that a return to dialectics—and the binarist scapegoating it entails—ultimately works against the critical desire to reaffirm the material conditions of literary production. Founded on negation and exclusion, dialectics mirrors theology in staging a struggle between matter and spirit, a struggle whose outcome is pre-scripted. What emerges from the battle can never be more than one: all sexual and historical others must finally be sacrificed to a univocal resolution.

At the heart of the dialectical impulse is the issue of transference or identification; the exclusionary agenda of canonical reading has its origin in the desire for (mis-) recognition and the illusory unity it promises. It is thus not surprising that the laughter and repudiation with which the *Troilus* closes is dense with intertextual resonance: sublimation works to repress the historical differences that disrupt the mirroring of poetic father and son by projecting that difference onto a feminized other. In rejecting Criseyde, the *Troilus* also rejects or annuls its own historical specificity, thus earning the right to stand beside "Virgile, Ovide, Omer, Lucan, and Stace." I identified a similar strategy on the part of the historicist reader who, committed to the binary opposition of public and private, structures that opposition along the lines of sexual difference. Within this mirroring logic, the political and public struggles of medieval men prefigure the discursive battles of academic men: the concerns of women, like those of Criseyde herself, are dismissed as private and ultimately irrelevant.

If there is to be a "new" historicism—or a new historical "thing-field"—it must contain a space for the marginalized other that dialectics necessarily excludes. I have argued that the question of literary-historical origins must first be an epistemological question; only then can a new historicism avoid merely repeating the historically-embedded ideological assumptions of philological or exegetical historicist reading. In pursuit of this admittedly elusive goal, we might do well to follow the lead of medieval writers themselves, who were no less obsessed with the problem of beginnings than are modern medievalists. The transgressive experimentalism of Chaucer, the excesses of the hagiographer and the lyricist, the fetishistic indeterminacy of *Sir Gawain*, the strategic inversions of Margery Kempe are attempts to come to terms with the past, the problem of origins, the limitations of figurative and conventional language. In bringing these admittedly incongruous texts together, I have attempted to open up a space within the critical language of medievalism, a field wherein feminism, psychoanalysis, and historicism might productively intersect without sublimation or repudiation. At the same time, I am aware that history itself merely haunts the periphery of this book—as it lurks beyond the walls of Troy in Chaucer's poem—exerting a lure that is potentially destabilizing, even threatening. For the feminist reader, the return to historical origins can be a return to silence—the history of women is, in some sense, a history of disappropriation. Nevertheless, I believe that feminists and historicists can and should begin to speak to one another, just as Margery Kempe and Chaucer have begun to do in these pages.

A careful reader will note that this putative dialogue is framed by yet another: a dialogue between two marginal women whose names are etymologically related to my own. The heterosexual—or heterotextual—dyad is finally contained by a homosexual and somewhat maternalist one: the dialogue between Margery Kempe and Morgan le Fay is the real (or, more accurately, imaginary) origin of my own narrative impulse. If there is a utopian element to this study, it lies, I suppose, in my own fetishistic refusal to choose between these two configurations, and in my belief that the laughing man and the weeping woman might find their way to a new kind of articulation, a language of plurality and apposition that is mindful of its limits, but always open to possibilities.

# *Appendix*

The lyrics reproduced here are taken from *Middle English Lyrics*, selected and edited by Maxwell S. Luria and Richard L. Hoffman (New York: Norton, 1974). Titles are borrowed from *The Harley Lyrics*, ed. G. L. Brook (Manchester: Manchester University Press, 4th ed. 1968). Translations are my own.

"Annot and John"

Ichot a burde in a bour ase beryl so bright,
Ase saphyr in selver semly on sight,
Ase iaspe the gentil that lemeth with light,
Ase gernet in golde and ruby well right;
Ase onycle he is on iholden on hight,
Ase diamaund the dere in day when he is dight;
He is coral icud with cayser and knight;
ase emeraude amorewen this may haveth might.
    The might of the margarite haveth this may mere;
    For charbocle ich hire ches by chin and by chere.

Hire rode is ase rose that red is on ris;
With lilie-white leres lossum he is;
The primerole he passeth, the perwenke of pris,
With alisaundre thareto, ache and anis.
Cointe ase columbine such hire cunde is,
Glad under gore in gro and in gris;
He is blosme opon bleo, brightest under bis,
With celydoine and sauge, as thou thyself sis.
    That sight upon that semly, to bliss he is broght;
    He is solsecle: to sauve is forsoght.

He is papeiay in pyn that beteth me my bale;
To trewe tortle in a tour I telle thee my tale;
He is thrustle thriven in thro that singeth in sale,

The wilde laueroc and wolc and the wodewale;
He is faucoun in frith, dernest in dale,
And with everuch a gome gladest in gale.
From Weye he is wisest into Wyrhale;
Hire nome is in a note of the nightegale.
>     In Annote is hire nome, nempneth it non?
>     Whose right redeth roune to Johon.

Muge he is and mondrake thourgh might of the mone,
Trewe triacle itold with tonges in trone;
Such licoris may leche from Lyne to Lone;
Such sucre mon secheth that saneth men sone;
Blithe iblessed of Crist, that baytheth me my bone
When derne dedes in day derne are done.
Ase gromil in greve grene is the grone,
Ase quibibe and comyn cud is the crone,
>     Cud comyn in court, canel in cofre,
>     With gingiure and sedewale and the gilofre.

He is medicine of might, mercie of mede,
Rekene ase Regnas resoun to rede,
Trewe ase Tegeu in tour, ase Wyrwein in wede,
Baldore then Byrne that oft the bor bede;
Ase Wylcadoun he is wis, doghty of dede,
Feyrore then Flores folkes to fede,
Cud ase Cradoc in court carf the brede,
Hendore then Hilde, that haveth me to hede.
>     He haveth me to hede, this hendy, anon;
>     Gentil ase Jonas, heo joyeth with Jon.

(I know a woman, in a bower, as bright as a beryl, / As fair to see as sapphire in silver / As the gracious jasper, that gleams with light / As a garnet in gold, and a ruby quite true; / As onyx, she is one well-esteemed / As the costly diamond when she is placed in the daylight / She is red coral, famous with emperor and knight / As an emerald in the morning, this maiden has might. / The might of the pearl has this excellent maiden; / I recognized [chose] her for a carbuncle, by her expression. / / Her complexion is like a rose that is red on a twig, / With lily-white cheeks, lovely she is; / She surpasses the primrose, the periwinkle in value / With parsley besides, celery and anise. /

Quaint as a columbine, such is her nature / Glad under skirts, in gray fur; / She is a blossom with regard to her face, brightest under fine linen, / With celandine and sage, as you yourself see. / He who looks on that seemly one, to bliss he is brought; / She is a marigold, sought out to heal. / / She is a parrot who cures my pain for me when I am in torment; / As to a true turtle-dove in a tower, I tell you my tale / / She is a thrush, doughty in contention, that sings in the hall, / The wild lark and hawk, and the singing bird / / She is a falcon in the wood, most hidden [discreet] in the dale, / And with every person, most glad in gaiety. / From the Wye until Wirral, she is the wisest; / Her name is in a note of the nightingale. / In Annote is her name, does that not name it? / Whoever guesses correctly, whisper to John. / / Nutmeg she is, and mandrake, through might of the moon, / True remedy, esteemed in speech in heaven; / Such licorice can heal from Lyn to Lune; / One seeks such sugar, that heals men quickly; / Happy one, blessed by Christ, who grants me my prayer, / When secret deeds are done secretly in the daylight. / As gromwell in a thicket, green is the seed, / As cubeb and cumin, known by its crown, / Cumin famous in court, cinnamon in a coffer, / With ginger and setwall and clove. / / She is a mighty medicine, a compassionate reward, / Ready as Regnas to advise reason, / True a Tegeu in a tower, as Wyrwein in clothing, / Bolder than Byrne, who often challenged the boar; / She is as wise as Wylcadoun, doughty in deeds, / Fairer than Flores to please people, / As famous as Cradoc in court, who carved the roast meat, / More gracious than Hilde, who has me to care for. / She cares for me, this fair one, at once; / As gracious as Jonas, she enjoys herself with John.)

"The Fair Maid of Ribbesdale"

Most I riden by Ribbesdale,
Wilde wimmen for to wale,
   And welde whuch I wolde,
Founde were the feirest on
That ever wes mad of blod and bon,
   In boure best with bolde.
Ase sonnebem hire bleo is bright;
In uche londe heo leometh light,
   Thourgh tale as mon me tolde.

The lilie lossum is and long,
With riche rose and rode among;
　　A fildor fax to folde.

Hire hed when ich biholde upon,
The sonnebeem aboute noon
　　Me thoghte that I seye;
Hire eyen aren grete and gray inogh;
That lussom, when heo on me logh,
　　Ibend wax either breye.
The mone with hire muchele maght
Ne leneth non such light anaght
　　That is in heovene heye
Ase hire forhed doth in day,
For wham thus muchel I mourne may,
　　For duel to deth I dreye.

Heo hath browes bend and heh,
Whit bitwene and nout too neh;
　　Lussum lif heo ledes;
Hire neose is set as it well semeth;
I deye, for deth that me demeth;
　　Hire speche as spices spredes;
Hire lockes lefly aren and longe,
For sone he mighte hire murthes monge
　　With blisse whem it bredes;
Hire chin is chosen and either cheke
Whit inogh and rode on, eke,
　　Ase roser when it redes.

Heo hath a mury mouth to mele,
With lefly rede lippes lele,
　　Romaunce for to rede;
Hire teth aren white ase bon of whal,
Evene set and atled all,
　　Ase hende mowe taken hede;
Swannes swire swithe well isette,
A sponne lengore then I mette,
　　That freoly is to fede.

Me were levere kepe hire come
Then beon Pope and ride in Rome,
  Stithest upon stede.

When I biholde upon hire hond,
The lilie-white lef in lond
  Best heo mighte beo;
Either arm an elne long,
Baloigne mengeth all bimong;
  Ase baum is hire bleo;
Fingres heo hath feir to folde;
Mighte ich hire have and holde,
  In world well were me.
Hire tittes aren anunder bis,
As apples two of parays,
  Youself ye mowen seo.

Hire gurdel of bete gold is all,
Umben hire middel small,
  That triketh to the to,
All with rubies on a rowe,
Withinne corven, craft to knowe,
  And emeraudes mo;
The bocle is all of whalles bon;
Ther withinne stont a ston
  That warneth men from wo;
The water that it wetes in
Iwis it wortheth all to win;
  That seyen, seyden so.

Heo hath a mete middel small,
Body and brest well mad all,
  Ase feines withoute fere;
Either side soft as silk,
Whittore then the moren milk,
  With leofly lit on lere.
All that ich you nempne noght
It is woner well iwroght,
  And elles wonder were.

He mighte sayen that Crist him seye
That mighte nightes negh hire leye:
   Hevene he hevede here.

(If I could ride through Ribbesdale, / To choose wanton women, / And possess the one I desired, / There might be found the fairest one / That ever was made of blood and bone; / In a bower, best with mighty ones. / Her complexion is as bright as a sunbeam, / In each land she gleams light, / According to the the tales I've been told. / The lily is lovely and long, / With a splendid rosy hue and blush here and there / A gold thread in her hair. / / When I behold her head, / It seemed to me I saw / The sunbeam at about noon; / Her eyes are large and grey enough; / That lovely one, when she laughs with me, / Each eyebrow arched. / The moon with her great power / Does not grant such light at night / That is high in heaven / As her forehead does during the day, / For whom thus I must mourn greatly, / On account of grief which I endure to death. / / She has brows both arched and high / white between and not too close together / / She leads a lovely life; / Her nose is set as well befits it; / I die, for the death that condemns me; / Her speech spreads like spices, / Her locks are lovely and long, / Forthwith she might mingle her joys / With bliss when it spreads [i.e., her hair]. / Her chin is beautiful, and either cheek / White enough and rosy as well, / As the rose-bush when it reddens. / / She has a merry mouth for speaking, / With lovely true red lips, / For reading a romance; / Her teeth are as white as whale bone, / Evenly arranged and set all, / As courteous people may notice; / A swan's neck, very well set, / A span longer than I [ever] found, / That is fair to give pleasure. / I would rather await her arrival / Than be Pope and ride in Rome, / Strongest upon steed. / / When I look upon her hand / The lily-white dear one in land, / The best she may be; / Either arm an ell long / Whalebone mingles all among; / Her complexion is like balsam / / She has fingers fair to fold; / If I might have her to hold / I would be doing well in the world. / Her breasts are under fine linen / As two apples of paradise— / You yourselves may see. / / Her girdle is all of beaten gold, / Around her small waist, / That hangs down to the toe, / All with rubies in a row, / Carved within, to reveal craft, / And more emeralds / The buckle is all of whalebone; / There within stands a stone, / That protects men from woe; / The water in which it is

dipped / Indeed, it turns all to wine; / Those who saw it said so. / /
She has a well-proportioned small waist, / Body and breast, well-
made all, / As a phoenix without peer; / Either side as soft as silk, /
Whiter than the morning milk, / With a lovely hue in her cheek. / All
that I haven't mentioned to you / It is wonderfully well-wrought /
Otherwise it would be a wonder. / He might say that Christ looked
on him [with favor] / Who might lie with her at night: / He would
have heaven here.)

## "The Poet's Repentance"

Weping haveth min wonges wet
For wikked werk and wone of wit;
Unblithe I be til I ha bet
Bruches broken, ase bok bit,
Of levedis love, that I ha let,
That lemeth all with luevly lit;
Ofte in song I have hem set,
That is unsemly ther it sit.
It sit and semeth noght
Ther it is seid in song;
That I have of hem wroght,
Iwis it is all wrong.

All wrong I wroght for a wif
That made us wo in world full wide;
Heo rafte us all richesse rif,
That durfte us nout in reines ride.
A stithie stunte hire sturne strif,
That is in heovene hert in hide.
In hire light on ledeth lif,
And shon thourgh hire semly side.
Thourgh hire side he shon
Ase sonne doth thourgh the glass;
Wommon nes wicked non
Sethe he ibore was.

Wicked nis non that I wot
That durste for werk hire wonges wete;
Alle heo liven from last of lot

And are all hende ase hawk in chete.
Forthy on molde I waxe mot
That I sawes have seid unsete,
My fikel fleish, my falsly blod;
On feld hem feole I falle to fete.
To fet I falle hem feole
For falslek fifty-folde,
Of alle untrewe on tele
With tonge ase I er tolde.

Thagh told beon tales untoun in toune,
Such tiding mey tide, I nul nout teme
Of brudes bright with browes broune,
Or blisse heo beyen this briddes breme.
In rude were ro with hem roune
That hem mighte henten ase him were heme.
Nis king, cayser, ne clerk with croune
This semly serven that mene may seme.
Semen him may on sonde
This semly serven so,
Bothe with fet and honde,
For on that us warp from wo.

Now wo in world is went away,
And weole is come ase we wolde,
Thourgh a mighty, methful may,
That us hath caste from cares colde.
Ever wimmen ich herie ay,
And ever in hyrd with hem ich holde,
And ever at neode I nickenay
That I ner nemnede that heo nolde.
I nolde and nullit noght,
For nothing now a nede,
Soth is that I of hem ha wroght,
As Richard erst con rede.

Richard, rote of resoun riht,
Rykening of rym and ron,
Of maidenes meke thou hast might;
On molde I holde thee muryest mon.

Cunde comely ase a knight,
Clerk icud that craftes con,
In uch an hyrd thin athel is hight,
And uch an athel thin hap is on.
Hap that hathel hath hent
Wit hendelec in halle;
Selthe be him sent
In londe of levedis alle!

(Weeping has wet my cheeks / On account of wicked deeds and lack
of wit; / I will be unhappy until I have atoned for / Broken breaches,
as the book bids / Of ladies' love, that I have abandoned, / Who all
gleam with a beautiful hue. / Often I have set them in song / That is
unsuitable where it suits [or, that is unsuitable where it is placed]. /
It is placed, and is not suitable / There where it is said in song; /
What I have written about them, / Indeed it is all wrong. / / All
wrong I wrought concerning a woman / That made woe for us in
the world full wide; / She robbed us of all abundant riches / She,
who shouldn't have dared to ride us in reins. / A strong and
excellent person put an end to her violent strife, / That [excellent
one] is hidden in heaven's heart. / [Having] alighted in her, one
leads life [i.e., lives] / And [he] shone through her excellent side
[i.e., through her body]. / Through her side he shone / As sun does
through glass; / There was never a [single] wicked woman/Since he
was born. / / Wicked are none that I know of / Who dared wet their
cheeks on account of [evil] deeds; / they all live free from vice / And
are all as gracious as hawks in a hall. / Therefore on earth I have
become sorry / That I have spoken unsuitable speeches, / My fickle
flesh, my deceptive blood; / I fall to the ground at their feet. / To
their feet I fall often / For fifty-fold falsehoods, / As I told before
with tongue / About all untrue ones in calumny. / / Though evil
tales be told in the world, / Such tidings [or events] may occur, I
will not vouch / Concerning fair women with brown brows, / Or
the bliss they buy, these excellent [or noisy?] women. / Among the
violent, it would be peace to whisper with them / So that one might
receive from them as were fitting to him [or, so that one might seize
them as were fitting to him]. / There is neither king, nor emperor,
nor tonsured clerk / Who would seem to be humiliated by serving
these seemly ones. / It is appropriate that he serve / This seemly one

as a messenger [or, on errand] / Both with feet and hands, / For the sake of one who rescued us from woe. / / Now worldly woe has disappeared, / And happiness has come as we wanted, / Through a might, gentle maid / Who cast us from cold cares. / I always praise women, / And I always defend them in the household, / And always, when necessary, I deny / Having said anything they did not wish. / I did not and will not [say] anything / For nothing now of necessity, / What I have written of them is true, / As Richard first did say. / / Richard, root of right reason, / Distinction of verse and poetry, / You have power over meek maidens; / I hold you to be the most pleasing man on earth. / As well-born and handsome as a knight, / Famous clerk, who knows skills, / In each household your nobility is mentioned, / and each noble is involved in your fate. / That splendid man has received [or seized] good fortune / With courtesy in the hall; / May happiness be sent to him / In all the lands of ladies!)

"De Clerico et Puella"

My deth I love, my lif ich hate,
For a levedy shene;
Heo is bright so dayes light
That is on me well sene.
All I falewe so doth the lef
In somer when it is grene.
If my thoght helpeth me noght,
To wham shall I me mene?

Sorewe and sike and drery mod
Bindeth me so faste
That I wene to walk wod
If it me lengore laste;
My serewe, my care, all with a word
He might awey caste
Whet helpeth thee, my swete lemmon
My lif thus for to gaste?

"Do wey, thou clerk, thou art a fol!
With thee bidde I noght chide.
Shalt thou never live that day
My love that thou shalt bide.
If thou in my boure art take,

Shame thee may bitide;
Thee is bettere on fote gon
Then wicked hors to ride."

"Weylawey! Why seist thou so?
Thou rewe on me, thy man!
Thou art ever in my thoght
In londe wher ich am.
If I deye for thy love,
It is thee mikel sham;
Thou lete me love and be thy lef
And thou my swete lemman."

"Be stille, thou fol—I calle thee right;
Cost thou never blinne?
Thou art waited day and night
With fader and all my kinne.
Be thou in my bour itake,
Lete they for no sinne
Me to holde and thee to slon,
The deth so thou maght winne!"

"Swete ledy, thou wend thy mod,
Sorewe thou wolt me kithe.
Ich am all so sory mon
So ich was whilen blithe.
In a window ther we stod
We custe us fifty sithe;
Feir biheste maketh mony mon
All his serewes mithe."

"Weylawey! Why seist thou so?
My serewe thou makest newe.
I lovede a clerk all paramours;
Of love he was full trewe;
He nes nout blithe never a day
Bote he me sone seye;
Ich lovede him betere then my lif—
Whet bote is it to leye?"

"Whil I wes a clerk in scole,
Well muchel I couthe of lore;

Ich have tholed for thy love
Woundes fele sore,
Fer from hom and eke from men
Under the wode-gore.
Swete ledy, thou rewe of me;
Now may I no more!"

"Thou semest well to ben a clerk,
For thou spekest so stille;
Shalt thou never for my love
Woundes thole grille;
Fader, moder, and all my kun
Ne shall me holde so stille
That I nam thin and thou art min,
To don all thy wille."

(My death I love, my life I hate, / On account of a beautiful lady; / She is as bright as the daylight / That's obvious as far as I'm concerned. / I wither quite as does the leaf / In summer when it is green. / If my thought doesn't help me, / To whom shall I complain? / / Sorrow and sighing and melancholy mind / Bind me so tightly / That I expect to toss about madly / If it lasts any longer for me; / My sorrow, my care, all with a word / She might cast away. / What good does it do you, my sweet lover, / Thus to ruin my life? / / "Get away, you clerk, you are a fool! / I don't want to wrangle with you. / You'll never see the day / That you'll get my love. / If you are caught in my chamber, / Shame may befall you; / It's better for you to go on foot / Than to ride a wicked horse." / / Alas! Why do you say such things? / Have pity on me, your servant! / You are always in my thoughts / Wherever I am. / If I die for your love, / It would be a great shame to you; / Let me live and be your love / And you my sweet lover." / / Be still, you fool—I call you correctly / Can you never cease? / You are spied on day and night / By my father and all my kin. / If you are caught in my chamber, / They won't refrain for any [fear of] sin / To hold me and slay you, / Thus may you earn your death!" / / "Sweet lady, change your mind, / Show some pity on me. / I am as sorry a man / As I was happy before. / In a window where we stood / We kissed fifty times; / A fair promise makes many a man / Conceal all his sorrows." / / "Alas! Why do you say such things? / You renew my sorrow. / I loved a clerk as a lover / In love he was full true; / He was

never happy a day / Unless he might see me quickly; / I loved him
better than my life— / What good is it to lie?" / / "While I was a
clerk in school, / I knew much of love-lore; / I have suffered for your
love / Very painful wounds, / Far from home and also from men /
Under the forest canopy. / Sweet lady, have pity on me; / Now I
can't say any more!" / / "You seem well-suited to be a clerk, / For
you speak so softly; / You shall never for my love / Suffer terrible
wounds; / Father, mother and all my kin / Shall not hold me so
firmly / That I am not yours, and you are mine, / To do all your
will.")

"The Meeting in the Wood"

In a frith as I con fare fremede,
I founde a well feir fenge to fere;
Heo glistnede ase gold when it glemede;
Nes ner gome so gladly on gere.
I wolde wite in world who hire kenede,
This burde bright, if hire will were.
Heo me bed go my gates lest hire gremede;
Ne kepte heo non hening here.

"There thou me now, hendest in helde,
Nav I thee none harmes to hethe.
Casten I wol thee from cares and kelde;
Comeliche I wol thee now clethe."

"Clothes I have on for to caste,
Such as I may weore with winne;
Betere is were thunne boute laste
Then side robes and sinke into sinne.
Have ye yor will, ye waxeth unwraste;
Afterward yor thonk be thinne;
Betre is make forewardes faste
Then afterward to mene and minne."

"Of munning ne munte thou namore;
Of menske thou were wurthe, by my might;
I take an hond to holde that I hore
Of all that I thee have bihight.

Why is thee loth to leven on my lore
Lengore then my love were on thee light?
Another might yerne thee so yore
That nolde thee noght rede so right."

"Such reed me might spacliche reowe
When all my ro were me atraght;
Sone thou woldest vachen an newe,
And take another withinne nye naght.
Thenne might I hongren on heowe,
In uch an hyrd ben hated and forhaght,
And ben icaired from all that I kneowe,
And bede clevien ther I hade claght.

Betere is taken a comeliche i'clothe,
In armes to cusse and to cluppe,
Then a wrecche iwedded so wrothe
Thagh he me slowe, ne might I him asluppe.
The beste red that I con to us bothe:
That thou me take and I thee toward huppe;
Thagh I swore by treuthe and othe,
That God hath shaped mey non atluppe.

Mid shupping ne mey it me aschunche;
Nes I never wicche ne wile;
Ich am a maide, that me ofthunche;
Luef me were gome boute gile."

(In a wood as I did walk, unfamiliar / I found a fair prize to
encounter; / She glistened as gold when it gleams; / There was never
a person so comely in clothes. / I would know who in the world
gave birth to her, / This bright maiden, if it were her will. / She
commanded me to go away, lest she be angry; / She did not want to
hear any insulting suggestions. // "Hear me now, most lovely one,
favorably. / I have no insults with which to scorn you. / I will protect
you from worry and sorrow; / I will clothe you becomingly." / "I
have clothes to put on, / Such as I may wear with pleasure; / It is
better to wear thin [clothing] without vice, / Than ample robes and
sink into sin. / If you have your will, you will become evil; /
Afterward your pleasure will be slight; / It is better to make secure
promises / Than afterward to lament and remember." // "Don't

think about memory anymore; / You would be worthy of honor, by my might; / I promise to be faithful until I grow grey, / In all that I have promised you. / Why are you reluctant to believe what I've said / Longer than my love might be settled on you? / Another might entreat you just as long / Who would not advise you so well." / /
"Such advice might I quickly rue / When all my peace is taken from me. / Soon you would fetch a new one, / And take another within nine nights; / Then might I lack a family; / In each household be hated and despised, / And be separated from all that I know, / And bid cling where I had embraced [i.e., beg my lover to be faithful to me]. / / It is better to take a person comely in clothes / To embrace in arms and kiss / Than to be wedded to a wretch so bad, / That though he beat me, I might not escape him. / The best advice I know for both of us is: / That you take me and I leap toward you; / Though I swore by oath, / What God has decreed, one may not escape— / With shape-shifting I may not escape him; / I was never a witch or a sorceress. / I am a maiden, and that displeases me; / Dear to me would be a man without guile.")

# Notes

## Preface

1. Connie Willis, *Doomsday Book* (New York: Bantam, 1992).
2. Fredric Jameson, *The Political Unconscious: Narrative as a Socially Symbolic Act* (Ithaca, NY: Cornell University Press, 1981), 9. Jameson's statement is discussed in detail by Geoff Bennington, "Demanding History," in *Post-Structuralism and the Question of History*, ed. Derek Attridge, Geoff Bennington, and Robert Young (Cambridge: Cambridge University Press, 1987), 20–21.
3. Lee Patterson, ed., *Literary Practice and Social Change in Britain 1380–1530* (Berkeley: University of California Press, 1990), 1.
4. David Aers, *Community, Gender, and Individual Identity: English Writing 1360–1430* (London: Routledge, 1988), 6, 10.

## Introduction

1. D. W. Robertson, *A Preface to Chaucer* (Princeton, NJ: Princeton University Press, 1962), 3.
2. There is, of course, a long tradition linking historical and aesthetic philosophy. Hegel's somewhat unwieldy *Aesthetics* is perhaps the best-known work in this genre; other, more contemporary examples include Theodor W. Adorno's *Aesthetic Theory* and Terry Eagleton's recent book, *The Ideology of the Aesthetic* (Cambridge, MA: Basil Blackwell, 1990).
3. See Lee Patterson, *Negotiating the Past: The Historical Understanding of Medieval Literature* (Madison: University of Wisconsin Press, 1987), and his introduction to the historicist anthology *Literary Practice and Social Change in Britain, 1380–1530*.
4. The so-called "*fort-da* game" is discussed in *Beyond the Pleasure Principle: The Standard Edition of the Complete Works of Sigmund Freud*, ed. James Strachey and trans. James Strachey et al. (London: Hogarth, 1953–74), vol. 18. All references to the *Standard Edition* will hereafter be cited as SE.
5. Jacques Lacan, "The Agency of the Letter in the Unconscious or Reason Since Freud," in *Écrits: A Selection*, trans. Alan Sheridan (New York: Norton, 1977), 154.
6. Writing about Juliet Mitchell's book *Psychoanalysis and Feminism*, Jane Gallop notes the problematic status of the conjunction in this particular context:

> This "and" bridges the gap between two combatants: it runs back and forth holding its white flag as high as possible. Although, of the two, feminism has

shown itself to be the most belligerent, psychoanalysis has not been known to come begging for forgiveness and reconciliation. The quiescent tradition of "and" as mainstay for peaceful coexistence is belied by the assertiveness of Mitchell's step. (1)

*The Daughter's Seduction: Feminism and Psychoanalysis* (Ithaca, NY: Cornell University Press, 1982).

7. See Jacqueline Rose, "Feminism and the Psychic," in her *Sexuality in the Field of Vision* (London: Verso, 1986).

8. I discuss the concept of *Nachträglichkeit* in more detail in Chapter Five. For more on the relation between psychoanalysis and history, see Kaja Silverman, "Back to the Future," *Camera Obscura* 27 (September 1991): 109–32, and Dominick LaCapra, "History and Psychoanalysis," in *Soundings in Critical Theory* (Ithaca, NY: Cornell University Press, 1989), 30–66.

9. SE 1: 356. Also quoted in LaCapra, "History and Psychoanalysis," 35.

10. Silverman, "Back to the Future," 118.

11. Jane Gallop, *Reading Lacan* (Ithaca, NY: Cornell University Press, 1985), 81. Gallop's chapter also deals with the chronology of Lacan's *Écrits*; she points out that

"The Mirror Stage" is the place to begin a study of Lacan's work. Yet not only does *Ecrits* not begin there, but it turns out that "there" may be a difficult place to locate exactly, a lost origin, one might say. (76)

12. Nationalist and racial concerns emerge clearly in the work of some of the early philologists, while sexual anxieties lurk just beneath the surface of much exegetical criticism. Some of these issues are addressed in Norman Cantor's *Inventing the Middle Ages: The Lives, Works and Ideas of the Great Medievalists of the Twentieth Century* (New York: William Morrow, 1991) and Lee Patterson's *Negotiating the Past*.

13. Julia Kristeva, *Powers of Horror: An Essay on Abjection*, trans. Leon Roudiez (New York: Columbia University Press, 1982), 55.

14. Rose, *Sexuality in the Field of Vision*, 219.

15. SE 8: 97–100.

16. See Eve Kosofsky Sedgwick, *Between Men: English Literature and Male Homosocial Desire* (New York: Columbia University Press, 1985).

17. This term derives from Gayle Rubin's analysis of the work of Claude Lévi-Strauss in her influential article, "The Traffic in Women: Notes on the 'Political Economy' of Sex," in *Toward an Anthropology of Women*, ed. Rayna R. Reiter (New York: Monthly Review Press, 1975), 157–210.

18. Perhaps the best known and most eloquent book-length study of the relationship between sexual difference and aesthetic theories is Naomi Schor's *Reading in Detail: Aesthetics and the Feminine* (New York: Methuen, 1987).

19. See Schor, 4.

20. See also Ross Chambers, "Irony and the Canon," *Profession 90* (New York: Modern Language Association of America): 18–24. Chambers voices concerns

similar to my own, arguing that "the traditional humanism whose ideology the canon encapsulates cannot be opposed . . . without challenging the structures of thinking that produce that system" (20).

## Chapter One

1. Caroline Walker Bynum, *Jesus as Mother: Studies in the Spirituality of the High Middle Ages* (Berkeley: University of California Press, 1982).

2. Karma Lochrie provides a much-needed corrective to the reductiveness with which the question of illiteracy has been addressed in some of the earlier discussions of Margery Kempe. See *Margery Kempe and Translations of the Flesh* (Philadelphia: University of Pennsylvania Press, 1991), 101–3. Lochrie's book is discussed in more detail below.

3. This and all subsequent quotations from the *Book* are taken from *The Book of Margery Kempe*, ed. Sanford Meech and Hope Emily Allen (London: Early English Text Society, 1940). All translations are my own.

4. The function of maternal desire and libidinal drives within the Christian signifying system is the leitmotif of Julia Kristeva's collection of essays, *Tales of Love*, trans. Leon Roudiez (New York: Columbia University Press, 1987).

5. According to both Paul de Man and Jacques Derrida, autobiography effaces borderlines and subverts binary oppositions. See de Man, "Autobiography as De-Facement," in his *The Rhetoric of Romanticism* (New York: Columbia University Press, 1984), 67–82, and Derrida, *The Ear of the Other: Otobiography, Transference, Translation*, trans. Peggy Kamuf (Lincoln: University of Nebraska Press, 1988).

6. Although most collections of work on the Middle English mystics now include chapters on Margery Kempe, she remains a troubling presence within them, an exception to the "rules" by which theologians and historians have learned to separate genuine mystics from those who don't quite measure up. One early reviewer, Martin Thornton, described her rather quaintly as "a club cricketer not quite good enough to play for England." See *Margery Kempe: An Example in the English Pastoral Tradition* (London: Talbot Press, 1960).

7. *The Book of Margery Kempe*, lxiv.

8. Herbert Thurston, S.J., "Margery the Astonishing," *The Month* (Nov. 1936): 452.

9. David Knowles, *The English Mystical Tradition* (London: Burns and Oates, 1961), 146.

10. Wolfgang Riehle, *The Middle English Mystical Tradition*, trans. Bernard Standring (London: Routledge & Kegan Paul, 1981), 11.

11. Maureen Fries, "Margery Kempe," in *An Introduction to the Medieval Mystics of Europe*, ed. Paul Szarmach (Albany: State University of New York Press, 1984), 233.

12. Hope Weissman, "Margery Kempe in Jerusalem: *Hysterica Compassio* in the Late Middle Ages," in *Acts of Interpretation: The Text in Its Contexts*, ed. Mary Carruthers and Elizabeth Kirk (Norman, OK: Pilgrim Books, 1982), 202.

13. Sarah Beckwith, "A Very Material Mysticism," in *Medieval Literature: Criticism, Ideology, History*, ed. David Aers (New York: St. Martin's Press, 1986), 54.

14. Weissman, "Margery Kempe in Jerusalem," 202.

15. Mary Jacobus, *Reading Woman* (New York: Columbia University Press, 1986) 108.

16. Katharine Cholmeley, *Margery Kempe: Genius and Mystic* (London: Longmans, Green and Co., 1947).

17. Eric Colledge, "Margery Kempe," *The Month* 28 (1962): 16–29.

18. E. I. Watkin, "In Defence of Margery Kempe" in his *Poets and Mystics* (London: Sheed and Ward, 1953).

19. Clarissa Atkinson, *Mystic and Pilgrim: The Book and the World of Margery Kempe* (Ithaca, NY: Cornell University Press, 1982).

20. Atkinson, *Mystic and Pilgrim*, 211.

21. Caroline Bynum, *Holy Feast and Holy Fast: The Religious Significance of Food to Medieval Women* (Berkeley: University of California Press, 1987), 209.

22. Bynum, *Holy Feast*, 206.

23. Bynum, *Holy Feast*, 296.

24. Bynum, *Holy Feast*, 294.

25. Jacques Lacan, "God and the *Jouissance* of the Woman," in *Feminine Sexuality: Jacques Lacan and the école freudienne*, trans. Jacqueline Rose, ed. Jacqueline Rose and Juliet Mitchell (New York: Norton, 1982), 140.

26. Lochrie, *Margery Kempe and Translations of the Flesh*, 62, 87.

27. See Jacques Derrida's critique of phonocentrism in *Of Grammatology*, trans. Gayatri Chakravorty Spivak (Baltimore: Johns Hopkins University Press, 1976), especially pages 30–44. Derrida makes explicit the connection between theology and metaphysics vis à vis the privilege of speech over writing:

> . . . writing, the letter, the sensible inscription, has always been considered by Western tradition as the body and matter external to the spirit, to breath, to speech, and to the logos. And the problem of soul and body is no doubt derived from the problem of writing from which it seems—conversely—to borrow its metaphors. (35)

28. I borrow this term from Luce Irigaray, "La Mystérique" in her *Speculum of the Other Woman*, trans. Gillian Gill (Ithaca, NY: Cornell University Press, 1985) 191–202.

29. Freud, SE 7.

30. Toril Moi, "Representation of Patriarchy: Sexuality and Epistemology in Freud's Dora," in *In Dora's Case: Freud—Hysteria—Feminism*, ed. Charles Bernheimer and Claire Kahane (New York: Columbia University Press, 1985), 198.

31. Jacqueline Rose, "Dora—Fragment of an Analysis," in *Sexuality in the Field of Vision*, 29.

32. SE 7: 118. Neil Hertz provides an interesting reading of the relationship between belated knowledge and sexual difference in the case of Dora, and in Freud's work in general. See "Dora's Secrets, Freud's Techniques," in *In Dora's Case*, 221–42.

33. In the essay "Female Sexuality," Freud makes explicit the connection be-

tween hysteria and the preoedipal "phase of attachment to the mother" (SE 21: 221), which retroactively redefines Dora's "gynaecophilic love" for Frau K.

34. SE 2: 7

35. SE 2: 160. This quotation is also discussed by Jacobus, *Reading Woman*, 197–204.

36. SE 22: 120.

37. Freud's abandonment of the seduction theory is the subject of Jeffrey Masson's controversial book, *The Assault on Truth: Freud's Suppression of the Seduction Theory* (New York: Farrar, Straus, and Giroux, 1984). The subsequent furor surrounding Masson's book and his character is discussed in detail by Jacqueline Rose, "Where Does the Misery Come From? Psychoanalysis, Feminism, and the Event," in *Feminism and Psychoanalysis*, ed. Richard Feldstein and Judith Roof (Ithaca, NY: Cornell University Press, 1989) 25–39.

38. The proponents of *écriture féminine* are in some sense the modern descendants of the medieval "mysterics," celebrating marginality through metaphor, or seeking transcendence through a return to primary narcissism. In privileging the feminine body as outside the patriarchal system of representation, *écriture féminine* refigures the medieval *via negativa*. As mysticism in the late Middle Ages represented a feminine and affective resistance to the androcentric intellectualism of the scholastics, so the French feminists' insistence on "writing the body" may be seen as a reaction to a philosophical post-structuralism which has been in large part an exclusionary discourse between men.

39. SE 2: 181.

40. At the height of her illness, Anna O. was only able to communicate in foreign languages.

41. See, for example, Fries, "Margery Kempe," 219, and Atkinson, *Mystic and Pilgrim*, 209.

42. The link between language and sexual difference in medieval readings of the creation myth is explored by R. Howard Bloch in his recent book, *Medieval Misogyny and the Invention of Western Romantic Love* (Chicago: University of Chicago Press, 1991), by Carolyn Dinshaw, *Chaucer's Sexual Poetics* (Madison: University of Wisconsin Press, 1989), 3–27, and by Alexandre Leupin, *Barbarolexis: Medieval Writing and Sexuality* (Cambridge, MA: Harvard University Press, 1989), 9–12.

43. My association of metonymy with materiality is based in part on Roman Jakobson's important paper, "Two Aspects of Language and Two Types of Aphasic Disturbances," in *Selected Writings II* (Paris: Mouton, 1971), 239–59. Jakobson points out that "it is generally realized that romanticism is closely linked with metaphor, whereas the equally intimate ties of realism with metonymy usually remain unnoticed." (258).

44. "The speaking body," writes Mary Jacobus, "cries out to be read metaphorically" (*Reading Woman*, 227).

45. In the Middle English legend of Saint Margaret, the saint explicitly states her willingness to be dismembered in order to protect her faith and her virginity:

Ich wulle bitechen mi bodi to eauer-euich bitternesse þat tu const onbi-þenchen, ne bite hit ne se sare, wið þon þet ich mote meidene mede habben in heovene . . . . ʒef mi lich is toloken, mi sawle schal resten wið þe rihtwise: sorhe & licomes sar is sawulene heale. (12; 14)

(I will deliver my body to every bitterness that you can devise, no matter how painful, provided that I may have a virgin's reward in heaven . . . . If my body is torn to pieces, my soul shall rest with the righteous; sorrow and bodily pain is the health of souls.)

*Seinte Marherete, Þe Meiden ant Martyr*, ed. Frances Mack (London: Early English Text Society, 1934).

46. Saint Margaret is, of course, the patron saint of childbirth.

47. *Seinte Katerine*, ed. S.R.T.O. d'Ardenne and E. J. Dobson (London: Early English Text Society, 1981). The Latin version in the *Legenda Aurea* is very similar:

Confiteor tamen meam progeniem non tumore iactantiae, sed humilitatis amore, ego enim sum Catharina Costi regis unica filia, quae, quamvis in purpura nata et liberalibus disciplinis non mediocriter instructa, haec tamen omnia contemsi et ad dominem Iesum Christum confugi.

48. See Michel Foucault, *Language, Counter-Memory, Practice*, ed. Donald Bouchard (Ithaca, NY: Cornell University Press, 1977), 139–64. According to Karma Lochrie, the notion of a "counter-canon" is incompatible with feminist critical praxis:

For the feminist project of delineating the position of women's writing, the paradigm of influence itself is suspect, since it is based on a male tradition of cultural patrilineage. This model already excludes women except as receptors or mediums of male culture. (*Margery Kempe and Translations of the Flesh*, 204)

It is nonetheless difficult to see how "women's writing" can be possible without a notion of tradition, a sense of history. It seems to me that "cultural patrilineage" is precisely the "given" that women's writing must call into question.

49. This section of my argument draws on Kaja Silverman's analysis of the "fantasy of the maternal voice," in *The Acoustic Mirror: The Female Voice in Psychoanalysis and Cinema* (Bloomington: Indiana University Press, 1988), 120–24.

50. SE 19: 33.

51. SE 20: 34; and Silverman, *Acoustic Mirror*, 121.

52. Silverman, *Acoustic Mirror*, 124.

53. Cf. Weissman's reading of Margery's maternalism as a manifestation of her Marian piety.

54. I derive this distinction from Lacan's essay "The Eye and the Gaze," in *The Four Fundamental Concepts of Psycho-Analysis*, trans. Alan Sheridan, ed. Jacques-Alain Miller (New York: Norton, 1977), 67–78, and from the exegesis of Kaja Silverman in her article "Fassbinder and Lacan: A Reconsideration of Gaze, Look, and Image," *Camera Obscura* 19 (1989), 54–84.

55. I say "interiorizes" because, in blurring the boundary between inside and

outside, private and public, autobiography calls the putative exteriority of both reader and writer into question.

56. Lochrie, *Margery Kempe and Translations of the Flesh*, 227.

57. Atkinson, *Mystic and Pilgrim*, 59.

58. Lochrie makes a similar point in suggesting that Margery's "discourse of tears cuts through language and silences it, leaving only the surplus of body and voice for people to marvel at—and the possibility of rapture" *Margery Kempe and Translations of the Flesh*, 197.

59. Jacobus, *Reading Woman*, 288.


## Chapter Two

This chapter is a revised version of an article that was published as "Desiring Narrative: Ideology and the Semiotics of the Gaze in the Middle English *Juliana*," *Exemplaria* 2, 2 (1990): 355–74. I am grateful to R. A. Shoaf and J. P. Hermann for their generous comments and suggestions in preparing the article for publication, and to *Exemplaria* for allowing me to reprint portions of the article here.

Quotations are taken from *Þe Liflade ant te Passiun of Seinte Iuliene*, ed. S.R.T.O. d'Ardenne (London: Early English Text Society, 1961). All translations and emphases are my own.

1. See d'Ardenne's Introduction and Appendix to *Iuliene*, especially xxvii and 178; the point is also made by Norman Blake, *The English Language in Medieval Literature* (London: J. M. Dent, 1977), 40, 53.

2. The sexual violence that characterizes medieval romance as a genre is also discussed by Kathryn Gravdal in her book *Ravishing Maidens: Writing Rape in Medieval French Literature and Law* (Philadelphia: University of Pennsylvania Press, 1991).

3. In his study of *La Vie de Saint Alexis*, Alexandre Leupin also discusses the significance of origins in structuring hagiography as a genre, albeit in somewhat different terms. See *Barbarolexis: Medieval Writing and Sexuality*, 39–58.

4. *Iuliene*, 178–79.

5. In *Powers of Horror: An Essay on Abjection*.

6. Kristeva, *Powers of Horror*, 161.

7. *Powers of Horror*, 54.

8. Kristeva discusses this phenomenon in the context of her analysis of the works of Louis-Ferdinand Céline:

> The conjunction of opposites (courtliness-sadism) is again encountered in all of Céline's feminine characters. To varying degrees, such ambivalence seems to show that genital fear can be kept within bounds by idealization as well as by the unleashing of partial drives (sado-masochistic, voyeurist-exhibitionist, oral-anal). (*Powers*, 162)

9. There is some inconclusive evidence for a continuous alliterative tradition in the West Midlands of England throughout the Anglo-Norman period: in addition to the Katherine texts, Laȝamon's *Brut*, the Harley Lyrics, and some of the

early Middle English romances are of West or North-West Midland origin. The West Midlands were later to become the center of the so-called alliterative revival of the fourteenth century.

10. See *Jokes and Their Relation to the Unconscious*, SE 8: 96 ff.

11. In *Powers of Horror*, Kristeva discusses the role of abjection in religious ritual:

> The various means of *purifying* the abject—the various catharses—make up the history of religions, and end up with that catharsis par excellence called art, both on the far and near side of religion. Seen from that standpoint, the artistic experience, which is rooted in the abject it utters and by the same token purifies, appears as the essential component of religiosity. (17)

12. The violence of Christian dualism is also discussed by J. P. Hermann in his innovative study of the Old English *Juliana*. See "Language and Spirituality in Cynewulf's *Juliana*," *Texas Studies in Literature and Language* 26, 3 (1984): 263–81.

13. Kristeva's work on abjection provides, I think, a much-needed theoretical dimension to Caroline Walker Bynum's fascinating studies of the conditions of representation in the writings of women mystics. See *Jesus as Mother* and the somewhat troubling concluding chapter of *Holy Feast and Holy Fast*, 277–96.

14. For example, see Christian Metz, *The Imaginary Signifier: Psychoanalysis and Cinema*, trans. Celia Britton, Annwyl Williams, Ben Brewster, and Alfred Guzzetti (Bloomington: Indiana University Press, 1982), 1–81.

15. See Mary Ann Doane, *The Desire to Desire: The Woman's Film of the 1940s* (Bloomington: Indiana University Press, 1987), 13–22; Kaja Silverman, *The Acoustic Mirror*, 1–41.

16. SE 21: 152–57.

17. The history of this concept within film theory is discussed by Silverman, *Acoustic Mirror*, 1–41.

18. This cinematic strategy was first theorized by Laura Mulvey in her essay "Visual Pleasure and Narrative Cinema," *Screen* 16, 3 (1975): 8–18. This essay virtually founded feminist film theory as a discipline, and its claims are still central to the feminist debate in the field.

19. Mulvey, Silverman, and Doane all discuss classic cinema's dependence on the fragmentation and interiorization of the feminine body in producing pleasure. In *The Acoustic Mirror*, Silverman argues that

> the female subject's involuntary incorporation of the various losses which haunt cinema, from the forclosed real to the invisible agency of enunciation, makes possible the male subject's identification with the symbolic father, and his imaginary alignment with creative vision, speech, and hearing. (32)

20. Jacques Lacan, *The Four Fundamental Concepts of Psycho-Analysis*, 67–78. My reading of *Seminar XI* is indebted to that of Kaja Silverman, "Fassbinder and Lacan," 54–84.

21. Lacan, *Concepts*, 72.

22. *Concepts*, 84.

23. *Concepts*, 85.

24. *Concepts*, 73.

25. Silverman, "Fassbinder and Lacan," 59.

26. See Paul Ricoeur, *The Rule of Metaphor*, trans. Robert Czerny (Toronto: University of Toronto Press, 1977), 131–32.

27. Metaphor's erasure of its own origins is the focus of Jacques Derrida's essay "White Mythology," in *Margins of Philosophy*, trans. Alan Bass (Chicago: University of Chicago Press, 1982), 207–271. It should be pointed out that the last chapter of Ricoeur's *Rule of Metaphor* is in part a response to this essay; Derrida continues the dispute in "The Retrait of Metaphor," *Enclitic* 2 (1978): 5–33. The dispute is discussed in detail by Dominick LaCapra in *Rethinking Intellectual History: Texts, Contexts, Language* (Ithaca, NY: Cornell University Press, 1983), 118–44.

28. The medieval notion of alienation from God as "unlikeness" derives from the seventh book of Augustine's *Confessions*; before his conversion Augustine describes himself as far from God "in the land of unlikeness" (7: 10)

29. Jane Gallop, *Reading Lacan*, 128 ff.

30. Lacan, "The Agency of the Letter," in *Écrits: A Selection*.

31. Lacan, "God and the Jouissance of the Woman," and "A Love Letter," in *Feminine Sexuality*, 137–61.

32. The Lacanian concept of the *objet petit a* or "little other" can be understood as the embodied substitute-object that stands in for that which can not be embodied, the inaccessible Other (sometimes called the "big Other") that underwrites or guarantees the meaning of all signifying acts. The *objet a* is the "cause" of desire, the (often feminine) object that is characterized precisely by its ability to be lost and replaced.

33. *Écrits*, 164.

34. *Écrits*, 154; 158. Cf. Gallop, *Reading Lacan*, 114–32.

35. *Écrits*, 154.

36. *Écrits*, 158.

37. *Feminine Sexuality*, 144.

38. *Feminine Sexuality*, 153–54.

39. See Roman Jakobson, "Two Types of Language and Two Types of Aphasic Disorders," in *Selected Writings II: Word and Language*.

40. Lacan, *Écrits*, 158.

## Chapter Three

Quotations from the Harley Lyrics are taken from *Middle English Lyrics*, selected and edited by Maxwell Luria and Richard L. Hoffman (New York: Norton, 1974). I have included the complete texts of all the poems I discuss, with my own translations, in an appendix at the end of this study.

1. See Jonathan Culler, "Changes in the Study of the Lyric," in *Lyric Poetry:*

*Beyond New Criticism*, ed. Chaviva Hosek and Patricia Parker (Ithaca, NY: Cornell University Press, 1985), 38–54.

2. Paul de Man, *The Rhetoric of Romanticism*, 78.

3. SE 18: 164–79.

4. See Nicolas Abraham and Maria Torok, "A Poetics of Psychoanalysis: The Lost Object—Me," *SubStance* 43 (1984): 3–18. The concept of "endocryptic identification," whereby the melancholic subject internalizes or encrypts the lost object provides a way into the problematic relationship between prosopopoeia and melancholia.

5. Derek Pearsall, *Old and Middle English Poetry* (London: Routledge and Kegan Paul, 1977).

6. Arthur K. Moore, *The Secular Lyric in Middle English* (Lexington: University of Kentucky Press, 1951), 66.

7. Moore's assessments are echoed by M. J. C. Hodgart, who contends that "the English medieval lyric, religious and secular, is a poor relation of the splendid Continental art-form," and by W. T. H. Jackson, who notes the "monotony of theme and lack of technical skill" in the Middle English texts. See Hodgart, "Medieval Lyrics and the Ballads," in *The Age of Chaucer*, ed. Boris Ford (Baltimore: Penguin Books, 1969), 159; and Jackson, *The Literature of the Middle Ages* (New York: Columbia University Press, 1960), 275.

8. G. L. Brook, ed., *The Harley Lyrics: The Middle English Lyrics of MS Harley 2253* (Manchester: Manchester University Press, 1968).

9. Brian Stone, trans., *Medieval English Verse* (Baltimore: Penguin Books, 1964), 179–80.

10. Possible sources for these literary allusions are discussed at length by Carleton Brown in his edited anthology, *English Lyrics of the XIIIth Century* (Oxford: Clarendon Press, 1932), 226–28.

11. Brown begins his discussion of this line by stating that it is "hardly a reference to the Hebrew prophet." Nevertheless, he is able to provide neither a justification for his assumption, nor a plausible alternative source for the reference itself. See Brown, *English Lyrics*, 228.

12. The prurient fascination elicited by these texts extends into the realm of critical discourse as well. In his analysis of "Annot and John," for example, Daniel Ransom suggests that the lines "cointe ase columbine such her cunde is / Glad under gore in gro and in gris" are but a code for talking about the woman's "cunt in its fine fur." "Once again," Ransom writes, "the author winks at his audience." The critic then winks at *his* audience, adding that "something is flourishing *under gore*, and it clearly is not synecdoche." See Daniel Ransom, *Poets at Play: Irony and Parody in the Harley Lyrics* (Norman, OK: Pilgrim Books, 1985), 38–39.

13. SE 8: 94–102.

14. SE 8: 97–98.

15. SE 8: 99.

16. "When the first person finds his libidinal impulse inhibited by the woman," Freud writes, "he develops a hostile trend against that second person and calls on the originally interfering third person [the rival] as his ally. Through the first person's smutty speech the woman is exposed before the third, who, as listener, has now been bribed by the effortless satisfaction of his own libido." (100)

17. SE 8: 137.

18. The phenomenon of "male homosocial desire" was first theorized by Eve Kosofsky Sedgwick in her influential book, *Between Men*.

19. See R. Howard Bloch, *Medieval Misogyny*. An interesting summary of the historical association of troping, errancy and sexual difference is also provided by Patricia Parker, *Literary Fat Ladies: Rhetoric, Gender, Property* (London: Methuen, 1987). I engage with Parker's work more specifically in chapter six.

20. Although the image of the sun passing through glass is, to my knowledge, seldom reversed as it is in the Harleian text, it often works in both directions at once, as in this lyric by the poet Rutebeuf dating from the mid thirteenth century:

Si com en la verriere
Entre et reva arriere
Li solaus que n'entame
Ainsinc fus virge entiere
Quant Diex, qui es ciex iere,
Fist de toi mere et dame.

See Rutebeuf, *Le Miracle de Théophile*, ed. Grace Frank (Paris: Éditions Champion, 1983), 20.

21. The theoretical implications of this particular paradox are explored by Kaja Silverman, "The Fantasy of the Maternal Voice: Paranoia and Compensation," in *The Acoustic Mirror*, 72–140.

22. The connection between the Fall and the alienation of the subject in language is eloquently argued by Carolyn Dinshaw in her reading of "Chaucers Wordes unto Adam, His Owne Scriveyn." See Dinshaw, *Chaucer's Sexual Poetics*, 3–27.

23. The pastourelle, like its literary descendant, the English pastoral, is obsessed with the dilemma of memory. The speaker's "story" is almost always presented in the past tense, and memory itself often either blocks or facilitates the sexual encounter. In several poems (the Harleian "De Clerico et Puella" among them) the woman yields after recognizing the man from a previous sexual encounter; in others, she rejects him for the same reason.

24. For examples of these various types, see the useful anthology compiled, edited, and translated by William D. Paden, *The Medieval Pastourelle*, 2 vols. (New York: Garland Publishing, 1987).

25. Kathryn Gravdal sees the continental pastourelle as a symptom of institutionalized violence against women rather than a space where the cultural and aesthetic problematic of feminine speaking is played out. See *Ravishing Maidens*, 104–21. Joan Ferrante makes the point that "the peasant [woman] actually speaks in too polished a way and with too much knowledge of courtly traditions and literature to be anything but a figure for the courtly lady; the courtly lady, when finally allowed to speak for herself, is more than a match for her would-be lover." See "Male Fantasy and Female Reality in Courtly Literature," *Women's Studies* 11 (1984): 70.

26. The most difficult of these problems is that presented by the word

"ashunche": the word is a *hapax legomenon* which may mean either "scare away," "escape," or neither of these. See G.L. Brook's textual note, *The Harley Lyrics*, 79. Similarly, "shupping" may mean "devising (counter) measures," "decree," or "shape-shifting." I have chosen to rely on the translation favored by Rosemary Woolf in her essay "The Construction of *In a Fryht As Y Con Fare Fremede*," *Medium Aevum* 38 (1969): 55–59.

27. A similar argument may be made about the rhetorical significance of conversion within the hagiographical tradition. It is, as I have argued in the previous chapter, the turning from the flesh to the spirit that constitutes the theological or paternal metaphor.


*Chapter Four*


An earlier version of this essay was published under the same title in *Feminist Approaches to the Body in Medieval Literature*, ed. Linda Lomperis and Sarah Stanbury (Philadelphia: University of Pennsylvania Press, 1993). All quotations from Chaucer's works in this and the following chapter are taken from *The Riverside Chaucer*, gen. ed. Larry D. Benson, 3d ed. (Boston: Houghton Mifflin, 1987).

1. The relationship between aesthetic judgment and the institution of patriarchy is discussed at length by Naomi Schor in her important study, *Reading in Detail: Aesthetics and the Feminine*. Schor argues that oppositions based on sexual difference have informed traditional aesthetic theory. As a result, the detail has been pathologized as feminine: like femininity itself, the detail at once sustains and subverts the aesthetic ideal of transcendence. Schor's work has interesting implications for the theoretical understanding of canons in general, since the canonicity of a given artifact depends to some extent on its ability to master the detail, or, as I suggest here, to elicit and contain the material and mundane within a quasi-theological system.

2. In her book, *The Critical Difference* (Baltimore: Johns Hopkins University Press, 1980), Barbara Johnson discusses the implications of this deconstructive assertion for the institution of literary criticism.

3. This assertion is anticipated by Lee Patterson in his most recent, and, to my mind, provocative book: *Chaucer and the Subject of History* (Madison: University of Wisconsin Press, 1991).

4. The relation between sleep and poetry is of course the metaphoric foundation for the medieval dream-vision from the Anglo-Saxon period onward. Sleep and/or dreaming is also evoked in this connection in works such as Shakespeare's *The Tempest*, Milton's *Paradise Lost*, Spenser's *Daphnaida* (modeled on the *Duchess*) and Keats's *Endymion*, to name but a few.

5. The last lines of Keats's poem in fact echo those of Chaucer's *Duchess*:

And up I rose refresh'd, and glad, and gay,
    Resolving to begin that very day
These lines; and howsoever they be done,
I leave them as a father does his son. (401–4)

6. It should be noted that medievalists have recently begun to explore the relationship between origins, loss, and representation more closely. Allen Frantzen's ground-breaking book, *Desire for Origins: New Language, Old English, and Teaching the Tradition* (New Brunswick, NJ: Rutgers University Press, 1990) offers a long-overdue analysis of the role of originary and nationalist fantasies in the foundation of Anglo-Saxon studies. Louise Fradenburg's excellent article on loss and reparation in Chaucerian poetics addresses the problem of loss—both in the field and in Chaucer's texts—by way of a reading of the psychoanalytic literature on mourning. See "'Voice Memorial': Loss and Reparation in Chaucer's Poetry," *Exemplaria* 2, 1 (Spring 1990): 169–202. Fradenburg's analysis centers on the Chaucerian elegy, with particular emphasis on the relation between "loss" and "authority" in a genre she sees a fundamentally "coercive" and misogynistic. Like many (of the few) psychoanalytically oriented medievalists, she is reluctant to accept the Lacanian-deconstructive reading of Freud's texts, and seems to bypass the question of loss as it relates specifically to the situation on the subject-in-language. For a more sustained reading of Fradenburg's essay, see the earlier version of this chapter in *Feminist Approaches to the Body in Medieval Literature*.

7. Very little has been made of the morphological similarity between "Lollius" and "Lollard." Several readers have suggested that the name Lollius derives from a medieval misreading of Horace's address to Maximus Lollius:

Troiani belli scriptorem, Maxime Lolli,
dum tu declamas Romae, Praeneste relegi.

*(Epist., 1, 2, 1)*

For a compilation of evidence supporting this idea, see Robert Armstrong Pratt, "A Note on Chaucer's Lollius," *Modern Language Notes* 65 (1950): 183–87. More recently, the Lollius issue has been reconsidered by Bella Millet, "Chaucer, Lollius, and the Medieval Theory of Authorship," in *Studies in the Age of Chaucer*, Proceedings no. 1 (1984): 93–103.

8. For an examination of Chaucer's problematic relation to the idea of paternal authority, and the effect this may have had on his own literary successors, see A. C. Spearing, *Medieval to Renaissance Poetry* (Cambridge: Cambridge University Press, 1985), 59–120.

9. See James Wimsatt, *Chaucer and the French Love Poets: The Literary Background of the Book of the Duchess* (Chapel Hill: University of North Carolina Press, 1968) and B. A. Windeatt, ed. and trans., *Chaucer's Dream Poetry: Sources and Analogues* (Totowa, NJ: D. S. Brewer-Rowman and Littlefield, 1982).

10. See Donald Howard, *Chaucer: His Life, His Works, His World* (New York: E. P. Dutton, 1987), 86–87.

11. SE 18: 14–17. In her reading of the *fort-da* scenario, Fradenburg attempts to circumvent the problem of language, in order to, as she puts it "release Freud's little child . . . from the bondage to mimesis to which he has been routinely subjected" (183). She offers a somewhat difficult reading of the scenario that emphasizes instead the "particularity" of *fort* and *da*. Her reading, which I find problematic but nonetheless interesting, reflects current the historicist insistence upon the "local and contingent" as a locus of resistance to "totalizing" political

and theoretical configurations. A persuasive critique of historicist "localism" is offered by Alan Liu in his essay, "Local Transcendence: Cultural Criticism, Postmodernism, and the Romanticism of Detail," *Representations* 32 (Fall 1990): 75–113.

12. Wayne Koestenbaum, "Privileging the Anus: Anna O. and the Collaborative Origin of Psychoanalysis," *Genders* 3 (Fall 1988): 57–80.

13. In *Studies on Hysteria*, Breuer calls Anna O. "the germ-cell of the whole of psychoanalysis." Her role in the genesis of psychoanalytic theory is also discussed by Mary Jacobus in *Reading Woman*, 205–28.

14. Koestenbaum, "Privileging the Anus," 67.

15. My argument, like Koestenbaum's, is here indebted to Eve Kosofsky Sedgwick's *Between Men*.

16. The homosocial aspects of the poem—but not their homoerotic implications—have also been noted by Maud Ellman in her essay, "Blanche" in *Criticism and Critical Theory*, ed. Jeremy Hawthorn (London: Arnold, 1984): 99–110, as well as by Elaine Tuttle Hansen, "The Death of Blanche and the Life of the Moral Order" in *Thought: A Review of Culture and Idea* 64, 254 (September 1989): 287–97.

17. The theoretical significance of Blanche's absence has been noted by Maud Ellman in her extremely suggestive but somewhat undeveloped essay, "Blanche." Ellman also notes the sense in which "Chaucer's poem intimates that mourning is native to narrative itself, which arises in and through the loss of origin" (104). She does not pursue this provocative comment, however; given that the *Duchess* is thought to be Chaucer's "originary" work, and that Chaucer himself is said to have metaphorically "originated" English poetry, the concept of the origin is a good deal more problematic for medievalists than her rather decontextualized reading allows.

18. In his analysis of the child's "artistic play," Freud explicitly states that the unpleasure of loss may be mitigated by the pleasures of representation:

> We are therefore left in doubt as to whether the impulse to work over in the mind some overpowering experience so as to make oneself master of it can find expression as a primary event, and independently of the pleasure principle. For, in the case we have been discussing, the child may, after all, only have been able to repeat his unpleasant experience in play because the repetition carried with it a yield of pleasure of another sort but none the less a direct one. (SE 18: 16)

19. See Bernard F. Huppé and D. W. Robertson, Jr., *Fruyt and Chaf: Studies in Chaucer's Allegories* (Princeton, NJ: Princeton University Press, 1963).

20. This is the position taken by Judith Ferster in her book *Chaucer on Interpretation* (Cambridge: Cambridge University Press, 1985), 69–93.

21. See Robert Edwards, "The *Book of the Duchess* and the Beginnings of Chaucer's Narrative," *New Literary History* (1982): 189–204.

22. A rather strained Boethian reading of the poem is offered by Michael D. Cherniss in his *Boethian Apocalypse* (Norman, OK: Pilgrim Books, 1987), 169–81.

23. Robert Jordan, *Chaucer's Poetics and the Modern Reader* (Berkeley: University of California Press, 1987), 75.

24. Robert Hanning, "Chaucer's First Ovid: Metamorphosis and Poetic Tradition in The Book of the Duchess and The House of Fame," in *Chaucer and the Craft of Fiction*, ed. Leigh Arrathoon (Rochester, MI: Solaris Press, 1986), 125.

25. Hanning sees the relationship between the dreamer and the Black Knight as analogous to that between critic and text:

> The text puts barriers between us and the truth —fictions, *integumenta*—and thus invites (or even coerces) us to respond by figuring out what the truth is. (Such a decorum of interpretation characterizes the dialogue between the dreamer and the black knight: the latter expresses his personal crisis through a series of verbal structures—lament, metaphor, stylized autobiography— while the former judges these structures and presses the knight for an ever clearer, more complete exposition of the nature and extent of his sorrow). Accordingly, when we divine a truth, no matter how terrible or moving it may be . . . we experience the satisfaction of discovery, plus the fact of closure in the fiction itself. (124)

26. Cf. John Fyler, *Chaucer and Ovid* (New Haven, CT: Yale University Press, 1979). For Fyler, these lines refer to a Golden Age of ideal love.

27. Fradenburg points out that "Chaucer's 'good women' are—like Anelida and Alcyone . . .—usually inconsolable, if not altogether dead; and the capacity of these women to generate narrative from their grief is either problematic or non-existent" (172).

28. The occlusion of reference in the poem is also noted by Terence Hoagwood in his article "Artifice and Redemption: Figuration and the Failure of Reference in Chaucer's *Book of the Duchess*," *Studia Mystica* 11 (Summer 1988): 57–68. For Hoagwood, the "failure of reference" in the poem serves an "ideational" or mystical end, ultimately affirming the transcendent value of art.

29. Here, as throughout this book, I draw on Kaja Silverman's *The Acoustic Mirror*. For the interiorization of femininity, see pages 42–71.

30. An interesting analysis of the use of conventional language in the *Duchess* is provided by Philip Boardman in his article "Courtly Language and the Strategy of Consolation in the *Book of the Duchess*," *English Literary History* 44 (1977): 567–79.

31. Boardman's analysis of the conventional moments in the poem is somewhat different in emphasis, though, I think, not inconsistent with my own; he sees the poem as Chaucer's "critique of the conventional language of love poetry," a critique which focuses specifically on the inability of courtly discourse to express the affect brought about by loss.

32. SE 21: 152–57.

33. The idea of a feminist Chaucer reflects, on the one hand, recent interest in feminist or quasi-feminist readings of Chaucerian texts, and on the other, a simultaneous concern to exculpate Chaucer the poet on the charge of phallocentrism. Some of the more politically problematic aspects of this phenomenon are discussed at length by Elaine Tuttle Hansen in her essay, "Fearing for Chaucer's Good Name," *Exemplaria* 2,1 (Spring 1990): 23–36. Many of Hansen's points are

well taken, particularly her indictment of what she calls the "post-feminist" trend in contemporary medievalism. Her essay is, however, based on some essentializing assumptions about the relationship between "male" versus "female" reading and writing that I find difficult to accept. Hansen defines feminist criticism in terms of "an insistence that the gender of the author and reader/critic matters." This definition carries with it decidedly empiricist assumptions, most notably the idea that writing bears an immediate and unproblematic relation to the experience of gender. If the gender of the *author* is so important, how can feminist criticism address the huge corpus of anonymous works from the Middle Ages? If the gender of the *critic* determines her/his capacity to read politically or not, how can feminism become more than a single-sex discourse? How can it address the equally problematic category of masculinity? Is the gender-category of "man" to remain unproblematic, while that of "woman" remains a site of contention, contradiction, and instability? More to the (political) point, what does Hansen's assumption promise for those for those of us who are *not* heterosexual, who have only a vexed relationship to our culturally-determined gender and the object-choice it mandates? These are difficult questions, which I obviously can't begin to answer here. I do think, however, that there is more at stake in the idea of a feminist Chaucer than merely "Chaucer's good name." For a provocative analysis of the discursive and cultural implications of gender as an epistemological category, see Nancy Armstrong, "The Gender Bind: Women and the Disciplines," *Genders* 3 (Fall 1988): 1–23.

34. My analysis of fetishism as it relates to the *Duchess* is indebted to the work of feminist film theorists Kaja Silverman and Mary Ann Doane. The subheading of this final section is borrowed from Doane's book *The Desire to Desire: The Woman's Film of the 1940s.*

35. SE 21: 152

36. SE 21: 152–53.

## Chapter Five

1. Again, this phenomenon was first noted by Louise Fradenburg in her fascinating study, "'Voice Memorial'." Some of the ideas put forth in this essay are developed further in a more recent essay, "'Our owen wo to drynke': Loss, Gender and Chivalry in *Troilus and Criseyde*," in *Chaucer's Troilus and Criseyde "Subjit to alle Poesye": Essays in Criticism*, ed. R. A. Shoaf (Binghamton, NY: Center for Medieval and Renaissance Studies, 1992), 88–106.

2. See "A Poetics of Psychoanalysis." Abraham and Torok's article is a rethinking of Freud's essay "Mourning and Melancholia" (SE 18: 164–79), focusing particularly on the issues of introjection and incorporation. Endocryptic identification is a process by which the boundary between mourning subject and lost object becomes utterly effaced. According to Abraham and Torok, "in endocryptic identification, the 'I' is understood as the phantasied ego of the lost object" (15). In simpler terms, the process of identification unfolds such that the subject imagines her-or himself to be the object—her or his desires, traumas, and so on are the *imagined* desires of the lost and incorporated object.

3. The resistance of Anglo-Saxon studies to methodological innovations and ideological re-orientation has been explored by Allen Frantzen and Charles Venegoni in their article "An Archeology of Anglo-Saxon Studies," *Style* 20, 2 (Summer 1986). Frantzen's book, *Desire for Origins*, offers a fuller treatment of these issues from both a theoretical and a historical perspective.

4. This association of woman, loss, and origin has been most precisely theorized by Julia Kristeva, in both her "maternalist" works and in her later exploration of the aesthetic implications of melancholia. This nexus also underwrites Freud's theorization of fetishism and the *fort-da* paradigm, as I suggested in the previous chapter.

5. Lee Patterson, *Negotiating the Past*.

6. Lee Patterson, ed., *Literary Practice and Social Change in Britain, 1380–1530*, 1.

7. Patterson's introduction to *Literary Practice* stages a confrontation between formalism and historicism at the expense, I think, of an honest assessment of the significant questions deconstructive theory raises for historicist practice. It seems to me that the works of Derrida and de Man, for example, have opened up the question of source and origin from a philosophical and rhetorical perspective in a way that history as a discipline has so far failed to do; to simply dismiss their contributions as "transhistorical" and therefore irrelevant is to turn away from a powerful challenge that could potentially re-define the relationship between literary and historical studies. This re-definition is already underway in the work of scholars both within and outside the field of literary studies. See, for example, Dominick LaCapra, *Rethinking Intellectual History*, and his essay "On the Line: Between History and Criticism," *Profession 89* (New York: Modern Language Association of America), 4–9; and *Post-Structuralism and the Question of History*, ed. Derek Attridge, Geoff Bennington, and Robert Young (Cambridge: Cambridge University Press, 1987).

8. There are too many recent essays on these topics to enumerate here. For example, see Susan Crane, "The Writing Lesson of 1381" in *Chaucer's England: Literature in Historical Context* ed. Barbara Hanawalt (Minneapolis: University of Minnesota Press, 1992), 201–21; Lee Patterson, "'No Man His Reson Herde': Peasant Consciousness, Chaucer's Miller, and the Structure of the Canterbury Tales," in *Literary Practice and Social Change in Britain 1380–1530*, 113–55; and Paul Strohm, "Saving the Appearances: Chaucer's *Purse* and the Fabrication of the Lancastrian Claim," in *Chaucer's England*, 21–40.

9. The Hegelian concept of sublimation or *Aufhebung* can be understood onto-theologically: by negating given or immediate being—by which we may understand nature, or body—one begins the dialectical process that holds out the promise of transcendence, of ascent to the realm of *das absolute Wissen*. Like the body of the mother in Freudian theory, given being stands outside the dialectical process, and therefore outside language and history; but see the reading of Alexandre Kojève, *Introduction to the Reading of Hegel: Lectures on the Phenomenology of Spirit*, assembled by Raymond Queneau, edited by Allan Bloom, and translated by James H. Nichols, Jr. (Ithaca, NY: Cornell University Press, 1989), 199, n.10.

10. G. F. W. Hegel, *Phenomenology of Spirit*, trans. A. V. Miller (Oxford: Ox-

ford University Press, 1977). See, in particular, pages 104–38. Hegel's theory of the dialectic is obviously much more complex and far-reaching than many historicist uses of it would suggest. A good portion of the *Phenomenology* is explicitly concerned with the relationship between perception and cognition; in his statement that "consciousness itself is the absolute dialectical unrest" (124), for example, Hegel prefigures Freud's theorization of the role of repression in the constitution of the knowing subject.

11. Patterson, "No Man His Reson Herde," in *Literary Practice*, 113–55. Patterson's very interesting reading turns on the Hegelian issue of *Anerkennung*: for Patterson, the Miller's Tale allegorizes the peasant struggle for recognition, only to contain that struggle within conventional tropes that effectively de-politicize and thus neutralize the challenge of Slave to Master.

12. See Paul Strohm, *Social Chaucer* (Cambridge, MA: Harvard University Press, 1989), and his essay "Politics and Poetics: Usk and Chaucer in the 1380s," in *Literary Practice*, 83–112.

13. Stephen Knight, *Geoffrey Chaucer* (Oxford: Basil Blackwell, Ltd., 1986), 3.

14. See Knight, 6, and Patterson's Introduction to *Literary Practice*, 13–14.

15. See Patterson, *Negotiating*, 70–71. Again, for an interesting critique of this "localism," see Alan Liu, "Local Transcendence."

16. The concept of expressive totality, also referred to a expressive causality, is something of a problem in Marxist literary thought. The term itself derives from Louis Althusser's critique of the Hegelian idealist strain in hermeneutic Marxism, that is, of the allegorical or theological reading of history which privileges one of the elements within a cultural or historical totality as the "master code" or key to the political/historical meaning of that phenomenon or period. In discussing Althusser's position, Fredric Jameson acknowledges that "interpretation in terms of expressive causality or allegorical master narratives remains a constant temptation . . . because such master narratives have inscribed themselves in the texts as well as in our thinking about them; such allegorical narrative signifieds are a persistent dimension of of literary and cultural texts precisely because they reflect a fundamental dimension of our collective thinking and our collective fantasies about history and reality" (*The Political Unconscious*, 34). See also the discussion offered by La Capra, *Rethinking*, 241–45; and that of Ted Benton, *The Rise and Fall of Structural Marxism: Althusser and His Influence* (Hong Kong: Macmillan, 1984), 62–65.

17. See Walter Benjamin, "Theses on the Philosophy of History," in *Illuminations*, trans. H. Zohn (New York: Schocken, 1969), 253. Benjamin's assertion of the dependence of historical materialism on theology is also discussed by Jameson, who notes that

> any comparison of Marxism with religion is a two-way street, in which the former is not necessarily discredited by its association with the latter. On the contrary, such a comparison may also function to rewrite certain religious concepts—most notably Christian historicism and the "concept" of providence, but also the pretheological systems of primitive magic—as anticipa-

tory foreshadowings of historical materialism within precapitalist social formations in which scientific thinking is unavailable as such." (*The Political Unconscious*, 285)

18. In *Chaucer and the Subject of History*, Patterson sees an epistemological distinction between the "secular and causal" historiography of the twelfth century—represented most notably by Geoffrey of Monmouth's *Historia Regum Britannie*—and the ecclesiastical and teleological histories of the earlier Middle Ages (95–96). In fact, Geoffrey's *Historia* is itself grounded in a teleology based on ecclesiastical models. For example, we are told that both Arthur and Mordred utilized divisions comprised of "six thousand, six hundred, and sixty-six armed men" at the final battle of Camblam. The fall of Arthur is allegorically linked to the apocalypse, and thereby to the inevitabilities of sacred history.

19. Knight, *Geoffrey Chaucer*, 35–36.

20. Knight, *Geoffrey Chaucer*, 37.

21. Knight, *Geoffrey Chaucer*, 52.

22. Patterson, "No Man," 150.

23. Dominick La Capra, *Soundings in Critical Theory*, 30–66.

24. This is not to assert that historicist thinking can or should take place without invoking the concept of the real; it is rather to suggest that we preface our gestures toward the real with some exploration of the epistemological limits of the category itself. It is here, it seems to me, that psychoanalytic theory has much to offer; the Lacanian idea of the Real as that which "resists symbolization absolutely" has been appropriated by Althusser in his theorization of the "absent cause," and by Jameson in his effort to articulate a theory of narrative and dialectics that might "[designate] the Real without claiming to coincide with it." See Jameson, "Imaginary and Symbolic in Lacan: Marxism, Psychoanalytic Criticism, and the Problem of the Subject," *Yale French Studies* 55–56 (1977): 338–95.

25. Patterson, Introduction to *Literary Practice*, 7, 8.

26. Patterson, Introduction to *Literary Practice*, 7. Patterson's assessment of deconstructive theory is somewhat disingenuous here. His reading in fact attributes to deconstruction an assumption which, according to Derrida, is central to the Western metaphysical tradition. It is precisely the privilege accorded the pre-or-extra-linguistic realm of the real that deconstruction calls into question. Deconstruction does not prescribe, but rather describes, the "sequestering" Patterson disparages. "Within this epoch," Derrida writes, "reading and writing, the production or interpretation of signs, allow themselves to be confined within secondariness. They are preceded by a truth, or a meaning already constituted by and within the element of the logos" (*Grammatology*, 14). In revealing the source to be an effect of the supplement, deconstruction works to overturn, *not* to affirm, the binary opposition between speech and writing.

27. Statius, *Thebaid*, with an English translation by J. H. Mozley, 2 vols., Loeb Classical Library (London: William Heinemann Ltd., 1928) 1: 347.

28. The poem's opening lines trace the Theban story back to the violence that led to its founding: the rape of Europa and the sowing of the dragon's teeth. See

*Thebaid*, 1: 3–14. My reading of Statius is indebted to the work of Winthrop Wetherbee, *Chaucer and the Poets: An Essay on Troilus and Criseyde* (Ithaca, NY: Cornell University Press, 1984), 111–44.

29. Eugene Vance points out that "the legend of Troy nourished the political identities of newly emerging European nations faced with the task of inventing their own historical past." See *Mervelous Signals: Poetics and Sign Theory in the Middle Ages* (Lincoln: University of Nebraska Press, 1986), 266.

30. Both Peter M. Sacks and Louise Fradenburg have noted the traditional connection between mourning and inheritance. See Sacks, *The English Elegy: Studies in the Genre from Spenser to Yeats* (Baltimore: Johns Hopkins University Press, 1985), 37; and Fradenburg, "Voice Memorial," 171. The issue of inheritance vis à vis Chaucer's debt to classical and continental precedent is also discussed by Vance, *Mervelous Signals*, 264–68.

31. Julia Kristeva, *Black Sun: Depression and Melancholia*, trans. Leon Roudiez (New York: Columbia University Press, 1989). Kristeva draws on Freud's "Mourning and Melancholia" (SE 14), as well as the works of Karl Abraham and Melanie Klein in exploring the connection between art and melancholia. For Kristeva, both mourning and melancholia are characterized by "intolerance for object loss and the signifier's failure to insure a compensating way out." (10)

32. What I am calling the real here is what Kristeva calls "the archaic Thing"—as in Freudian theory, the thing is the lost maternal object, cast into the foreclosed realm of the real by the paternal prohibition. I discuss the concept of the thing in more detail in the afterword to this book. For a more critical reading of Kristeva's theory—and the psychoanalytic theory of loss in general—see Louise Fradenburg, "'Our owen wo to drynke'," 90–93.

33. Freud distinguishes mourning and melancholia thus:

> In one class of cases it is evident that melancholia [like mourning] may be the reaction to the loss of a loved object; where this is not the exciting cause one can perceive that there is loss of a more ideal kind. The object has not actually died, but has become lost as an object of love. In yet other cases one feels justified in concluding that a loss of the kind has been experienced, but one cannot see clearly what has been lost, and may the more readily suppose that the patient too cannot consciously perceive what it is he has lost. . . . This would suggest that melancholia is in some way related to an unconscious loss of a love-object, in contradistinction to mourning, in which there is nothing unconscious about the loss. (SE 14: 166)

34. The controversial concept of the death drive (*Todestrieb*) is articulated in Freud's *Beyond the Pleasure Principle* (SE 18). The death drive represents what Freud held to be the fundamental tendency of living beings to reduce tensions absolutely, that is, to return to an inorganic state.

35. In his recent analysis of the poem, Lee Patterson sees Troilus and Criseyde equally implicated in the poem's disavowal of the historical world; for Patterson, the *Troilus* explores "the nature of subjectivity itself." In its emphasis on a "human" and "universal" understanding of subjectivity, however, his analysis effec-

tively erases sexual difference as an issue in the text. See *Chaucer and the Subject of History*, 142.

36. My argument here draws on that of David Anderson, "Theban History in Chaucer's *Troilus*," *Studies in the Age of Chaucer* 4 (1982): 125–28.

37. The function of the male gaze in the *Troilus* is also discussed by David Aers in his book *Community, Gender and Individual Identity: English Writing 1360–1430*, 117–52; and by Sarah Stanbury in two closely related essays: "The Voyeur and the Private Life in *Troilus and Criseyde*," *Studies in the Age of Chaucer* 13 (1991): 141–58; and "The Lover's Gaze in *Troilus and Criseyde*," in *Chaucer's Troilus and Criseyde "Subjit to alle Poesye"*, 224–38.

38. A different—and very provocative—reading of this exchange is offered by Stanbury in her essay "The Lover's Gaze." See, in particular, pages 230–33.

39. Again, Kristeva's discussion in *Powers of Horror* of the coincidence of abjection and veneration in the works of Céline can help us to understand this seeming paradox. The rise and fall of Criseyde in medieval and renaissance literature can be understood in terms of the conjunction of courtliness and sadism that Kristeva notes in Céline's feminine characters: the fetishized object and despised abject are but two sides of the same coin. This conjunction accounts for the religious significance of the abject as the focus of purification rituals, and explains why Henryson might have seen the abjection and moral purification of Cresseid as an appropriate epilogue to Chaucer's poem.

40. That Troilus's pre-coital invocations are fantasies of rape is noted by David Aers, *Community*, 129. Fradenburg discusses the ambiguity surrounding the issue of rape in "'Our owen wo to drynke'," 99–101. Winthrop Wetherbee has pointed out to me that it is by no means clear that Troilus sees himself as the aggressor here. I agree that Troilus seems decidedly uncertain as to whether he identifies with the objects of desire or the desiring subjects in this passage. The matter is further complicated by the inclusion of the somewhat strange Ovidian tale of Mercury, Herse, and Aglauros—a story whose resonance for the *Troilus* is difficult to ascertain. See Wetherbee, *Chaucer and the Poets*, 104.

41. For a feminist reading of the politics of exchange in the poem, see Carolyn Dinshaw, *Chaucer's Sexual Poetics*, 28–64.

42. This tendency is also noted by Stanbury, "The Lover's Gaze," 234. Most of the "Criseydan" readings of the poem see Criseyde as victim. For example, see David Aers, "Criseyde: Woman in Medieval Society," *Chaucer Review* 13 (1979): 177–200; Dinshaw, *Sexual Poetics*, 28–64; Maureen Fries, "'Slydyng of Corage': Chaucer's Criseyde as Feminist and Victim," in *The Authority of Experience: Essays in Feminist Criticism*, ed. Arlyn Diamond and Lee Edwards (Amherst: University of Massachusetts Press, 1977) 45–59; and Monica McAlpine, *The Genre of Troilus and Criseyde* (Ithaca, NY: Cornell University Press, 1978), 182–217.

43. Judith Ferster, "'Your Praise is Performed by Men and Children': Language and Gender in the *Prioress's Prologue and Tale*," *Exemplaria* 2, 1 (Spring 1990): 149–68.

44. Ferster, 150.

45. "From the History of an Infantile Neurosis," SE 17: 7–122.

46. SE 17: 14. An interesting re-reading of the sister's role in Freud's case

history is provided by Nicolas Abraham and Maria Torok in their study *The Wolf Man's Magic Word: A Cryptonymy*, trans. Nicholas Rand (Minneapolis: University of Minnesota Press, 1986). Abraham and Torok argue for a different interpretation of the Wolf Man's dream, and a different "primal scene"—a scene of incest between the father and the sister.

47. SE 17: 52.

48. SE 17: 51

49. SE 17: 96.

50. Freud appended a footnote to the case study in 1923—five years after the case history was published, and nine years after the analysis itself—in which he attempted to lay out the chronology of events in linear fashion. This last effort to chronicle the traumas—both oneiric and waking—that led to the Wolf Man's illness merely accentuates the extent to which the case history unfolds tropologically rather than chronologically, ultimately resisting linearity. See SE 17: 121.

51. The infantilization of Troilus and maternalization of Criseyde in Book III are discussed in Kleinian terms by Aers in *Community*, 139–42.

52. D. W. Robertson, Jr., "Chaucerian Tragedy," *ELH* 19 (1952): 26.

53. Donald Howard, *The Three Temptations* (Princeton, NJ: Princeton University Press, 1966), 137.

54. Wetherbee, *Chaucer and the Poets*, 72.

55. Dinshaw, *Sexual Poetics*, 61.


## Chapter Six

Translations and citations of the *Aeneid*, except where noted, are taken from the Loeb Classical Library edition, trans. H. R. Fairclough (London: Heinemann, repr. 1986). Citations from *Sir Gawain and the Green Knight* are taken from the edition of J. R. R. Tolkien and E. V. Gordon, second edition ed. Norman Davis (Oxford: Oxford University Press, 1967). Translations of the latter are my own.

1. Two of the most important studies of the relationships between literary epic and national origins are R. Howard Bloch's *Etymologies and Genealogies: A Literary Anthropology of the French Middle Ages* (Chicago: University of Chicago Press, 1983) and Eugene Vance, *Mervelous Signals*. See, in particular, Bloch's chapter "Literature and Lineage," pages 92–127, and Vance's chapter on Roland and Charlemagne, pages 51–85.

2. Most of the book-length studies of the poem, such as those by Benson and Burrow, simply ignore this initial crux in the text.

3. The most notable studies of the Troy frame to date are Alfred David, "Gawain and Aeneas," *English Studies* 49 (1968): 402–9; SunHee Kim Gertz, "*Translatio studii et imperii*: Sir Gawain as Literary Critic," *Semiotica* 63 (1987): 185–203; Malcolm Andrew, "The Fall of Troy in *Sir Gawain and the Green Knight* and *Troilus and Criseyde*," in *The European Tragedy of Troilus*, ed. Piero Boitani (Oxford: Clarendon Press, 1989), 75–93.

4. It should be noted that the Troy opening has traditionally been seen as a

reference to the medieval versions of the Troy story—specifically Benoit's *Roman de Troie* and Guido della Colonna's *Historia Destructionis Troiae*—rather than to the *Aeneid* itself. The critical and editorial history of the problem is detailed by David, 402–4. Gertz notes in passing the importance of the Virgilian epic for medieval literary culture, but does not pursue the matter further; see Gertz, 186–89.

5. Here, as throughout this chapter, I draw on Patricia Parker's important book *Literary Fat Ladies: Rhetoric, Gender, Property*. Parker sees the "narrative topos of overcoming a female enchantress or obstacle en route to completion and ending" as the expression of authorial anxiety about narrative control and closure. She identifies the *Aeneid* as one of the prototypes for this characteristic romance narrative strategy. See Parker, 11–17.

6. The word *barathrum*, meaning "abyss" or "pit," is often used to describe parts of the body as well.

7. See Lee Patterson, "'Rapt with Pleasaunce': Vision and Narration in the Epic," *ELH* 48 (1981): 455–75. The quotation in the title is from Book VI of Spenser's *Faerie Queene*.

8. Patterson, 458.

9. This is precisely the strategy that Chaucer foregrounds in his own reading of the *Aeneid*, *The House of Fame*; in unveiling the symbiotic relation between public Fame and private Rumor, Chaucer subverts the classical poet's insistence upon this distinction, thereby opening up a space for a new kind of "auctoritee."

10. Lynn Staley Johnson is one of the few readers to note that "Aeneas' journey to Italy may lie behind Gawain's journey to the north and his experiences there." See Johnson, *The Voice of the Gawain-Poet* (Madison: University of Wisconsin Press, 1984), 71.

11. Gawain's continental reputation as a womanizer is noted by many readers. See, for example, Larry D. Benson, *Art and Tradition in Sir Gawain and the Green Knight* (New Brunswick, NJ: Rutgers University Press, 1965), 95, 103–4; A. C. Spearing, *The Gawain-Poet: A Critical Study* (Cambridge: Cambridge University Press, 1970) 198–99; W. R. J. Barron, *Trawthe and Treason: The Sin of Gawain Reconsidered* (Manchester: Manchester University Press, 1980) 21.

12. The Arthurian epic context of the poem has been discussed most recently by Sheila Fisher, "Leaving Morgan Aside: Women, History, and Revisionism in *Sir Gawain and the Green Knight*," in *The Passing of Arthur: New Essays in the Arthurian Tradition*, ed. Christopher Baswell and William Sharpe (New York: Garland, 1988) 129–51 and by Ivo Kamps, "Magic, Women, and Incest: The Real Challenges in *Sir Gawain and the Green Knight*," *Exemplaria* 1, 2 (Fall 1989): 313–36.

13. See Parker, *Literary Fat Ladies*, 9.

14. Benson notes that "in the First Continuation of *Perceval*, in which Gawain is generally a model of chivalric virtue, he is guilty of two characteristic crimes, lechery and rape" (*Art and Tradition*, 103).

15. R. A. Shoaf, *The Poem as Green Girdle: "Commercium" in Sir Gawain and the Green Knight* (Gainesville: University Presses of Florida, 1984).

16. Kristeva, *Powers of Horror*, 99–102.

17. Like the Troy frame, the belated insertion of Morgan into the romance has been generally ignored by many of the poem's readers. There are, however,

notable exceptions: in addition to the recent essay by Sheila Fisher, cited above, are much earlier studies by Denver Ewing Baughan, "The Role of Morgan le Fay in *Sir Gawain and the Green Knight*," *ELH* 17 (1950): 241–251; Albert B. Friedman, "Morgan la Fay in *Sir Gawain and the Green Knight*," *Speculum* 35 (1960): 260–74; Mother Angela Carson, "Morgain la Feé as the principle of Unity in Gawain and the Green Knight," *MLQ* 23 (1962): 3–16; Douglas Moon, "The Role of Morgain la Feé in *Sir Gawain and the Green Knight*," *NM* 67 (1966): 31–57. A more recent study is undertaken by Dennis Moore, "Making Sense of an Ending: Morgan le Fay in *Sir Gawain and the Green Knight*," *Mediaevalia* 10 (1984): 213–33.

18. Benson, *Art and Tradition*, 34.

19. Friedman, "Morgan la Fay," 274.

20. Geraldine Heng uncovers a "feminine narrative folding into and between the masculine." See "Feminine Knots and the Other *Sir Gawain and the Green Knight*," *PMLA* 106, 3 (May 1991): 500–14.

21. See Bloch, *Medieval Misogyny*, 26.

22. Bloch, 14.

23. Heng points out that "Morgan and the Lady figure the ease of misrecognition and the concomitant difficulty of anchoring textual significance and responsibility" ("Feminine Knots," 503).

24. Kristeva, *Powers*, 32–55.

25. SE 21:154.

## Afterword

1. Jacques Lacan, "The Freudian Thing, or The Meaning of the Return to Freud in Psychoanalysis," *Écrits*, 114–45.

2. Lacan, *The Seminar of Jacques Lacan, Book VII: The Ethics of Psychoanalysis 1959–1960*, ed. Jacques-Alain Miller, trans. Dennis Porter (New York: Norton, 1992).

3. As I noted earlier, a similar point is made by Julia Kristeva in her study of Céline's female characters.

4. One of the best studies of the medieval understanding of what we would call anachronism is to be found in V. A. Kolve's early work, *The Play Called Corpus Christi* (Stanford, CA: Stanford University Press, 1966).

5. See SE 8:26

6. Sir Thomas Malory, *Works*, ed. Eugène Vinaver (Oxford: Oxford University Press, 1971), 681.

7. Malory, *Works*, 681.

8. When Mordred besieges Guenevere in the Tower of London, Malory writes that he "layde a myghty syge aboute the Towre and made many assautis, and threw engynnes unto them, and shotte grete gunnes" (707). This is the first and only mention of firearms in the work, to my knowledge.

9. My assessment of this moment draws on Slavoj Žižek's reading of Lacan. See Žižek, *The Sublime Object of Ideology* (London: Verso, 1989). See pages 69–75 in particular.

# Bibliography

Abraham, Nicolas and Maria Torok. "A Poetics of Psychoanalysis: The Lost Object—Me." *SubStance* 43 (1984): 3–18.

———. *The Wolf Man's Magic Word: A Cryptonomy*. Trans. Nicholas Rand. Minneapolis: University of Minnesota Press, 1986.

Aers, David. *Community, Gender and Individual Identity: English Writing 1360–1430*. London: Routledge, 1988.

———. "Criseyde: Woman in Medieval Society." *Chaucer Review* 13 (1979): 177–200.

Anderson, David. "Theban History in Chaucer's *Troilus*." *Studies in the Age of Chaucer* 4 (1982): 125–128.

Andrew, Malcolm. "The Fall of Troy in *Sir Gawain and the Green Knight* and *Troilus and Criseyde*." In *The European Tragedy of Troilus*. Ed. Piero Boitani. Oxford: Clarendon Press, 1989. 75–93.

Armstrong, Nancy. "The Gender Bind: Women and the Disciplines." *Genders* 3 (Fall 1988): 1–23.

Atkinson, Clarissa. *Mystic and Pilgrim: The Book and the World of Margery Kempe*. Ithaca, NY: Cornell University Press, 1982.

Attridge, Derek, Geoff Bennington, and Robert Young, eds. *Post-Structuralism and the Question of History*. Cambridge: Cambridge University Press, 1987.

Augustine of Hippo. *The Confessions of St. Augustine*. Trans. John K. Ryan. New York: Doubleday, 1960.

Barron, W. R. J. *Trawthe and Treason: The Sin of Gawain Reconsidered*. Manchester: Manchester University Press, 1980.

Baughan, Denver Ewing. "The Role of Morgan le Fay in *Sir Gawain and the Green Knight*." *ELH* 17 (1950): 241–51.

Beckwith, Sarah. "A Very Material Mysticism: The Medieval Mysticism of Margery Kempe." In *Medieval Literature: Criticism, Ideology, History*. Ed. David Aers. New York: St. Martin's Press, 1986. 34–57.

Benjamin, Walter. "Theses on the Philosophy of History." *Illuminations*. Trans. H. Zohn. New York: Schocken Books, 1969.

Bennington, Geoff. "Demanding History." In *Post-Structuralism and the Question of History*. Ed. Derek Attridge, Geoff Bennington, and Robert Young. Cambridge: Cambridge University Press, 1987. 15–29.

Benson, Larry D. *Art and Tradition in Sir Gawain and the Green Knight*. New Brunswick, NJ: Rutgers University Press, 1965.

Benton, Ted. *The Rise and Fall of Structural Marxism: Althusser and His Influence*. Hong Kong: Macmillan, 1984.

Blake, Norman. *The English Language in Medieval Literature*. London: J. M. Dent, 1977.

Bloch, R. Howard. *Etymologies and Genealogies: A Literary Anthropology of the French Middle Ages*. Chicago: University of Chicago Press, 1983.

———. *Medieval Misogyny and the Invention of Western Romantic Love*. Chicago: University of Chicago Press, 1991.

Boardman, Philip. "Courtly Language and the Strategy of Consolation in the *Book of the Duchess*." *ELH* 44 (1977): 567–79.

Brook, G. L., ed. *The Harley Lyrics: The Middle English Lyrics of MS Harley 2253*. Manchester: Manchester University Press, 1968.

Brown, Carleton, ed. *English Lyrics of the XIIIth Century*. Oxford: Clarendon Press, 1932.

Bynum, Caroline Walker. *Holy Feast and Holy Fast: The Religious Significance of Food to Medieval Women*. Berkeley: University of California Press, 1987.

———. *Jesus as Mother: Studies in the Spirituality of the High Middle Ages*. Berkeley: University of California Press, 1982.

Cantor, Norman. *Inventing the Middle Ages: The Lives, Works, and Ideas of the Great Medievalists of the Twentieth Century*. New York: William Morrow, 1991.

Carson, Mother Angela. "Morgain le Feé as the Principle of Unity in *Sir Gawain and the Green Knight*." *MLQ* 23 (1962): 3–16.

Chambers, Ross. "Irony and the Canon." *Profession 90*. New York: Modern Language Association of America, 1990. 18–24.

Chaucer, Geoffrey. *The Riverside Chaucer*. Gen. ed. Larry D. Benson. 3rd ed. Boston: Houghton, 1987.

Cherniss, Michael. *Boethian Apocalypse*. Norman, OK: Pilgrim Books, 1987.

Cholmeley, Katharine. *Margery Kempe: Genius and Mystic*. London: Longmans, Green and Co., 1947.

Colledge, Eric. "Margery Kempe." *The Month* 28 (1962): 16–29.

Culler, Jonathan. "Changes in the Study of the Lyric." *Lyric Poetry: Beyond New Criticism*. Ed. Chaviva Hosek and Patricia Parker. Ithaca, NY: Cornell University Press, 1985.

David, Alfred. "Gawain and Aeneas." *English Studies* 49 (1968): 402–9.

De Man, Paul. *The Rhetoric of Romanticism*. New York: Columbia University Press, 1984.

Derrida, Jacques. *The Ear of the Other: Otobiography, Transference, Translation*. Ed. Christie McDonald. Trans. Peggy Kamuf. Lincoln: University of Nebraska Press, 1985.

———. *Margins of Philosophy*. Trans. Alan Bass. Chicago: University of Chicago Press, 1982.

———. *Of Grammatology*. Trans. Gayatri Chakravorty Spivak. Baltimore: Johns Hopkins University Press, 1976.

———. "The Retrait of Metaphor." *Enclitic* 2 (1978): 5–33.

Dinshaw, Carolyn. *Chaucer's Sexual Poetics*. Madison: University of Wisconsin Press, 1989.

Doane, Mary Ann. *The Desire to Desire: The Woman's Film of the 1940s*. Bloomington: Indiana University Press, 1988.

Edwards, Robert. "The *Book of the Duchess* and the Beginnings of Chaucer's Narrative." *New Literary History* (1982): 189–204.

Ellman, Maud. "Blanche." *Criticism and Critical Theory*. Ed. Jeremy Hawthorn. London: Arnold, 1984. 99–110.

Ferrante, Joan M. "Male Fantasy and Female Reality in Courtly Literature." *Women's Studies* 11 (1984): 67–97.

Ferster, Judith. *Chaucer on Interpretation*. Cambridge: Cambridge University Press, 1985.

———. "'Your Praise is Performed by Men and Children': Language and Gender in the *Prioress's Prologue and Tale*." *Exemplaria* 2, 1 (Spring 1990): 149–68.

Fisher, Sheila. "Leaving Morgan Aside: Women, History, and Revisionism in *Sir Gawain and the Green Knight*." In *The Passing of Arthur: New Essays in the Arthurian Tradition*. Ed. Christopher Baswell and William Sharpe. New York: Garland, 1988. 129–51.

Foucault, Michel. *Language, Counter-Memory, Practice*. Ed. Donald Bouchard. Trans. Donald Bouchard and Sherry Simon. Ithaca, NY: Cornell University Press, 1977.

Fradenburg, Louise O. "'Our owen wo to drynke': Loss, Gender, and Chivalry in *Troilus and Criseyde*." In *Chaucer's Troilus and Criseyde 'Subjit to alle Poesye': Essays in Criticism*. Ed. R. A. Shoaf and Catherine S. Cox. Binghamton: State University of New York Press, 1992. 88–106.

———. "'Voice Memorial': Loss and Reparation in Chaucer's Poetry." *Exemplaria* 2, 1 (Spring 1990): 169–202.

Frantzen, Allen. *Desire for Origins: New Language, Old English, and Teaching the Tradition*. New Brunswick, NJ: Rutgers University Press, 1990.

Frantzen, Allen and Charles Venegoni. "An Archaeology of Anglo-Saxon Studies." *Style* 20, 2 (Summer 1986): 142–56.

Freud, Sigmund. *Beyond the Pleasure Principle. The Standard Edition of the Complete Psychological Works of Sigmund Freud*. Ed. James Strachey. Trans. James Strachey et al. London: Hogarth, 1953–74. Vol. 18 of 24.

———. "Female Sexuality." *The Standard Edition* 21.

———. "Fetishism." *The Standard Edition* 21.

———. "Fragment of an Analysis of a Case of Hysteria." *The Standard Edition* 7.

———. "From the History of an Infantile Neurosis." *The Standard Edition* 17.

———. *Jokes and Their Relation to the Unconscious. The Standard Edition* 8.

———. "Mourning and Melancholia." *The Standard Edition* 14.

———. *New Introductory Lectures on Psycho-Analysis. The Standard Edition* 22.

———. *Project for a Scientific Psychology. The Standard Edition* 1.

———. "Screen Memories." *The Standard Edition* 3.

———. "Some Psychical Consequences of the Anatomical Distinction Between the Sexes." *The Standard Edition* 19.

Freud, Sigmund and Josef Breuer. *Studies on Hysteria. The Standard Edition* 2.

Friedman, Albert B. "Morgan la Fay in *Sir Gawain and the Green Knight*." *Speculum* 35 (1960): 260–74.

Fries, Maureen. "Margery Kempe." In *An Introduction to the Medieval Mystics of*

*Europe*. Ed. Paul Szarmach. Albany: State University of New York Press, 1984.

———. "'Slydyng of Corage': Chaucer's Criseyde as Feminist and Victim." In *The Authority of Experience: Essays in Feminist Criticism*. Ed. Arlyn Diamond and Lee Edwards. Amherst: University of Massachusetts Press, 1977.

Fyler, John. *Chaucer and Ovid*. New Haven, CT: Yale University Press, 1979.

Gallop, Jane. *The Daughter's Seduction: Feminism and Psychoanalysis*. Ithaca, NY: Cornell University Press, 1982.

———. *Reading Lacan*. Ithaca, NY: Cornell University Press, 1985.

Gertz, SunHee Kim. "*Translatio Studii et Imperii*: Sir Gawain as Literary Critic." *Semiotica* 63 (1987): 185–203.

Gravdal, Kathryn. *Ravishing Maidens: Writing Rape in Medieval French Literature and Law*. Philadelphia: University of Pennsylvania Press, 1991.

Hanawalt, Barbara A., ed. *Chaucer's England: Literature in Historical Context*. Minneapolis: University of Minnesota Press, 1992.

Hanning, Robert. "Chaucer's First Ovid: Metamorphosis and Poetic Tradition in the Book of the Duchess and the House of Fame." In *Chaucer and the Craft of Fiction*. Ed. Leigh Arrathoon. Rochester, MI: Solaris Press, 1986.

Hansen, Elaine Tuttle. "The Death of Blanche and the Life of the Moral Order." *Thought: A Review of Culture and Ideas* Guest ed. Thelma Fenster. vol. 64, no. 254 (September 1989): 287–97.

———. "Fearing for Chaucer's Good Name." *Exemplaria* 2, 1 (Spring 1990): 23–36.

Hegel, G. W. F. *Phenomenology of Spirit*. Trans. A. V. Miller. Oxford: Oxford University Press, 1977.

Heng, Geraldine. "Feminine Knots and the Other *Sir Gawain and the Green Knight*." *PMLA* 106, 3 (May 1991): 500–514.

Hermann, J. P. "Language and Spirituality in Cynewulf's *Juliana*." *Texas Studies in Literature and Language* 26, 3 (1984): 263–81.

Hertz, Neil. *The End of the Line: Essays on Psychoanalysis and the Sublime*. New York: Columbia University Press, 1985.

Hoagwood, Terence. "Artifice and Redemption: Figuration and the Failure of Reference in Chaucer's *Book of the Duchess*." *Studia Mystica* 11 (Summer 1988): 57–68.

Hodgart, M. J. C. "Medieval Lyrics and the Ballads." In *The Age of Chaucer*. Ed. Boris Ford. Baltimore: Penguin Books, 1969.

Howard, Donald. *Chaucer: His Life, His Works, His World*. New York: E. P. Dutton, 1987.

———. *The Three Temptations*. Princeton, NJ: Princeton University Press, 1966.

Huppé, Bernard and D. W. Robertson, Jr. *Fruyt and Chaf: Studies in Chaucer's Allegories*. Princeton, NJ: Princeton University Press, 1963.

Irigaray, Luce. *Speculum of the Other Woman*. Trans. Gillian Gill. Ithaca, NY: Cornell University Press, 1985.

Jackson, W. T. H. *The Literature of the Middle Ages*. New York: Columbia University Press, 1960.

Jacobus, Mary. *Reading Woman*. New York: Columbia University Press, 1986.

Jakobson, Roman. "Two Aspects of Language and Two Types of Aphasic Disturbances." *Selected Writings II: Word and Language*. Paris: Mouton, 1971.

Jameson, Fredric. "Imaginary and Symbolic in Lacan: Marxism, Psychoanalytic Criticism, and the Problem of the Subject." *Yale French Studies* 55–56 (1977): 338–95.

———. *The Political Unconscious: Narrative as a Socially Symbolic Act*. Ithaca, NY: Cornell University Press, 1981.

Johnson, Barbara. *The Critical Difference*. Baltimore: Johns Hopkins University Press, 1980.

Johnson, Lynn Staley. *The Voice of the Gawain-Poet*. Madison: University of Wisconsin Press, 1984.

Jordan, Robert. *Chaucer's Poetics and the Modern Reader*. Berkeley: University of California Press, 1987.

Kamps, Ivo. "Magic, Women, and Incest: The Real Challenges in *Sir Gawain and the Green Knight*." *Exemplaria* 1, 2 (Fall 1989): 313–36.

Kempe, Margery. *The Book of Margery Kempe*. Ed. Sanford Meech and Hope Emily Allen. London: Early English Text Society, 1940.

Knowles, David. *The English Mystical Tradition*. London: Burns and Oates, 1961.

Koestenbaum, Wayne. "Privileging the Anus: Anna O. and the Collaborative Origin of Psychoanalysis." *Genders* 3 (Fall 1988): 57–80.

Kojève, Alexandre. *Introduction to the Reading of Hegel: Lectures on the Phenomenology of Spirit*. Assembled by Raymond Queneau. Ed. Allan Bloom. Trans. James H. Nichols, Jr. Ithaca, NY: Cornell University Press, 1980.

Kolve, V. A. *The Play Called Corpus Christi*. Stanford, CA: Stanford University Press, 1966.

Knight, Stephen. *Geoffrey Chaucer*. Oxford: Basil Blackwell, 1986.

Kristeva, Julia. *Black Sun: Depression and Melancholia*. Trans. Leon Roudiez. New York: Columbia University Press, 1989.

———. *Powers of Horror: An Essay on Abjection*. Trans. Leon Roudiez. New York: Columbia University Press, 1982.

———. *Tales of Love*. Trans. Leon Roudiez. New York: Columbia University Press, 1987.

Lacan, Jacques. *Écrits: A Selection*. Trans. Alan Sheridan. New York: Norton, 1977.

———. *Feminine Sexuality: Jacques Lacan and the école freudienne*. Ed. Jacqueline Rose and Juliet Mitchell. Trans. Jacqueline Rose. New York: Norton, 1982.

———. *The Four Fundamental Concepts of Psycho-Analysis*. Ed. Jacques-Alain Miller. Trans. Alan Sheridan. New York: Norton, 1977.

———. *The Seminar of Jacques Lacan, Book VII: The Ethics of Psychoanalysis 1959–1960*. Ed. Jacques-Alain Miller. Trans. Dennis Porter. New York: Norton, 1992.

LaCapra, Dominick. "On the Line: Between History and Criticism." *Profession 89*. New York: Modern Language Association of America. 4–9.

———. *Rethinking Intellectual History: Texts, Contexts, Language*. Ithaca, NY: Cornell University Press, 1983.

————. *Soundings in Critical Theory*. Ithaca: Cornell University Press, 1989.

Leupin, Alexandre. *Barbarolexis: Medieval Writing and Sexuality*. Cambridge, MA: Harvard University Press, 1989.

Þe Liflade ant te Passiun of Seinte Iuliene. Ed. S.R.T.O. d'Ardenne. London: Early English Text Society, 1961.

Lochrie, Karma. *Margery Kempe and Translations of the Flesh*. Philadelphia: University of Pennsylvania Press, 1991.

Lomperis, Linda and Sarah Stanbury, eds. *Feminist Approaches to the Body in Medieval Literature*. Philadelphia: University of Pennsylvania Press, 1993.

Liu, Alan. "Local Transcendence: Cultural Criticism, Postmodernism, and the Romanticism of Detail." *Representations* 32 (Fall 1990): 75–113.

Luria, Maxwell S. and Richard L. Hoffman, eds. *Middle English Lyrics*. New York: Norton, 1974.

Malory, Sir Thomas. *Works*. Ed. Eugène Vinaver. Oxford: Oxford University Press, 1971.

Margherita, Gayle. "Desiring Narrative: Ideology and the Semiotics of the Gaze in the Middle English *Juliana*." *Exemplaria* 2, 2 (Fall 1990): 355–74.

Masson, Jeffrey. *The Assault on Truth: Freud's Suppression of the Seduction Theory*. New York: Farrar, Straus, and Giroux, 1984.

McAlpine, Monica. *The Genre of Troilus and Criseyde*. Ithaca, NY: Cornell University Press, 1978.

Metz, Christian. *The Imaginary Signifier: Psychoanalysis and Cinema*. Trans. Celia Britton, Annwyl Williams, Ben Brewster and Alfred Guzzetti. Bloomington: Indiana University Press, 1982.

Millet, Bella. "Chaucer, Lollius, and the Medieval Theory of Authorship." *Studies in the Age of Chaucer*. Proceedings no. 1 (1984): 93–103.

Moi, Toril. "Representation of Patriarchy: Sexuality and Epistemology in Freud's Dora." In *In Dora's Case: Freud—Hysteria—Feminism*. Ed. Charles Bernheimer and Claire Kahane. New York: Columbia University Press, 1985.

Moon, Douglas. "The Role of Morgain la Feé in *Sir Gawain and the Green Knight*." *NM* 67 (1966): 31–57.

Moore, Arthur K. *The Secular Lyric in Middle English*. Lexington: University of Kentucky Press, 1951.

Moore, Dennis. "Making Sense of an Ending: Morgan le Fay in *Sir Gawain and the Green Knight*." *Mediaevalia* 10 (1984): 213–33.

Mulvey, Laura. "Visual Pleasure and Narrative Cinema." *Screen* 16, 3 (1975): 8–18.

Paden, William D. *The Medieval Pastourelle*. 2 vols. New York: Garland, 1987.

Parker, Patricia. *Literary Fat Ladies: Rhetoric, Gender, Property*. London: Methuen, 1987.

Patterson, Lee. *Chaucer and the Subject of History*. Madison: University of Wisconsin Press, 1991.

————, ed. *Literary Practice and Social Change in Britain, 1380–1530*. Berkeley: University of California Press, 1990.

————. *Negotiating the Past: The Historical Understanding of Medieval Literature*. Madison: University of Wisconsin Press, 1987.

————. "'No Man His Reson Herde': Peasant Consciousness, Chaucer's Miller, and the Structure of the *Canterbury Tales*." In *Literary Practice and Social Change in Britain 1380–1530*. Ed. Lee Patterson. Berkeley: University of California Press, 1990. 113–55.

———. "'Rapt with Plesaunce': Vision and Narration in the Epic." *ELH* 48 (1981): 455–75.

Pearsall, Derek. *Old and Middle English Poetry*. London: Routledge and Kegan Paul, 1977.

Pratt, Robert Armstrong. "A Note on Chaucer's Lollius." *MLN* 65 (March 1950): 183–87.

Ransom, Daniel. *Poets at Play: Irony and Parody in the Harley Lyrics*. Norman, OK: Pilgrim Books, 1985.

Ricoeur, Paul. *The Rule of Metaphor*. Trans. Robert Czerny. Toronto: University of Toronto Press, 1977.

Riehle, Wolfgang. *The Middle English Mystics*. Trans. Bernard Standring. London: Routledge, 1981.

Robertson, D. W., Jr. "Chaucerian Tragedy." *ELH* 19 (1952).

———. *A Preface to Chaucer*. Princeton, NJ: Princeton University Press, 1962.

Rose, Jacqueline. *Sexuality in the Field of Vision*. London: Verso, 1986.

———. "Where Does the Misery Come From? Psychoanalysis, Feminism, and the Event." In *Feminism and Psychoanalysis*. Ed. Richard Feldstein and Judith Roof. Ithaca, NY: Cornell University Press, 1989.

Rubin, Gayle. "The Traffic in Women: Notes on the 'Political Economy' of Sex." In *Toward an Anthropology of Women*. Ed. Rayna R. Reiter. New York: Monthly Review Press, 1975. 157–210.

Rutebeuf. *Le Miracle de Théophile*. Ed. Grace Frank. Paris: Champion, 1983.

Sacks, Peter. *The English Elegy: Studies in the Genre from Spenser to Yeats*. Baltimore: Johns Hopkins University Press, 1985.

Schor, Naomi. *Reading in Detail: Aesthetics and the Feminine*. New York: Methuen, 1987.

*Seinte Katerine*. Ed. S.R.T.O. d'Ardenne and E. J. Dobson. London: Early English Text Society, 1981.

*Seinte Marherete, Þe Meiden ant Martyr*. Ed. Frances Mack. London: Early English Text Society, 1934.

Sedgwick, Eve Kosofsky. *Between Men: English Literature and Male Homosocial Desire*. New York: Columbia University Press, 1985.

Shoaf, R. A. *The Poem as Green Girdle: "Commercium" in Sir Gawain and the Green Knight*. Gainesville: University Presses of Florida, 1984.

Silverman, Kaja. *The Acoustic Mirror: The Female Voice in Psychoanalysis and Cinema*. Bloomington: Indiana University Press, 1988.

———. "Back to the Future." *Camera Obscura* 27 (Sept. 1991): 109–32.

———. "Fassbinder and Lacan: A Reconsideration of Gaze, Look, and Image." *Camera Obscura* 19 (1989): 54–84.

*Sir Gawain the the Green Knight*. Ed. J. R. R. Tolkien and E. V. Gordon. 2nd ed. Norman Davis. Oxford: Oxford University Press, 1967.

Spearing, A. C. *The Gawain-Poet: A Critical Study*. Cambridge: Cambridge University Press, 1970.

————. *Medieval to Renaissance Poetry*. Cambridge: Cambridge University Press, 1985.

Stanbury, Sarah. "The Lover's Gaze in *Troilus and Criseyde*." In *Chaucer's Troilus and Criseyde 'Subjit to alle Poesye': Essays in Criticism*. Ed. R. A. Shoaf and Catherine S. Cox. Binghamton: State University of New York Press, 1992. 224–38.

————. "The Voyeur and the Private Life in *Troilus and Criseyde*." *Studies in the Age of Chaucer* 13 (1991): 141–58.

Statius. *Thebaid*. Trans. J. H. Mozley. 2 vols. London: Loeb Classical Library, 1928.

Stone, Brian, trans. *Medieval English Verse*. Baltimore: Penguin Books, 1964.

Strohm, Paul. *Social Chaucer*. Cambridge: Harvard University Press, 1989.

————. "Saving the Appearances: Chaucer's *Purse* and the Fabrication of the Lancastrian Claim." In *Chaucer's England: Literature in Historical Context*. Ed. Barbara Hanawalt. Minneapolis: University of Minnesota Press, 1992. 21–40.

Thornton, Martin. *Margery Kempe: An Example in the English Pastoral Tradition*. London: Talbot Press, 1960.

Thurston, Herbert, S. J. "Margery the Astonishing." *The Month* (November 1936): 446–56.

Vance, Eugene. *Mervelous Signals: Poetics and Sign Theory in the Middle Ages*. Lincoln: University of Nebraska Press, 1986.

Virgil. *Aeneid*. Trans. H. R. Fairclough. 2 vols. London: Loeb Classical Library, repr. 1986.

Watkin, E. I. *Poets and Mystics*. London: Sheed and Ward, 1953.

Weissman, Hope. "Margery Kempe in Jerusalem: *Hysterica Compassio* in the Late Middle Ages." In *Acts of Interpretation: The Text in Its Contexts*. Ed. Mary Carruthers and Elizabeth Kirk. Norman, OK: Pilgrim Books, 1982.

Wetherbee, Winthrop. *Chaucer and the Poets: An Essay on Troilus and Criseyde*. Ithaca, NY: Cornell University Press, 1984.

Willis, Connie. *Doomsday Book*. New York: Bantam, 1992.

Wimsatt, James. *Chaucer and the French Love Poets: The Literary Background of the Book of the Duchess*. Chapel Hill: University of North Carolina Press, 1968.

Windeatt, B. A., ed. and trans. *Chaucer's Dream Poetry: Sources and Analogues*. Totowa, NJ: D.S. Brewer-Rowman and Littlefield, 1982.

Woolf, Rosemary. "The Construction of *In a Fryht As I Con Fare Fremede*." *Medium Aevum* 38 (1969): 55–59.

Žižek, Slavoj. *The Sublime Object of Ideology*. London: Verso: 1989.

# Index

This book has been set in Linotron Galliard. Galliard was designed for Mergenthaler in 1978 by Matthew Carter. Galliard retains many of the features of a sixteenth-century typeface cut by Robert Granjon but has some modifications that give it a more contemporary look.

Printed on acid-free paper.